Savage Girls and Wild Boys
A HISTORY OF FERAL CHILDREN

Michael Newton

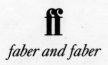

faber and faber

First published in 2002
by Faber and Faber Limited
3 Queen Square London WC1N 3AU

Typeset by Faber and Faber Ltd
Printed in England by Clays Ltd, St Ives plc

A CIP record for this book is available from the British Library

ISBN 0–571–20139–3

10 9 8 7 6 5 4 3 2 1

For my mother and father

Contents

List of Illustrations

Acknowledgements

I am indebted to the team at Faber and Faber: Julian Loose for being both an inspiring and a patient editor, and, above all, for allowing me a second opportunity, and to Angus Cargill, Kate Ward and Ron Costley; Professor Philip Horne for keeping me at it and seeing me through; Professor Karl Miller for his support, for teaching me a thing or two, and for giving me the benefit of his scholarship and critical skills; Professor Roy Porter and (the much missed) Professor Tony Tanner for telling me it was good; Julia Jäkel for her all-too-necessary patience with the German passages; Hilary Cook and John Collingwood; Adrian Garvey; Annie Cooper; Dr Cheryce Kramer for giving me the invaluable help of believing in me; Dr Chris Hamilton for his encouragement, and for taking things seriously; Dr Lorna Gibb for her knowledge of both linguistics and Burt Bacharach; Dr Emma Widdis for being a brilliant amateur detective; Sara Dane, who said exactly the right thing; Olivia Goodwin for helping me to write, and especially for providing the kindness, support and wisdom that made all the difference; Jane and Phil Cole for putting a roof over my head; and my mother and father, without whose love and immense generosity this book would never have been completed.

Other people also read this book before it was a book, and offered excellent advice: Dr Stephen James; Dr Christine Göttler; the incomparable Lee Sands; Catherine McLoughlin; Miranda Davies; Debbie Humphry; Dr Anne Button; and Sarah Lusznat, who saved me, as ever, from making a terrible mistake.

Thanks to Linda Garmon and Jay Shurley, who told me fascinating things about Genie and helped enormously with picture research; Seamus Heaney; Simon Elliott at the Department of Special Collections at UCLA; Colonel Richard Brook and the Board of Trustees at the Chevening Estate.

Thanks to Helen Hayward and John Armstrong for their generosity. And thanks to Cris Popa, Thalia Thompson and Vivienne Hammond for never asking me if I'd finished it yet, and to Richard Allen and Jason Whiston for never giving up on asking me the same question.

Thanks to Debbie Brown, for taking me to Ireland and giving me a clue to the whole thing.

I would also like to thank the following institutions for financial support given during the inordinately long time I spent writing this book: The British Academy; the Department of English at University College, London; the Irwin Fund of the University of London; Harvard University; The Charles Lamb Society; The Fabian Society. This book wouldn't have been finished without the support of the five people who generously kept me in work: Professors John Sutherland, David Trotter, Michael Wood, and Caroline Dakers, and my unofficial agent, Roger Sabin.

I want to acknowledge my indebtedness to four people I have never met, but whose books on the same subject as my own have provided me with patterns of excellence in their research and writing: Harlan Lane, author of *The Wild Boy Of Aveyron* (also for some very useful advice on picture research); Jeffrey Masson, author of *Wild Child: The Unsolved Mystery of Kaspar Hauser*; Charles Maclean, author of *The Wolf Children*; and Russ Rymer, author of *Genie, A Scientific Tragedy*.

Finally, I thank my teachers: John Smithies; David Akers; Professor Henry Woudhuysen; Professor Stanley Cavell; and Brother Edwin.

Foreword

These are tales of pursuit. The pursuers are various: the young French surgeon flushed with the possibilities of a great enterprise; the wearied, sardonic Scottish doctor; the village priest willing to believe; the eccentric judge; the gentleman of leisure; the errant aristocrat. Yet the object of their pursuit is constant. All of them seek the truth, one that is embodied in another human being; and, for each one, that truth is something that can only be found in the exceptional fate of *this* boy, of *this* girl. That is the end of their quest: to fix for a moment the fleeting truth glimpsed within the life, the eyes, the soul, of the wild child.

'Wild child' or 'feral child': the phrase covers a multitude of stories. Mostly it describes children brought up by animals; but over the last few centuries these words have been applied to children who have grown up alone in the wilderness, lost in the woods and forests. More strangely the same phrases are also used for those few children who have lived through another, perhaps crueller kind of loneliness, locked for long years in solitary confinement in single rooms. What unites all these stories is the image of a human life developing in complete isolation, cut off from all human contact.

Such stories have afforded generations of scholars, writers and philosophers insights into the very essence of humanity. These children raise the deepest and most insoluble of questions: what is human nature? Does such a thing even exist? How do we differ from other animals? Where does our identity come from? And the inevitable silence of these children provokes a further mystery: what part does language play in creating our humanity?

Behind all these questions lies one final source of uncertainty and intrigue: what makes us human? Somehow these stories of abandoned children, suffering children, of savage girls and wild boys, always bring us back to this implacable and insoluble source of fascination. It is a fascination that this book will set out to explore, doing so through the fragmented and disrupted biographies of children whose histories are partially lost.

Come on, poor babe
Some powerful spirit instruct the kites and ravens
To be thy nurses! Wolves and bears, they say,
Casting their savageness aside, have done
Like offices of pity.
    William Shakespeare, from *The Winter's Tale*

CHAPTER ONE

The Child Of Nature

'Men saye that we have bene begotten miraculously, fostered and geven sucke more straungely, and in our tendre yeres were fedd by birdes and wilde beasts, to whom we were cast out as a praye. For a wolfe gave us sucke with her teates . . .' Nowe amongst the warders, there was by chaunce one that was the man to whom the children were committed to be cast awaye, and was present when they were left on the bancke of the river to the mercie of fortune.

From North's translation of Plutarch's *Life of Romulus*

In the years since the fall of communism, as the social fabric of Russia was rent and fell apart, street kids became a common sight in Moscow or St Petersburg. Like the homeless in London, they were both ever present and subtly invisible – a backdrop to city life; an irritating intrusion into the process of simply getting on with things. But one of these Moscow street kids was different. He was actually to find the visibility that had so long been denied to him.

In 1996, Ivan Mishukov left home. He was four years old. Ivan's mother could not cope with him or with her alcoholic boyfriend, so the little boy decided that life on the streets was better than the chaos of their apartment; and just as Moscow has its homeless, so it has its wild dogs, an inevitable consequence of the inability to create facilities for the city's many strays. Dogs are abandoned with mournful regularity, and quickly turn feral, rummaging through bins for scraps, running around the streets in packs in order to survive. Out on the streets, Ivan began to beg, but gave a portion of the food he cadged each time to one particular pack of dogs. The dogs grew to trust him; befriended him; and, finally, took him on as their pack leader.

The relationship worked perfectly, far better than anything Ivan had known among his fellow humans. He begged for food, and shared it with his pack. In return, he slept with them in the long

winter nights of deep darkness, when the temperatures plummet-
ed. The heat of the animals kept him warm and alive, despite the
snow, the ice, the bitter cold; and if anyone should try to molest him
or thieve from him, the dogs were there on hand to attack them.

The police came to know of Ivan's life, but could not wrest him
from the streets. Three times he fled from them, or the dogs savagely defended their leader. Eventually the police managed to separate
the dogs from Ivan by laying bait for them inside a restaurant
kitchen. Deprived of his animal guards, the savagely snarling boy
was quickly trapped.

He had been living on the street for two years. Yet, as he had had
four years within a human family, he could talk perfectly well. After
a brief spell in the Reutov children's shelter, Ivan started school. He
appears to be just like any other Moscow child. Yet it's said that at
night he dreams of dogs.

After many months of hunting, a friend of mine, Emma Widdis, a
lecturer in Russian at Cambridge University, managed to track
down Tamara Novikova, the woman who runs the Reutov children's shelter. So one February morning of 2001, we phoned her
office at Reutov. The call did not begin well. Tamara Novikova was
suspicious, edgy, and – even allowing for the customary Russian
directness – dismissively brusque. We asked what had happened to
Ivan in the last few months. He was with a foster-family, she told us,
and though there had been difficulties, he was very happy there. We
explained that, although I had no wish to intrude on Ivan's privacy,
I did wonder if she and I could perhaps meet in order to discuss his
story. It was impossible, she said. She could not talk to anyone
about the story – nobody at all. And particularly not anyone who
was not Russian.

When his story was released in July 1998, Ivan's case was extraordinary enough to gain the attention of the world's press. Yet his
experience is not unique. Over the last four hundred years, a few
such children have been discovered and brought back into civilized

life. As soon as he appeared in the newspapers, journalists made links between Ivan and these other cases. They saw him as a living, contemporary example of what are called 'feral children', or 'wild children'. Many of their stories are even more remarkable and unexpected than Ivan's own. This book will explore these other stories, revealing levels of human experience that are stranger still. The curiosity that greeted Ivan's story is itself strong evidence of a continuing preoccupation, a desire to know about such children, that has persisted throughout human history. But what are the furthest origins of these stories? And where does that sense of intrigue begin?

The fascination with the wild child goes back a long way, and Ivan's story has many counterparts in the myths of antiquity. Again and again we find legendary tales of the hero abandoned at birth and brought up by animals or in isolation: the wild education of Cyrus; the river-borne abandonment of Moses; the infancy of Semiramis, founder of Babylon, fostered by birds; the story of Oedipus, lamed and left in the wilderness of Kithairon; the childhood of the twins, Amphion and Zethos, forsaken on a mountain side; the exposure of Paris on the slopes of Mount Ida, where for five days he was suckled by a bear; the story of Tyro, and Neleus and Pelias; infant Aleas fed by a doe; even, the nativity of Christ.[1] Often these heroes go on to become the founders of cities – such as Amphion, whose music charmed the very stones to build by themselves the walls of Thebes.[2]

The most famous of all Ivan's mythic progenitors, however, are Romulus and Remus, the founders of Rome. Their story offers us a template that would fit equally well many of these other versions of the myth. The twins' mother was Rhea Silvia, daughter of Numitor, once the King of Alba Longa, but now deposed by Amulius, his wicked brother. In order to prevent his niece, Rhea Silvia, from having offspring and so continuing Numitor's lineage, Amulius forced her to become a Vestal Virgin. However, one night a ghostly and very large phallus appeared in the Vestals' temple and impregnated

Rhea. Amulius was maddened with rage, but Rhea protested that it
was the god Mars who was responsible for her pregnancy. On her
giving birth to twin sons, Amulius ordered that the infants should be
exposed. They were taken to the River Tiber, where they were left to
'the mercy of fortune', as Thomas North's sixteenth-century translation of Plutarch puts it. Death seemed imminent, but help came
from an unexpected quarter: a she-wolf suckled the young infants,
and a woodpecker fetched food for them. The twins lived on in this
way until a shepherd, named Faustulus, discovered them.

Faustulus and his wife, Acca Larentia, brought up the children,
who turned out to be noble, virile and courageous. The twins grew
up to lead a band of outlaws who raided the countryside, until eventually their true identity was discovered. They overthrew Amulius
and restored Numitor, their grandfather, to the throne of Alba
Longa. The twins then set out to found a city of their own. However,
according to some versions of the story, in the course of building
this city, Romulus and Remus argued and came to blows, and in a
fury Romulus slew his brother. The city was founded on the earth
soaked by the dead brother's blood, and populated by brigands. As
these brigands were all men, Romulus feared that the colony would
fail, and so, to ensure the continuation of the city, he abducted a
large number of women from the Sabine tribe.

This story has always seemed a strange one. It systematically
strays into the discreditable and forbidden, so that some scholars
(probably wrongly) have even seen it as evidence of anti-Roman
propaganda.[3] Still there is so much in the story that embroils the
myth in shamefulness: the Romulan colonists are all criminals; the
brothers spend their youth as bandits; Romulus populates his city
through a mass abduction; and the twins' mother conceives
through the disgraceful intervention of a large and spectral phallus
or, if that is too fantastic to believe, by some other more credible
and only slightly less scandalous means. Moreover, while some
Roman writers disputed whether Romulus actually murdered

Remus, the killing nonetheless remains an inescapable part of the story.

Yet the transgressive element that most scandalized the Romans was precisely the one that concerns us here; that is, the twins' suckling from the she-wolf. Curiously, it led the Roman historian Ennius to cover up this part of the tale by introducing what might be thought of as an equally shameful link. Ennius realized that the word *lupa* can mean either 'she-wolf' or 'prostitute', and so deftly replaced the wolf with a prostitute, Acca Larentia, the wife of Faustulus the shepherd.[4]

This desire to remove the wolf from the story may lead us to wonder why she was there in the first place. Restorations and substitutions are at the very heart of the Romulus and Remus story: brothers take the rightful place of others, foster-parents bring up other people's children, the god Mars stands in for a human suitor. Yet the crucial substitution occurs when the she-wolf saves the lost children. In that moment, when the infants' lips close upon the she-wolf's teats, a transgressive mercy removes the harmful influence of a murderous culture. The moment is a second birth: where death is expected, succour is given, and the children are miraculously born into the order of nature.

The story is more than shameful: its strangeness unsettles us, leaving a sense of wonder. In Plutarch's account of the tale, Remus himself confesses astonishment at the marvel of his own life, and Ovid also exclaims at the twins' unexpected fate: 'A she-wolf which had cast her whelps came, wondrous to tell, to the abandoned twins: who could believe that the brute would not harm the boys? Far from harming, she helped them; and they whom ruthless kinsfolk would have killed with their own hands were suckled by a wolf!'[5]

Nature's mercy admonishes humanity's unnatural cruelty: only a miracle of *kindness* can restore the imbalance created by human iniquity. From this experience the city may begin over again, refounded in the building of Rome.

There are other legendary parallels to Ivan's strange history. The stock of stories of abandoned infants certainly did not end with the fall of Rome; writers in the medieval period also witness in story wild animals that come to the rescue of such children. The folk tales of the period saw 'swan-children', and *Märchen* where children are suckled by a hind, or a goat, a lioness, a wolf, ravens, or even rats.[6] Sometimes the beast steals the child away from its human mother; in other tales a wild animal rescues the child from the outrages of human cruelty. In the popular romance *Octavian*, another set of twin boys is nurtured by, in one case, an ape, and in the other, a lioness. In the romance of *Sir Gowther*, a malignant child who tears his mother's nipple while feeding from her breast voluntarily chooses the wild life, and so suffers a penance of literally living out this wildness, as he is fed from the mouths of dogs while locked speechless in an atoning silence.[7]

The most famous such tale, however, was that of Valentine and Orson, twin boys lost in the forest, the children of outcast Bellyssant. One boy, Valentine, is quickly rescued and returned to civilization; while Orson, his brother, remains behind in the woods, where he is snatched by a bear and taken back to her lair to be fed to her cubs. There, 'God that never forgeteth his frendes shewed an evydent myracle.'[8] The bear-cubs, rather than devouring the baby, stroke it softly. The bear takes pity on the child and brings him up as one of her own.

All this reads like an old tale. The brothers separate: Valentine grows up civilized; Orson metamorphoses into that medieval bogeyman, the 'wild man'. Such wild men haunted the woods of medieval and Renaissance romance: irrational, carnivorous, danger-ous, untamed. They lived and died out in the wild woods, far from the sound of church bells; hairy as demons, or sometimes leafy; always solitary; moving alone through the wilderness; sometimes snatching children or, more often, women from the beleaguered villages; marauding, angry, violent, though (if tamed) useful and loyal servants to the wandering knights given up to adventure in the trackless forests. They were without speech.[9]

Valentine and Orson, the parted twins, meet, fight, recognize each other, are reunited. Perhaps stories such as this are fables of the necessity for civilization and the wild to be reconciled with each other. It is as though the contradictions that sustain each person – that tension between our primal, animal natures and our civilized, social selves – are here acted out, embodied in identical and yet utterly different selves. Hence, perhaps, why so many of these early myths are tales of twins: Amphion and Zethos, Romulus and Remus, Valentine and Orson. The wild man and the found child face each other as enemies and allies, as strangers and brothers.

Such wild men are the fictional ancestors of our real wild children; the genealogy of the feral child passes through them. The imaginative roots of the historical, documented cases we shall be exploring throughout this book are in these fables, these tales of miracles.

All these tales, from the Roman twins to Valentine and Orson, point to a fabulous order within the natural world. When, in North's translation, Plutarch described the giving up of Romulus and Remus to 'the mercy of fortune', we must accept this phrase in two distinct and contradictory senses. He both suggests with wry irony that there is no mercy in fortune and that this was precisely why the twins were left to its dark power, and yet he seems to affirm that there is indeed a miraculous compassion in the very order of things. This feeling for the marvellous is even clearer in the Christianized medieval forms of the 'wild child' story. Now a belief in the providential nature of the world is there, and the suffering of the abandoned child becomes a form of patience in which all wrongs will be righted, all crimes met with appropriate justice and the unlooked for addition of grace.

So these are the mythic and literary origins of the wild children, the spectral figures of folklore that stand behind the real figure of

Ivan, begging for food among Moscow's wild dogs; but what were the origins of my own interest in these children?

The impulse that drives any book is necessarily obscure even to the writer. Writing is often a matter of choosing not to inquire into one's own motivations: to learn the motive may remove the necessity for the writing of the work. Books grow best in the dark. Yet inevitably there are clues. Every child dreams of escape. As a child I was feckless, timid and hopelessly over-imaginative. What I imagined most of all was myself caught up in an adventure, often an intrepid quest, or on the run from danger. In these moods, abandonment meant being let loose. I saw an image of Romulus and Remus in a book of myths. It was the Capitoline Wolf, now in the Palazzo dei Conservatori, the standing she-wolf and the infant twins sitting up to suckle milk from her teats. I never forgot it. Then I read, as many children do, Rudyard Kipling's *The Jungle Books*, and fell in love with them. On the outskirts of Brighton, on the south coast of England, I longed to be Mowgli, alone yet animal-befriended in the Indian jungle. Saturday morning Tarzan films followed; I watched them and carried on dreaming.

Every child fears abandonment. The displaced, unspoken anxieties of family life fed those familiar, petty losses, the sense that home rested on insubstantial foundations – that my own presence there might go unrecognized, punishingly unnoticed – and if a fear of my own abandonment partly informs this book, a sense of a faltering relationship with someone implacably remote, then here is also the guilty terror of abandoning. Perhaps behind everything in this book is the desire to rescue someone lost, to restore the wounded-hearted, to look after another as though they were myself. Of course, these desires are immodest, self-aggrandizing, and ultimately futile. Yet they have the singular advantage to the writer of being shared by many of the 'heroes' of this book. My failing was their failing.

More substantially, one image from my own life echoes for me through the book. When I was myself a child, a little withdrawn and blushingly shy, my mother worked at a speech therapy clinic for young children. I would sometimes go with her to work, and sit and watch among the other children. All of them were silent, all of them somehow wrapped up in their own speechless worlds. Each child possessed the ability to speak; yet none of them ever did so. I can still see those quietened figures moving around the toys, the sand-pit, or splashing at the water basin. And I wonder how much of that silent playroom stole into this book.

At the end of my undergraduate career, I started, in a rather desultory way, a doctoral thesis on late-Victorian ghost stories. My chief reason for doing so was simply to avoid the dreary necessity of finding a job. I spent the first few years of my studies behaving exactly as a postgraduate student is supposed to: I stayed up, slept late, frequented cafés in the long afternoons, wrote an unpublish-able novel and an unperformable play, watched far too many old movies, and diligently avoided my supervisor. On principle, I never read any ghost stories.

Then, I took another look at *The Jungle Books*. To my surprise, I found that I still loved them, that they still moved me; and I won-dered if there were any real cases like Mowgli's. At that time I knew nothing about any of the children in this book, and the impulse to find out more might have died as soon as it was born, if it had not been for two things. Late one night, I watched François Truffaut's film, *L'Enfant Sauvage*, the story of Itard and Victor, the Wild Child of Aveyron. The film was elegant, beautiful, rationally delicate in its calm delineation of the central relationship between the young physician and the speechless wild child he sought to educate. It captivated me, agitated me: it woke me up.

Then, in a house in Ireland, a beautiful, ramshackle, irresponsible Georgian house, beneath the mountains and close to the sea, where I learnt more about living than I had ever done before, I was told a family story. Some decades before, one of the family, a wise and humorous woman, had been working as a district social worker in the Northern Irish countryside. As part of her work she had been involved in a strange and disturbing case. A young boy had been kept, almost from birth I was told, in a hen-house. He had grown up there, among the chickens, never learning language, never having much human contact, never receiving love – a silent, strange, nightmarish world.

It caught me. I changed the topic of my dissertation, and began proper research, working on in London and, for a while, at Harvard; but it was nine years before I finally met, face to face, a wild child, like Ivan, or Victor, or Romulus, or Orson, or the henhouse boy.

I thought he would look like everyone else. Even though by then I'd read all the books, knew every story off by heart, I hadn't quite believed that there would be this unquantifiable, unmistakable difference. But I was wrong: I knew him instantly, picked him out the moment I walked into the room. He was sitting with the others, on the rows of new wooden chairs, just there on the other side. In a moment he sensed that I was looking at him and shot me a troubled, suspicious glance – the look of someone all too used to being stared at. It disturbed me, that look of his. Was it just that I was foreign to him – strange, threatening, linked only with those who sought to question or verify his seemingly unbelievable story? There was a challenge in that glance, a question that I wasn't sure I could justifiably answer. Suddenly shy, I dropped my gaze and did not look at him again for a long time.

On the face of things, he was the one who should have been feeling strange and out of place. Instead it seemed to be me that was ill at ease and absurdly, inappropriately uncomfortable. The area of London was one I hardly knew: a conglomeration of wide arterial roads, where forlornly faded nineteenth-century houses seemed lost and desperate among blank-faced modern buildings, ceaseless traffic, and the loose skeins of dust and litter blown about by a fierce, sunshiny autumnal wind.

I knew the church where I would find him was down a ramshackle side road of houses converted into cheap flats. Here, off the main road, the wind dropped and there, just along the street, was an imposing church of municipal Gothic. Was this the place? On the steps young women in brilliant orange robes and Nike trainers sprawled with their cigarettes in the Sunday afternoon quietness. 'The Destiny Church?' No; this wasn't it. They pointed to an alleyway across the road. The place I wanted was over there.

Eventually I found it: a concrete-and-brick sixties-looking community centre, all frosted windows meshed with wire, orange plastic signs, graffiti and drifting piles of dried-up leaves. I tried the ground-floor public hall. No – the place I wanted was upstairs. A walkway curved round and upwards, over the tarmac front with hopscotch squares and teenage messages promising romance chalked on it. So, here was the place – a plain, unadorned room filled with natural light, with rows of chairs, a microphone at the front, a space for the church band – just like those solidly unpretentious, drearily functional baptist church halls where I'd spent my childhood but which I hadn't set foot in for over twenty years. All was just as it had been: just the same scent of Bibles and paint, that same atmosphere of quiet piety, those same blue shirts and ties, those floral dresses; the same hatted, elderly women, the same bored, awkwardly reverent youths – and there, in the sudden force of reminiscence, I scanned the room and, without hesitation or doubt, knew that I had found him.

I had been thinking about him for nearly nine years, although I'd only heard of him a few months before. It was impossible not to see echoes in him of those others that I had only read about, and each moment I found myself fighting against an insidious double take in which he – this particular boy, sitting there in the crowded pew of a Ugandan church in south London – threatened to vanish, absorbed by those ancestral ghosts: Peter the Wild Boy, the Savage Girl, the Wild Boy of Aveyron, Kaspar Hauser. So I sat in the church and watched him where he sat, there among the other orphans.

The service began. The pastor rose to his feet. David Kateeba is a neat, self-possessed man; talking to him on the phone I had pictured a late-middle-aged patriarch, a massive and imperturbable point of masculine calm. I was surprised to find him young and slight in build, as though in our brief conversation I had glimpsed some possible future for him rather the person that he actually was. The small crowd hushed while the pastor welcomed Paul and Molly Wasswa and their orphans, the Pearl of Africa Choir. A murmur of welcome passed around the room. The pastor's sister rose to her feet and led the congregation in a song praising God for beloved Africa; she dedicated the song to me, a visitor to their church. It was my turn to feel the centre of attention; self-consciously I nodded my thanks and tried to join in, untunefully, with the singing.

We sat down again, and Paul Wasswa walked to the front of the church. He really did look as I had imagined the pastor would. Broad-shouldered, confident, strongly handsome, he seemed the very epitome of authority. He nodded to his daughter and his wife Molly, beautiful as a model, sitting there in the front row; and with conscious dignity, he began to tell the story of John Ssabunnya, the boy that I had come to see.

John is an orphan, just fourteen years old, and apparently like the other 1500 or so children who live in the Kamuzinda Christian Orphanage run by Paul and Molly Wasswa. Uganda is a country of orphans, children left without parents following the ravages of war and AIDS. That John's parents were both dead was almost a commonplace fact in such a world. Yet John is not quite an orphan like those others.

Eleven years before, in 1988, John's father had murdered his mother in the family's little house. John had fled the hut, running off into the bush. In normal circumstances, he would probably have died there; too frightened to go home, too young to survive in the wilds on his own. But John had not died. Instead, perhaps something miraculous had happened. Paul Wasswa told us that a family of monkeys had found and fed John, taking him into the group, nurturing him, saving him. For three years he had lived there among the monkeys, eating their food, acting according to the rules of their family. Then, in 1991, John had been discovered by local villagers, captured, and taken to the Wasswas' orphanage. There, through the kindness and care of Paul, Molly and their family, John had recovered from his ordeal, had been reclaimed for God, restored to the happiness of human community.

Paul Wasswa knew what John's story meant: here was the evidence of the curious proving of God's love. Love had preserved John in the bush; love had brought him back into the human fold. Paul Wasswa himself seemed for that moment a man touched by the love of God: the meaning was Love, he was saying; and the congregation in that little church hall murmured back its approval. Yes, the meaning was love.

The congregation was there to worship; but why was I there? I had come to look at a boy who might perhaps have been brought up by monkeys. Had I turned the church into a freak-show? Was my curiosity at fault? Was I a voyeur or a witness?

The choir began to sing – John taking the solo part – standing out even then from the warm faces of the chorus. Unfairly, I thought how there seemed a kind of showiness about him – an all-too-understandable teenage self-consciousness. He, after all, was the centre of attention; people must have been looking at him curiously, with expectation, for as long as he could remember. Was it simply this that had made me notice him so quickly? I began to rethink my impression of him. Suddenly he seemed knowing, a little full of himself. Could his story even be true?

John was the star. His name had appeared everywhere in the British press; he had appeared on national news; a BBC documentary dedicated to his story had been shown on television only the week before. It would be a strange teenager whose head was not turned a little by such intense interest. Yet for a moment John seemed to relish the eyes upon him, was clearly loving his moment playing to the crowd. Only he had not liked my eyes upon him. His first look of distrust and strange suspicion came back to me. There was, after all, something beyond expectation about him, something unidentifiably odd, for which those three years in the bush living with the monkeys might be the right, the amazing justification.

It was hard to think of what his life must have been like – his parents dead, and him abandoned, alone. With such a background, what right had I to judge his reaction to his own fame? And this fame was, after all a welcome, unaccountable gift. Without John's uniqueness, how much interest would the world have taken in the plight of those 1500 other orphans, forgotten and far away, the victims of a plague that most wanted to ignore, in a country and a continent that seem synonymous with the extremes of human suffering?

Yet that was not why I was there. Voyeur or witness, I had come to see John because of what might be true about him. I had come to see a living wild child.

Everyone I told about the meeting asked me the same question: did I think his story was true? It did seem far-fetched. In the weeks following the screening of the documentary about John, a controversy was thrashed out in the pages of the BBC's *Ariel* on-line magazine and in the *BBC Forum*. Ian Garrard, assistant web producer of *Science*, wrote about the programme's 'flimsy proof'; Tony Todd of Radio Merseyside talked of its 'embarrassing approach'. The editor of *Living Proof* (the series in which the documentary had been shown) was moved to defend the programme in the same letters pages.

Yet such stories are not necessarily impossible, and John Ssabunnya is far from the only such child to have made headlines around the world in the last few centuries, as Ivan Mishukov's story shows. This book will trace those other stories – wild Peter, poor Memmie Le Blanc, Victor of Aveyron, Kaspar Hauser, the wolf-girls of India, and sad Genie – and through these tales perhaps another narrative will emerge, the fragmented and haunting story of our continuing relationship with the savage image of ourselves.

CHAPTER TWO

Bodies Without Souls

I: An Unnatural Nursing

The same unnaturall nursing had Cyrus, the same incredible fostering had
Semiramis, the one by a Bitch, the other by Birds.
  Sir Walter Raleigh, *The History of the World*

Nothing separates us so much from the past as our inability to
believe in wonders. Caught in the web of a strange magic, the wandering courtiers of Shakespeare's *The Tempest* seem to encounter
curious and monstrous islanders, and old Gonzalo remarks to the
Duke how things that seemed improbable to earlier generations are
being proved daily by travellers' reports. Now that we turn to our
first fully documented account of a wild child, it is well to remind
ourselves just how easily tales of the miraculous might once have
been believed. Peter the Wild Boy, a silent and savage child, an
inhabitant of cold Germanic woods, came to London in the spring
of 1726. Only one year after his arrival news of a wonderful birth
gripped the capital: a woman, Mary Toft, was said by reliable
observers to have given birth to a warren of rabbits.

It is hard now to see how anyone could ever have given credit to
such stories, and we recoil slightly from the extravagance of such
gullibility. Everyone knows now that no fantasy is quite innocent.
Our irony and our self-possession intact, we sense how belief in the
incredible only exposes us, and flinch from such exposure as from
the recounting of a troubled and repellent dream. Yet what have we
lost in committing ourselves so tepidly to probabilities? The sense
of the marvellous imbues that apparently so rational eighteenth-
century world. The need that such tales fulfilled might still hunger
inside us. In reading, then, of Peter the Wild Boy, we must first
imagine ourselves back to a world where the marvellous was so

commonplace that it could turn with ease into a high-spirited joke. For all those who wrote of Peter transmuted his story into an occasion for frivolity. Yet it would be our shallowness, the sign of just how engrained our scepticism is, to see such wit as a sign of disbelief. Only in one instance (though it is a telling one) did anyone express a doubt concerning the truth of the tale of Peter. Such a miracle of survival, such a challenge to accepted notions of the self and its place in society, hardly stirred the majestic complacency of their world. There the boy was – that was all – like a lost son in a fantastic tale; and so all questions concerning him could turn at once to other matters. No one felt the need for verification. Those who would pay money to see a dead Indian would fall at once for a savage European, scrutinizing either with an equally fervid and transient wonder.

We have travelled down a long road, stretching from Voltaire to Richard Dawkins and beyond, and each step of the way we have scratched out some miracle. Yet are we so different from those witnesses who once beheld Peter, who, in the court of a king, watched his buffoonish tricks with civilized delight?

In the summer when I was writing this book, I visited a Protestant chapel in the once fashionably shabby area of London that lies north of Notting Hill. It was a Sunday, but the chapel was empty. It had been empty, in fact, for many years, a sad relic of that same declining faith in the miraculous and the wonderful. Yet the building, not quite abandoned, had been brought back to life for a few weeks by an arts group, and an exhibition was in progress.

The interior of the white-fronted building was murkily dark after the brightness of the June afternoon outside. I walked over the space where the congregation had once prayed, and a guide took a torch and, walking ahead, led me up winding steel steps in a narrow stairwell where the dirty white walls pressed close. The stairway opened out on to a darkened room lit feebly by blue attic windows; but in the centre of the room, among long wires hanging from the spokes of an overhead wheel, a brighter light cast crazy shadows on the bare floor. The room was full of murmuring voices, a babel of strange beliefs; for at the end of each wire hung a round-framed, cross-shaped speaker. I walked into the circle and, one after another, pressed the speakers to my ear: in each one a story was being told, tale after tale – from Plymouth, Northumberland, Wisconsin, Provence: from practically anywhere – of flying saucers and meetings with aliens from distant worlds.

Each story was perhaps the defining moment of a life, but one somehow too fantastic to be fitted into the ordinary shape of things. Somehow those endlessly looped monologues telling their tales over and over indicated the double predicament of our removal from the people who met the Wild Boy. Yes, we too believe in wonders – in aliens, table-tappings, telekinesis, out-of-body experiences, ghosts and monsters. Yet such marvels are distinct from the frame of our lives: wonder has departed from the universe and instead become localized, individual and therefore insignificant. For those earliest witnesses of the wild child the miraculous still pointed to a greater miracle that was everywhere, though the seeds of our own mechanical and senseless universe were being first sown right then.

However, Peter the Wild Boy wasn't the first savage child to receive the attention of wondering and rational inquirers. In the later seventeenth century, the new impetus for experimental science (or 'natural philosophy', as it was then called) had already begun to impact upon the long-prevailing mythic and fabulous approach to the wild child. Philosophers and writers began to describe what they saw in plain terms, and therefore, for the first time, we find factual accounts of wild children.

Sir Kenelm Digby's account of 'John of Liège' is the first such consideration in English of a wild child. Digby is a typically outré and extravagant seventeenth-century character – a noted philosopher and literary critic, his chief fame now rests on his marriage to the infamous Venetia, whose death he is supposed to have accidentally caused by having her drink snake's venom in the belief that it would preserve her beauty. When not engaged in such activities, Digby was a keen philosopher, and it is in a philosophical work on the relation between body and soul published in 1644 that he presents the story of John of Liège. During the religious wars in Europe, John, a young boy, fled with his fellow villagers into the nearby woods. When the soldiers finally left the area, the villagers returned to their homes, but John,

> being of a very timorous nature, had images of feare so stronge in his fansie; that first, he ranne further into the wood than any of the rest; and afterwardes apprehended that every body he saw through the thickets, and every voyce he hearde was the souldiers: and so hidd himselfe from his parents, that were in much distresse seeking him all about, and calling his name as loud as they could.[1]

Not finding him, his parents returned to the village, and John remained alone in the woods for many years, living on roots and wild fruits. In the woods, John's senses sharpened; he could scent food from improbably great distances. He lived in this way until one very sharp winter, he was forced to steal food from the outlying houses in his village:

> He could not do this so cunningly, but that returning often to it, he was upon a time espyed: and they who saw a beast of so strange a shape (for such they tooke him to be; he being naked and all ouer growne with haire) beleeving him to be a satyre, or some such prodigious creature as the recounters of rare accidents tell us of; layed wayte to apprehend him. But he that winded them as farre off, as any beast could do, still avoyded them, till att the length, they layed snares for him; and tooke the wind so advanta-giously of him, that they caught him: and then, soone perceived

he was a man; though he had quite forgotten the use of all language: but by his gestures and cryes, he expressed the greatest
affrightednesse that might be.[2]

Digby only hears of wild John; Bernard Connor meets his savage
boys face to face. Connor, a young Irishman, and the private doctor
to the King of Poland, published *Medicina Mystica* in 1697, a work
describing how the miracles of scripture might accord with the
apparently unchanging nature of scientific truth. This book briefly
mentions wild children, and Connor returned to the subject at
greater length in his next work, *The History of Poland* (1698).

Here Connor describes several wild children, among them a
Lithuanian bear-boy, who was found in what was then a wild,
remote and forested province of Poland. The abduction of children
by bears was popularly thought to be a common occurrence in this
region. In a Polish convent Connor himself saw a boy supposedly
brought up by bears:

He was about ten Years of Age (which might be guessed only by
his Stature and Aspect) of a hideous Countenance, and had neither the use of Reason, nor Speech: He went upon all four, and
had nothing in him like a Man, except his Human Structure: But
seeing he resembled a Rational Creature, he was admitted to the
Font, and christen'd; yet still he was restless and uneasy, and
often inclined to flight.[3]

Here the Irish physician hits every note habitually struck by early
witnesses to such wild children. Is the boy human or not human
('nothing in him like a Man')? A soul to be saved, or a creature outside the body of Christendom?

Connor tells how the child was trained to stand upright 'by clap-
ping up his Body against a Wall, and holding him after the manner
that Dogs are taught to beg . . . '[4] The boy was successfully taught to
speak a little, 'but being ask'd concerning his course of Life in the

Woods, he could not give much better account of it, than we can do of our Actions in the Cradle'.[5] Lack of language buries his experience in forgetfulness.

Connor also presents an earlier case, reported to him in a letter from J. P. Van den Brande de Cleverskerk, the Dutch Ambassador to London, relating to a boy he had seen in 1661:

Coming to this City of Poland with design to be Present at the Election of a King after John Casimir, who had abdicated the Crown, I enquir'd what was worth seeing in or about this Place: whereupon I was inform'd, among other things, that there was in the Suburbs of the City (which go towards King Casimir's Palace) in a Nunnery, a certain Male Child, who had been brought up among Bears, and who had been taken some time before at a Bear-hunting. Upon this Information I went immediately to that place to satisfy my Curiosity, where I found the aforesaid Boy playing under the Pent-house before the Nunnery Gate. His Age, as well as I remember, I guess'd to be about twelve or thirteen. As soon as I came near him he leap'd towards me as if surpriz'd and pleas'd with my Habit. First, he caught one of my Silver Buttons in his hand with a great deal of eagerness, which he held up to his Nose to smell; Afterwards he leap'd all of a sudden into a Corner, where he made a strange sort of Noise not unlike Howling. I went into the House, where a Maid-servant inform'd me more particularly of the Manner of his being taken. But having not with me the Book wherein I wrot [sic] my observations in my Travels, I cannot possibly give you an exact Account of it. This Maid call'd the Boy in, and show'd him a good large piece of Bread; which when he saw, he immediately leap'd upon a Bench that was joyn'd to the Wall of the Room, where he walk'd about upon all-four: After which, he rais'd himself upright with a great Spring, and took the Bread in his two Hands, put it up to his Nose, and afterwards leap'd off from the Bench upon the Ground, making the same

> odd sort of Noise as before. I was told that he was not yet brought to speak, but that they hop'd in short time he would, having his Hearing good. He had some Scars on his Face, which were commonly thought to be Scratches of the Bears.[6]

Cleverskerk conjectures that the fates of such children are the result of raids by the marauding Tartars, in which parents are taken into slavery before they are able to save their children.

The ambassador's account of his meeting with the wild child provides a fascinating example of the conditions in which these wild children were at first approached. That he goes to see the boy at all confirms an obvious curiosity concerning such children; however, it is clear that Cleverskerk, unlike later witnesses, visits the child in a state of mind that is comparatively empty of expectations. The boy is for him simply a traveller's 'curiosity'. Such 'curiosities' would then have included natural phenomena and sites of cultural interest or beauty, such as a volcano, a grotto, or a physic garden; but in the case of human beings the term 'curiosity' meant freaks of nature, those individuals marked out by the extraordinary. The ambassador is simply sightseeing in a manner that remains remarkably fixed throughout the various accounts of wild children; but, as often happens with visits to such children, the bear-boy quickly turns the tables on his visitor, transforming the civilized observer himself into an object of curiosity.

Connor offers one more wild child for our attention. In 1669, two children were surprised by huntsmen in the woods of Poland. One of the children escaped the hunters, but the other was trapped and taken to Warsaw. There he was christened Joseph, and attempts were made to educate him:

> He was about twelve or thirteen years old, as might be guest by his height, but his Maners were altogether bestial; for he not only fed upon raw Flesh, wild Honey, Crab-Apples, and such like Dainties which Bears are us'd to feast with, but also went, like them, upon

all-four. After his Baptism he was not taught to go upright without a great deal of difficulty, and there was less hope of ever making him learn the *Polish* Language, for he always continu'd to express his Mind in a kind of Bear-like Tone. Some time after King *Casimir* made a Present of him to *Peter Adam Opalinski*, Vice-Chamberlain of *Posnan*, by whom he was employ'd in the Offices of his Kitchin, as to carry Wood, Water, &c but yet could never be brought to relinquish his native Wildness, which he retain'd to his dying-day; for he would often go into the Woods amongst the Bears, and freely keep company with them without any fear, or harm done him, being, as was suppos'd, constantly acknowledg'd for their Fosterling.[7]

Wildness has reduced the boy to an inhuman level, and yet an almost magical belonging in the company of bears recompenses his human losses, his roughness, maladroitness, and wild incomprehensibility. Among the bears, his subhuman status, signalled most clearly by his becoming a gift between a king and a politician, is healed into a relationship that is free of fear and coercion.

As Connor closes these brief accounts, mere interludes in a work primarily devoted to political and historical matters, he declares that perhaps 'the History of *Romulus* and *Remus* is not so fabulous as it is generally conjectured to be'.[8] He remarks that such stories touch on 'Philosophical Matters', and alludes to his earlier discussion of innate Ideas in *Medicina Mystica*. Yet Connor effectively passes up the chance of initiating the philosophical speculation that would transform the subject. That was an opportunity not grasped until the late 1720s, with the arrival of Peter the Wild Boy in the royal palaces of London.

II: Mere Nature

It would indeed be a terrible Satyr upon the present inspir'd Age, first to
allow this Creature to have a Soul, and to have Power of thinking . . . he
should see it reasonable to chuse to continue silent and mute, to live and
converse with the Quadrupeds of the Forest, and retire again from human
Society, rather than dwell among the inform'd Part of Mankind; for it must
be confess'd he takes a Leap in the Light, if he has Eyes to see it, to leap
from the Woods to the Court; from the Forest among Beasts, to the
Assembly among the Beauties; from the Correction House at Zell, (where,
at best, he had convers'd among the meanest of the Creation, viz the Alms-
taking Poor, or the Vagabond Poor) to the Society of all the Wits and Beaus
of the Age . . .

    Daniel Defoe, *Mere Nature Delineated*[9]

The story begins with a witness, and the only private record of the
marvel in the midst of the city. In London, on the evening of 16 April
1726, Jonathan Swift finally went to one of the Prince and Princess of
Wales's hectic open evenings at Leicester House, at the north of the
square known as Leicester Fields (now Leicester Square). It was
there, among the chic and the artfully gracious, that Swift first
encountered the Wild Boy.

    The ostensible object of his visit was to meet Caroline, the plump
Princess of Wales, an energetic collector of European intellectuals
who had long had her acquisitive eye on Swift. (She had befriended
Handel; Leibniz, Isaac Newton's mathematical rival, often saw her
for long, chatty, philosophical discussions; and Swift's friends the
writers Pope and Gay were frequent visitors.) Since his coming to
London from Ireland one month before, Caroline had courted Swift
through the intermediary of her physician and his old friend, Dr
John Arbuthnot. Caroline sent for him – as many as eleven times,
Swift later claimed – but on each occasion he politely declined the
invitation and refused to make the short journey to swanky
Leicester House. Perhaps Swift enjoyed being wooed; perhaps he
had long since acquired the perverse pride of the insufficiently

rewarded. He had been an outsider too long not to relish such an emphatic social triumph.

But on the evening of the 16th, after these long preliminaries, the introduction was a real success, Swift behaving with his customary elegant self-deprecation: he had been informed, he told the Princess, that she loved to see odd persons, and that having sent for a Wild Boy from Germany, she had a curiosity to see a Wild Dean from Ireland.[10]

It was a Saturday night: on Sunday, Monday, Wednesday and Friday the young royals had to attend King George's arid open evenings at the rival palace of St James's. Tuesday, Thursday and Saturday were their own days to entertain. On returning from the elegant mayhem of the royal party, Swift sat down alone in his lodgings in Bury Street and wrote a letter to his Irish friend, Thomas Tickell. Tickell was about to be married and, perhaps fortuitously, was therefore to come into a large property in County Kildare brought him by Clotilda Eustace, his bride-to-be.[11] Swift wrote:

I am here now a Month, picking up a Remnant of my old Acquaintance, and descending to take new ones. Your People are very civil to me, and I meet a thousand times better Usage from them than from that Denomination in Ireland. [Tickell's 'people' are the Whigs. Swift refers here to party schisms: a great Tory himself, he had recently dined with Walpole, the arch-Whig and infamous corrupt politician.] This night I saw the wild Boy, whose arrivall here hath been the subject of half our Talk this fortnight. He is in the keeping of Dr Arbuthnot, but the King and Court were so entertained with him, that the Princess could not get him till now. I can hardly think him wild in the Sense that they report him.[12]

So Swift did not think him wild in the sense that was said of him. It is perhaps fitting that the finest purveyor of wonder that year in

London, the man who wrote the tale of a traveller tied down on an island where pygmies no more than four inches high lived, should be the one person to our certain knowledge to introduce a note of doubt into the story. Yet Swift writes '*our* Talk'; so that spring the Wild Boy had been the focus of attention for the brightest and sharpest wits of the Augustan period – that is, Swift and his friends: Alexander Pope, the midget poet; John Arbuthnot, the Scottish physician who had the boy in his care; the ambitious and witty playwright, John Gay; and the once disgraced statesman, Bolingbroke. The boy had strayed from the dark, silent forests of Hanover to the core of both fashionable and intellectual English life.

In a smaller way, Swift himself had made such another journey, in his case from 'exile' in his native country of Ireland back to the London where he had, thirteen years previously, been one of the established literary and political figures of the day. Not that Swift's influence had diminished while away: his writings on Irish affairs had made him a hero in that country and a thorn in the side of the English establishment. As Dean of St Patrick's, Swift now lived a retired but sociable life, exaggerating the hardships of Dublin both to himself and to his friends in comfortable London and Surrey.

These friends, in particular Arbuthnot, had been trying to persuade Swift to return to London for years, foreseeing the old gang reunited again 'like mariners after a storm'. Maybe it was the recent completion of his masterpiece, *Gulliver's Travels*, that prompted Swift finally to make the trip. Also he felt old: increasingly deaf, his ears filled with a continual noise as of rolling oceans, he both treasured and feared an encroaching isolation. He needed his friends, while clearly preferring them at the controlled distance of a correspondence. His letters to London prior to his arrival express both unease and impatience for the much-deferred meeting. Yet time was passing and death was increasingly on his mind: in late September 1725 he wrote to Pope in the midst of a severe illness of John Arbuthnot's: 'Mr Lewis sent me an account of Dr Arbuthnot's illness, which is a very sensible affliction to me, who by living so long out of the world have lost that hardness of heart contracted by years and general conversation. I am daily losing friends, and neither seeking nor getting others.' The idea that living in society hardens one to sensitive feeling is a typically Swiftian aside: since youth La Rochefoucauld, the prince of cynics, had been Swift's literary master.

He arrived in London around 16 March, and settled into his lodgings at Bury Street, next door to the Royal Chair. Pope joined him on the 20th, and over the next few days Swift travelled the countryside around London, making short visits at the houses of the arrogant Lord Chesterfield and the Tory politician William Pulteney. He saw Bolingbroke at his country estate at Dawley (near Uxbridge), a centre of Tory opposition to Whig rule, and then went to stay briefly with Pope at Twickenham. Soon he was back in London, and the object of those continuing requests from Arbuthnot and the Princess of Wales to visit her at Leicester House. So it was that on 16 April he responded at last and thus met the curious Wild Boy.

Arbuthnot had named him Peter – Peter the Wild Boy. They had found him in the woods near Hameln in Hanover, either at high summer or at Christmas time. As we shall see, the Christmas dating may be a mythic interpolation: as we have already noted, the wild child could be linked to the birth of a god; also children born at Christmas were popularly felt to be uncanny. Much of what we know about Peter is just as confused and uncertain as this. Was he found sucking milk from a cow in the fields, or caught roaming wild in the forests, trapped by hunters in the hollow of a tree, cracking nuts and eating acorns? Had he really lived on a diet of herbs and nuts (by some accounts, grass and moss)? Where had he come from? Was he left by gypsies who had passed that way some twelve years before? The only certain thing was that there he was – naked, dark-haired, tanned by constant exposure to the sun. Completely silent, he could tell them nothing of himself or of his history.

They reckoned him to be between twelve and fifteen years old. He was taken to the House of Correction at the nearby town of Zell, and from there brought by the House's Intendant to the Herrenhausen, King George I of Great Britain's court in Hanover and the summer residence of the royal family (suggesting that it *was* most probably July when the boy was found), a grand, imposing palace built in conscious imitation of Versailles. At dinner the boy was led before the King, and George placed him, with a napkin tied to his throat, at the table, to see how he would eat: 'He had no notion of behaviour, or manners, but greedily took with his hands out of the dishes, what he liked best, such as asparagus, or other garden-things, and after a little time, he was ordered to be taken away, by reason of his daubing undecent behaviour.'[13]

In the following spring of 1726, Peter the Wild Boy came to London, where he lived for a time with George I in St James's Palace, the King's usual winter residence. (Whitehall Palace had been burnt down in 1698 and there still wasn't enough money to rebuild it; St James's was a poor and unspectacular substitute.) Once in London, the Wild Boy rapidly became the object of an intense rivalry between the King and his son and daughter-in-law.

Father and son stood anyway in uneasy opposition – a traditional stand-off between youth and age in the royal politics of the period. The King resided in boring splendour at St James's; his son and daughter-in-law held court only a short distance across London at prestigious Leicester House. The court was the fulcrum of social advance: here a select group met, flirted, plotted, promised and deceived. St James's was impeccably dull, and it was now the young royals who drew the crowd – a situation that probably pleased George I, who longed to escape from the limelight of monarchy.

The King was a private, shy man, honest but tedious, clumsily kind in his unregal reticence; he was short, and slim in build – his lean figure being the consequence of much riding and his preference for walking. His son George, the Prince of Wales, is in many ways a less attractive figure: fiery in temperament and dull in understanding. Famously stupid, he was, on principle, uninterested in literature and philosophy. However, the bright, quick-witted presence of his wife Caroline leavened his lumpen, aristocratic boorishness. Some nineteen years before when first married, young George had stuck by her as she suffered the ravages of smallpox, at that time an unconventional act of kindness. Their courtship had been similarly unorthodox. The young George, anxious to get a glimpse of his future wife, had gone to see her in disguise as 'Monsieur de Busch', and romantically fell in love with her during the masquerade.

Since their marriage he had followed the more customary path of taking a mistress, in this case Henrietta Howard, the wife of Henry Howard, an irritable, dissolute drunk. Yet Caroline and Henrietta, an attractive, lively woman of George's own age, got on well with each other and the affair was amiably indulged.

On his first appearance at St James's Palace, on the night of Friday 8 April, Peter the Wild Boy charmed the assembled company. The King held court to visiting ambassadors in his apartments in the palace, in a fine stateroom with a rich canopy; but less formal occasions were generally held in the Great Drawing Room, where the nobility and ministers would meet, and where strangers could come to ogle the King, his son and daughter-in-law and their young children.[14] That night Peter was dressed in a bright-blue suit (despite his aversion to all clothing) and carried into this drawing room before the King and the young royals. There the Wild Boy played with a glove of Caroline's; grew fascinated by a pocket watch that struck the hours; and, as was usual with him, attempted some minor pick-pocketing. Gossips outside the court speculated as to what else had gone on that evening. The ladies in waiting, maliciously suspected to be disappointed that Peter was too young for an intrigue, were supposedly nonetheless amused to see him attempt to kiss the young Lady Walpole, the plain-featured daughter of the immensely

fat and continually scheming politican Robert Walpole. Furthermore, rumours spread that he had, in breach of all civilized deco-
rum, seized the Lord Chamberlain's staff and put his hat on before
the King. The boy fascinated Caroline: she made up her mind that
she would get Peter from her father-in-law and install him at
Leicester House. For a week the King hesitated to comply with her
wish: he too enjoyed the boy's company, and his antics provided
welcome relief in the formal and stultifying atmosphere of the
palace. At last he relented, and Peter made the short journey from
the Mall to the West End.

So there was Peter in the midst of these royal plots and this mod-
ish life. He was straight-backed and upright in posture; his dark-
brown hair was thick and bushy; his eyes roved endlessly, without
rest; yet he was of a merry disposition and laughed frequently.[15] A
healed wound on his left hand had left the middle and fourth fingers
welded together like the webbing of a duck's foot. Caroline dressed
him up in courtly clothes, in a coat of forest-green faced with red,
with scarlet stockings; by now fine clothes delighted him. At nights,
however, he could not be made to sleep in a bed, but instead would
go and lie in a corner of the room.[16]

Either on his arrival or, more likely, on his move to Leicester
House, the Wild Boy was put in the charge of Dr John Arbuthnot,
Swift's close friend. It is hard to think of a happier choice for a tutor.
Arbuthnot was a convivial, gently sarcastic man, an easy scholar, a
careless wit, an indiscreet gossip, an industrious player of cards and
a slouching walker. His mind worked in wayward flashes and he set
no great store by his literary achievements, letting ideas and jests
slip from him with negligent abundance. Famously vague and inat-
tentive in company, he meandered through social life in a pleasant
and concealing mist of happy inconsequentiality. He ate glut-
tonously and without remorse. A Scotsman, a physician and a
friend of the best writers of his day, as well as a writer himself,
Arbuthnot lived an enviably ordered life, surrounded by his family,

bolstered by his religion, and diversified by his wit. Cheerfulness kept breaking in; characteristically he once wrote to Swift: 'I really think there is no such good reason for living till seventy, as curiosity.' Yet the appearance of the humorous observer must mask a quiet, unignorable ambition: the genuinely retired do not end up by becoming physician to two queens. Arbuthnot was one of those men who advance on the merit of being a good fellow, a still point of genuine lightness on which the more strained stoicism of his friend Pope, or the good-humoured bile of Swift, could rest. Though once again appearances may be deceptive: for his friendship with Swift to have developed, Arbuthnot must have understood something of the other man's innate misanthropy from within.

Arbuthnot shared with Swift, and with the other writers of his circle – even we might say with the culture in which he lived – a desultory, deprecatory habit of self-portrayal. As with Pope's famous poem addressing him, 'An Epistle to Dr Arbuthnot', with its ironic self-descriptions and its poses ('this long Disease, my Life', 'I lisp'd in numbers'), Arbuthnot's own letters often involve the same indulgence:

> As for your humble servant, with a great stone in his right kidney, and a family of men and women to provide for, he is as cheerful as ever in public affairs . . . He never rails at a great man, but to his face; which I can assure you, he has had both the opportunity and licence to do. He has some few weak friends, and fewer enemies; if any, he is low enough to be rather despised than pushed at by them. I am faithfully, dear Sir, your affectionate humble servant,

J. ARBUTHNOTT.

The mixture of playful self-pity and proud self-assertion here is typical. Arbuthnot wore a mask even in the closest of friendships.

In the summer of 1711, when Swift and Arbuthnot first met, their
relationship appeared simple; the two men dined together often as
part of the literary, satirical group, the Scriblerus Club (other members including the same inner circle of Pope, Gay and the poet
Thomas Parnell) or rode together around Windsor Park, flirting
with Queen Anne's young maids of honour. Yet a strange, mutual
insecurity marks their friendship. Their correspondence echoes
with expressions of yearning, repeated protestations of continuing
affection; a needy doubt about themselves and the other joined
with the strongest declarations of admiration. Arbuthnot was
Swift's exact contemporary: both were born in 1667 and were near
the end of an unillusioned middle-age at the time when they were
introduced to the strange figure of the Wild Boy. However,
Arbuthnot had other simpler friendships: he knew Handel well and
enjoyed a general acquaintance with the best society in London and
Bath. The overall impression is of a complex man himself reclining
upon, even hiding within, the honourable pose of an effortlessly
congenial bonhomie.

Despite Arbuthnot's professed delight in curiosity he revealingly
wrote nothing of his involvement in educating the Wild Boy. For
this reason, our knowledge of their relationship is sketchy and
dependent upon the insecure authority of contemporary pamphlets. These tell us that he attempted to teach the boy language by
instructing him how to mouth the letters of the alphabet, and then
endeavouring to join these isolated sounds together.[17] Unsurprisingly,
perhaps, this method (if it was even used) appears to have gone
nowhere: Peter never did learn to speak for himself, although he
could, in time, pronounce words of one syllable at Arbuthnot's
prompting.

The Wild Boy seems to have lived with Arbuthnot for at least part
of his stay in London: on Thursday 5 July, Peter was baptized at
Arbuthnot's house near Burlington Gardens. We learn that
Arbuthnot was uncharacteristically strict with the boy; restraining

his 'Passions of Mind' by fear, and correcting him by striking his legs with a broad leather strap.[18] This may not fit our image of the gentle Scottish doctor, but it makes perfect sense in the context of child-rearing within the period. In any case, Arbuthnot's methods may have had some limited success: in those first months at Leicester House Peter learnt to fetch and carry by rote, to greet people by making a bow and kissing his fingers in imitation of the faddish beaus of the day.[19] Such accomplishments were, no doubt, improvements; but what did Arbuthnot or the other wits and writers of the day actually make of Peter? What thoughts might that fortnight's talk of him have led to?

III: The History of Silence

He is now, as I have said, in a State of Meer Nature, and that, indeed, in the literal Sense of it. Let us delineate his Condition, if we can: He seems to be the very Creature which the learned World have, for many Years past, pretended to wish for, viz. one that being kept entirely from human Society, so as never to have heard any one speak, must therefore either not speak at all, or, if he did form any Speech to himself, then they should know what Language Nature would first form for Mankind.

    Daniel Defoe, *Mere Nature Delineated*

The spring and summer of 1726 were a period of calm unease. Rumours of imminent war in Europe spread unchecked, and the sense that peace was fragile pushed stocks down and slowed trade. London life was its usual orderly chaos. Where to walk was a preoccupation: the streets were perpetually muddy, and to avoid being splashed everyone wanted to walk close by the wall and furthest from the road, creating an elaborate etiquette of whom one should 'give the wall to'. The busiest streets were the dirtiest, but also the safest: alleys were quieter, cleaner and emptier at night – and hence more dangerous. The London squares too were hazardous places after dark: the threat of assault was perhaps even greater then than it is now. The Thames was the true heart of the town: the quickest way to cross London was still by boat, though one had to risk the rudeness of the watermen, who were popularly reputed to be irrepressible con-men.

Each evening there was, as now, a rush hour as the workers went home in the evening twilight. Each evening, they would head back to their districts: in the east dwelt the sailors and dockers and their families; the urban poor congregated east of the city walls and in the area around the infamous Grub Street; affluent merchants and tradesmen lived in the centre of the City; and the nobility occupied prosperous Westminster. Here new squares were being built, with houses of fine brick, where the gentry could live free from the smoke, noise and stench of the City's older narrow streets and little lanes.

London was obsessed with style, a city compounded of fashion and unhappiness. When Peter first moved to the King's palace at St James's, he was inadvertently being brought to one of the trendiest areas in town. St. James's Park itself was a centre for illicit sex: on the island in the middle of the lake couples resorted to its 'private recesses' to carry on their affairs. A famous brothel stood on the north side of the park, near the Palace, and 'by Rosamond's pond are stalking, rogues and whores by couples, as the beasts went into Noah's Ark'.[20] On the Mall, the pretty young milk-sellers were known to offer more refreshment than just milk to the passing beaus and fashionable gentry wandering up and down the avenue, anxious to see and be seen.

In the capital Peter quickly became the object of enormous popular curiosity: pamphlets were printed, books written, a wax effigy exhibited in the Strand, another half-length figure of him displayed then – and for many years afterwards – at Mrs Salmon's in Fleet Street.[21] Such exhibitions were, like the pamphlets that described him, alternative ways of displaying to the public a figure hidden from the view of the masses by the rarefied life of the court. Usually exhibition of such 'freaks' was more direct, taking place at fairs or on the street. We hear of a girl without fingers with a prophetic spirit, who can be observed stitching ('She toucheth gratis'); of a boy with female breasts instead of legs; and, most aptly, of a wild child, 'The Bold Grimace Spaniard', supposed to have lived fifteen years among savage beasts in the Pyrenees, now the master of such tricks as contracting his face as small as an apple, sticking out his tongue a foot long, and assuming the face of an owl, or a corpse, as well as singing to the lute.[22]

In such a climate of credulity and naive wonder it is remarkably difficult to discover the facts about Peter. The chief reason for this is that the pamphlets that describe him simply do not have much interest in the circumstances of his discovery and education. In most cases, they even fail to investigate where he might first have come from. The pamphlets written on Peter – with titles such as 'It Cannot Rain But It Pours', 'The Most Wonderful Wonder That Ever Appear'd To The Wonder of the British Nation', 'The Devil To Pay At St. James's', or 'The Manifesto of Lord Peter' – are basically skits, impromptu 'witty' variations on the latest news. They mock Peter, the court, aristocrats, women; and, in the most interesting cases, they mock human beings at the expense of the nobility of animals.

It is tempting to say that here we have the case of a wild child before the cultural equipment and curiosity exists that could properly describe him. However, this simply condemns another culture for failing to have the same interests as our own. In fact, there was a great deal of interest in the boy; but its nature was, for the most part, quite different from what might be expected.

For those satirical pamphleteers who wrote on Peter he would prove, first and foremost, a convenient means of attacking the vagaries of fashion. None could resist the strange conjunction of his being himself fashionable, living at the very hub of the newfangled, with his own utter disregard for the values of appearance and impressiveness. There was a bitter, levelling joke too in making out that someone as wretched as Peter was akin to the nobility who so ostentatiously lived out the best of London life. Some years later, in his masterpiece of materialism, *Man A Machine*, La Mettrie was to remark in the same spirit that apes could easily be turned into perfect men around town.[23] Yet the pamphleteers were conscious that the peculiar aptness of the case stemmed from the fact that Peter's absolute silence confined him to surface appearances, like the beaus whose meaning resided in the cut of a coat or their presence in the right streets. In neither case could anything be discerned of the 'real person' within.

However, their next area of interest is one that is still present in our own reaction to contemporary wild children, like Ivan, the Moscow boy: it is the human–animal divide that is central to these pamphlets. Over and over they return to the idea that, in order to survive, Peter must have been nurtured by wild animals, in particular by a bear. This fascination with the idea that his wild parents were bears had its own local stimulus: bears were a common sight in London, as baiting was still popular – there was a famous bear pit at Hockley-in-the-Hole in the City.

So anxiety about the relation of human beings to animals pervades these texts. Why should this have been of such concern? To understand those witnesses who watched Peter the Wild Boy play right there in the heart of fashionable London we need to unlearn so many of our habitual responses to the world. It requires a feat of imagination to put ourselves back into the larger world of the 1720s. A journey then across England could take days on end, and South America or the Caribbean Islands must have felt as distant as the moon. Distance was a fact of life; and distance produced strangeness. The people encountered in those far-flung places could seem barely human, so foreign was their appearance, so strange their ways. William Dampier, a travel writer, remarked of the inhabitants of New Holland: 'The Inhabitants of this Country are the miserablest People in the World . . . And setting aside their human Shape, they differ but little from Brutes.'[24] The dissemination of such travel writing at a time when Britain was expanding its

colonial enterprises into far-flung countries inevitably led to doubts
about our common human nature. Of course, this doubt was far
from a new thing. In classical times, Pliny had told his tales of
Atalantes that 'degenerate from the rites and manners of all men'
and of 'the Satyre [that] besides their shape only, have no properties
nor fashions of men';[25] and in *The City of God*, St Augustine had
written of a fantastic array of freaks and human monsters, worrying
over whether or not these could count as human.[26] Just over a century before, in *The Tempest*, Shakespeare's Caliban, himself a kind
of 'salvage man', had embodied on stage our dizzying, potential
diversity. The cultural presence of the savage and the growing
knowledge of human variety were weakening the sense of what it
meant to be human.

Confusions arose, but the men of the Enlightenment loved to
define and order. Only a decade after Peter first appeared, Charles
Linnæus, the hugely influential natural historian, began his great
work of classifying the animal kingdom. His *Systema Naturæ* (1735)
begins with the following distinctions:

> MAMMALIA, covered with hair, walk on the earth, speaking.
> BIRDS, covered with feathers, fly in the air, singing.
> AMPHIBIA, covered with skin, creep in warm places, hissing.
> FISHES, covered with scales, swim in the water, smacking.
> INSECTS, covered with armour, skip on dry ground, buzzing.
> WORMS, without skin, crawl in moist places, silent.[27]

Linnæus then commences the section on mammals with the ordering of primates, describing two kinds of primate, 'Homo' and
'Simia'. Moving on, he then turns to a consideration of the first kind,
'Homo', the human being. This section on the kinds of humanity
begins with the typically Enlightenment injunction: 'Nosce te
ipsum', or 'Know thyself'. Linnæus then distinguishes six distinct
species of human beings: 'Ferens' [wild], 'Americanus', 'Europæus',
'Asiaticus', 'Afer', and 'Monstrosus'. Proceeding, he presents his

first subdivision of the human, the 'wild man' or 'Homo Feri', consisting purely of individual instances of wild children. Linnæus further divides this sub-species of humankind into nine examples (some of them added in later editions):

> Wild Men – a – H.Feri.
> Walk on all fours, are dumb, and covered with hair.
> 1 A youth found in Lithuania, in 1761, resembling a bear.
> 2 A youth found in Hesse, in 1544, resembling a wolf.
> 3 A youth in Ireland resembling a sheep. Tulp. Obs. iv. 9.
> 4 A youth in Bamberg resembling an ox. Camerarius.
> 5 A wild youth found, in 1724, in Hanover.
> 6 Wild boys found, in 1719, in the Pyrenees.
> 7 A wild girl found, in 1717, in Overyfel.
> 8 A wild girl found, in 1731, in Champagne.
> 9 A wild lad found near Leyden. Boerhaave.[28]

Peter, the wild youth found in Hanover, is, of course, the fifth child on this list; in the next chapter we shall hear more about the eighth example, the wild girl discovered in Champagne. In 1792, Robert Kerr, the translator of the text into English, adds the following note to Linnæus's classification: 'These instances of wild men, and their similitudes, are partly to be attributed to imposture, and in part to exaggeration. Most probably idiots who had strayed from their friends, and who resembled the above animals only in imitating their voices.'[29]

While Kerr's scepticism is understandable, it also raises an interesting series of questions. Why did Linnæus begin his classification of the human race in this way? Why should he wish to show these humans as sometimes resembling an animal species? Why, in this one instance, does an individual human being hold the position elsewhere occupied in Linnæus's system by a whole 'race' or human species? Why is 'homo ferens' the only type of human to be manifested in individuals?

These questions all return us to the central problem of the wild child first felt by those who saw Peter in the flesh: how is it that we can recognize another human being as human? What essential quality unites us all?

Swift himself had explored this very issue only a few months before while writing the bleak fourth book of *Gulliver's Travels*. Here his hero, Lemuel Gulliver, lives among the Houyhnhnms, horses that possess what appears to be the ideal human quality of rigorous rationality; but on their island he also encounters the terrible Yahoos, bestial creatures of human shape, without reason or language, filthy, disgusting and, in Gulliver's eyes, irredeemably vicious. Through some perversion of his instincts, Gulliver withdraws from the clearly human Yahoos in order to ally himself to the equine dignity of the Houyhnhnms. On his eventual return to England, the sight of his wife and children makes Gulliver literally swoon. He recoils from their embrace with an insane repugnance; their very smell disgusts him, so much so that he prefers to spend his time among horses in the stables.

Intriguingly it is possible that, following that encounter at the Princess of Wales's house, Swift himself wrote directly about the Wild Boy. Might he have taken time to write something on Peter, so soon after the completion of his greatest work, *Gulliver's Travels*? Swift might well be one person whom we would imagine to possess something of our own interest in the Wild Boy: we have seen, after all, how he and his literary friends talked of little else for the first fortnight of Peter's arrival in London.

'It Cannot Rain But It Pours' and 'The Most Wonderful Wonder' are the two pamphlets that may have been written by Swift. Both explore at length the relationship between human beings and animals, perhaps with the classical model of Plutarch's *Gryllus* in mind, in which Gryllus, one of Odysseus's sailors, transformed into a beast by Circe, the witch, describes how he prefers to live as an animal, rather than as a human being. As we have seen, in *Gulliver's*

Travels, the idea that animals might possess reason, while human beings may be purely irrational, fascinates Swift. Again in the pamphlets on Peter, we find this same inversion, by which human existence appears bound by arbitrary custom and sinful hypocrisy, while animal life reveals itself as formed by the dictates of reason.

The author of the pamphlets uses the satirical device by which the familiar becomes unfamiliar by being seen through the eyes of an outsider. Peter's existence beyond civilized life allows him to be used as just such an outsider. Seeing London through Peter's eyes estranges us from the place we thought we knew, and the town becomes a nightmare scene of cruelty, hypocrisy and idiocy. Peter was not the only exotic traveller to the court that year: George had already entertained ambassadors from Arabia and recently received visits from the savage inhabitants of the Cape of Good Hope and the wild Americas. Like these other visitors, Peter offered a slantwise perspective on the known. However, those outsiders belonged to cultures that could be perceived by ourselves as strange in turn. Peter, on the other hand, belonged nowhere, and looked on all human cultures from an edge, a liminal place, where even the fact of his being human at all stood in doubt.

Other means of estranging perception were proving popular in London at that time. Scientific instruments such as the microscope and telescope had literally discovered new ways of seeing. Scales of vision changed; nothing was stable and intrinsically itself; everything could be felt to be relative and dependent on the perspective from which it was seen. Sixty years before, Robert Hooke's *Micrographia* (1665) had opened up the new world of the tiny, showing for eager readers such wonders as the compound eyes of the housefly or the teeth of the snail. These microscopic delights were far from hackneyed in the 1720s – in fact, enthusiasm for microscopes persisted throughout the eighteenth century – and there were other ways of realizing the differences of perception. One talismanic anecdote expressed this new-found strangeness of the world for writers of the period, appearing in works by Voltaire, Burke and Buffon. The anatomist William Cheselden performed eye surgery on a young man who had been blind since birth. His sight restored, it was discovered that he now had to learn how to see. At first, he could not grasp the sense of perspective, understand scale, or even delineate the outlines of objects. His world was a flat and brilliant tapestry; he could find in the surprising gift of a landscape picture a whole new method of seeing. Slowly, the man, newly endowed with sight, learnt to see with eyes like the rest of us, moving beyond his vision of a one-dimensional world, inhabited with men like trees, walking. The world we take for granted, the world of our vision, could through this example suddenly seem surprising, tenuous, a construct of custom and use. Similarly, might not Peter make our social world, apparently fixed and certain, seem a ramshackle contraption, without sense, order or meaning?

So did Swift write those pamphlets on Peter? Daniel Defoe certainly thought so. During that summer of 1726 , he wrote his own book on Peter the Wild Boy, within which he attacks Swift for the insensitive nature of the two pamphlets described above. Resolutely middle-class, Defoe was far from a literary insider in Swift's circle and may well have jumped to a false conclusion in supposing Swift to be their author. (Swift famously dismissed Defoe as 'that fellow who was pilloried, I forget his name', alluding to Defoe's punishment in 1703 for his satirical pamphlet *The Shortest Way With Dissenters*.) However, in seeking to correct Swift's imagined approach to Peter's fate, Defoe produced the one work on Peter that really begins to express the philosophical complexity that might be glimpsed in the wild child.

Some critics doubt that we should take Defoe's speculations on Peter seriously. There has long been a tendency to see Defoe as a hack writer and only an unconscious genius, producing three or four great works of literature (*Robinson Crusoe*, *Moll Flanders*, *The Journal of the Plague Year*, *The Fortunate Mistress*) almost by accident in a lifetime of hack writing. Defoe certainly produced a phenomenal amount of books and journalism: he wrote at least five books (on trade, literature, inventions, and the Devil, among other topics) in the year that Peter arrived in London alone.

One of these was a substantial work on Peter the Wild Boy. The title page reads: '*Mere NATURE Delineated: or, A BODY without a SOUL. Being OBSERVATIONS Upon the Young FORESTER Lately Brought to Town from GERMANY. With Suitable APPLICATIONS. Also, A Brief Dissertation upon the Usefulness and Necessity of FOOLS, whether Political or Natural.*' Defoe's pamphlet was published on 23 July 1726, and sold at the price of one shilling and six pence.[30]

Little is known about Defoe's involvement with Peter, though one biographer conjectures that Defoe must have visited the boy prior to writing his text.[31] His *Mere Nature Delineated* has either been dismissed by his critics or simply ignored: the most recent biographies of Defoe have oddly failed to mention his involvement in the case at all. In *Memoirs of the Life and Times of Daniel De Foe* (London, 1830), Walter Wilson devotes six pages to the subject, the majority of which are given over to a summary of the work. William Lee's two-volume Victorian biography of Defoe considers the whole story to be an imposture on a gullible public.[32] Thomas Wright's biography of 1894 is even more dismissive, regarding Defoe's motives for writing the text as exclusively pecuniary, thereby accounting for its supposedly perfunctory nature, and declaring that he exhibits 'a more common-sense view of the subject than his contemporaries'.[33] Both points are debatable. In the first place, though not written *exclusively* for money, the tract was certainly written at great speed (as were nearly all Defoe's works), but it is precisely the speed of composition that gives the work one of its chief sources of interest: that is, the sense of Defoe's discovering as he goes along what he thinks about and finds important in Peter's case. Improvisation leads him down some hitherto unsuspected paths. In the second place, it is apparent that in fact Defoe was unusual in taking the case seriously

– his contemporaries plainly regarded Peter as, first and foremost, a joke. That Wright goes on to suggest that Defoe's speculations on language in the text amount to 'a little bit of fooling', and his parting shot – that Defoe only stops short of calling the boy an idiot as this would court unpopularity – miss the point entirely.[34] That Peter was an idiot was both a popular charge and one that Defoe specifically shields the boy from. William Lee's comment that *Mere Nature* is Defoe's most speculative work is nearer the mark.[35]

On confronting Peter, one overwhelming question came to Defoe: could this creature have a soul, and is he properly human? The idea of the soul's existence was one hotly debated in the period: mortalists had worried over the immortality of the soul and the materiality of the body; theologians had speculated on whether animals had souls, while natural philosophers increasingly depicted animals as biological machines. John Locke influentially described the infant child as a *tabula rasa* – a blank slate waiting to be inscribed with the impressions of its senses.

For Defoe, Peter, in being both child and beast in human shape, embodies 'mere nature': that is, he is entirely, supremely and exclusively natural (this is the old meaning of 'mere'), a human being without any admixture of art or culture. To our modern ears this may sound an enviable state. However, Defoe is clear that without the artifice of human culture, Peter must remain locked in the blank of childhood, trapped in being a mere animal machine:

Mere Nature receives the vivifying Influence in Generation, but requires the Help of Art to bring it to the perfection of living: The Soul is plac'd in the Body like a rough Diamond, which requires the Wheel and Knife, and all the other Arts of the Cutter, to shape it, and polish it, and bring it to shew the perfect Water of a true *Brilliant*. If Art be deficient, Nature can do no more . . . Thus the Soul, unpolish'd, remains bury'd under the Rubbish and Roughness of its own Powers . . . [36]

Without artifice, particularly the shared human artifice of speech, an unmeaning silence traps Peter in an endless, unvarying bestiality.[37] Within this limited world, Peter exists without knowing that he does so, and looks on at a world that to him is a senseless picture, a meaningless theatre. He sees the surface of things, but, truly apathetic, nothing impresses him: everything flattens out under his steady, unconcerned gaze, and he would watch a woman burnt at the stake as unmoved as if he were watching a dance at the theatre.[38]

Without a soul, Peter lives set apart in a no-man's-land, being neither a rational human being nor an instinctive animal. Defoe defines the human through the soul, and in declaring that Peter has none, and is a body without a soul, he inevitably comes to the conclusion that, despite the evidence of shared appearances, Peter is not yet truly human.

Peter's unique position also renders him uniquely alone. Isolation was Defoe's great subject, the *leitmotif* that runs through his entire writing; and in Peter, Defoe found the most extreme expression of a loneliness that had haunted him all his life. In later Romantic studies of such wild children, this loneliness would come to seem enviable; but in the 1720s, Peter's isolation clearly scares Defoe. How could Peter have wilfully chosen the lonely life of the woods? What could have made him flee from human society, and, even after his capture, attempt to escape back into that silent wilderness? The perversity of it shocks the ageing writer, a man for whom a realized life can only be found in the pleasures of society.

Contemporary social life enforces the solitude of Defoe's heroines, Moll Flanders, the thief, and Roxana, the courtesan. Defoe's portrayals of criminals, pirates and whores all express a fascination with societies bound together only by the thinnest threads of self-interest and mutual fear. London could be seen as another such society, one where a lost child might easily disappear: the exposure of children was all too common in London (and elsewhere). In

Defoe's novels, the drive for money – for survival – isolates every-one. Relationships are casual and can end as quickly as they begin. Nothing is stable; people come and go; even husbands and wives might casually disappear.

Yet it is a shallow reader who does not detect in Defoe's consider-ation of Peter the mingled horror and desire that characterizes all his explorations of human solitude. The loneliness that envelops everyone can be less fearful than the terrible presence of others. The closing pages of Defoe's novel, *Roxana, or the Fortunate Mistress* act out this fear with hallucinatory intensity, as Roxana, his heroine, is pursued and plagued by her lost daughter, the only person who might end her awful alienation; until, driven wild by her continual presence, she contemplates the killing by her servant, Amy, of her own child.

Of course, *Robinson Crusoe* is our culture's greatest myth of lone-liness. Crusoe lives for years separate from all others, before return-ing to human relationships through an encounter with the person most completely estranged from himself: that is, a pagan savage. Defoe's intention is to show Crusoe's distance from the savage who ends his solitude. Crusoe is a point of civilized life in a wild place; Peter the Wild Boy is his opposite and his mirror: he is similarly alone, but embodies the lonely state of nature isolated within the very centre of the social world.

It is Peter's silence that symbolizes this isolation and is the ulti-mate cause of it. Defoe's family life was anyway leading him to think increasingly about the mute. His beloved youngest daughter Sophia was being courted by Henry Baker, an astute and financially canny teacher of the deaf and dumb. Since 1724, Baker had been visiting Stoke Newington, Defoe's home village on the outskirts of London, in order to teach a boy named White to lip-read and speak. In 1726, Defoe was on good terms with Baker, who often visited the Defoes' family house to take tea (though their relationship would later go sour): the book on Peter includes a brief puff for the ingenious Mr

Baker's 'surprizing Dexterity in Teaching such as have been born Deaf and Dumb'.[39]

Peter's silence evokes another crucial question for Defoe: how can Peter think without words? And if Peter cannot think, then how can he have a consciousness of his self? In thinking about Peter, Defoe seizes upon the problem that would fascinate all later investigators of such wild children. He reasons that we live through language:

> Words are to us, the Medium of Thought; we cannot conceive of Things, but by their Names . . . we cannot muse, contrive, imagine, design, resolve, or reject; nay, we cannot love or hate, but in acting upon those Passions in the very Form of Words; nay, if we dream 'tis in Words, we speak every thing to ourselves, and we know not how to think, or act, or intend to act, but in the Form of Words; all our Passions and Affections are acted in Words, and we have no other Way for it.[40]

But if that is the case, then 'what do these silent People do?' What goes on in Peter's mind?

As a way of thinking about this question, Defoe recounts the true story of a young hearing girl brought up in a family in which everyone else was deaf and dumb. The girl, an orphan, was raised by her mute siblings, who communicated among themselves by means of a silent system of gestures and nods. When people who could speak came to the house, the girl discerned in their voices nothing but a 'confused Jargon or Medley of Sounds'.[41] When she was fourteen, it was discovered by accident that the girl had the ability to hear. Random and uncoordinated attempts were made to teach the girl language, but all these trials failed. After three years she could speak only haltingly, and as if with a foreign accent.

In the story of this girl Defoe draws close to our contemporary understanding of the acquired nature of language. In talking of her, Defoe reverses the terms elsewhere employed in his account of

Peter. The body's gestures become the girl's natural mode of communication, while vocalized speech becomes animalistic, senseless, strange, thus taking on the characteristics of Peter's condition in the state of nature:

Nothing could be more natural than for the Child to conclude, that this Finger Language was the true, and the only Way to understand one another, and converse together; that the other was of no Signification, but meer Noise, not to be imitated or understood: Nay, when she first began to learn to speak, she had no Relish of Words, no Taste; she did not soon conceive how Words could be understood, but thought the conversing by Signs, and by Motions of the Body, pointing and making Figures, and the like, infinitely more agreeable, more significant, easier to be done, more decent and handsomer to do, than to make a Gaping with her Mouth, and a Noise from it with her Tongue . . . the Servants, though they made the like Noises among themselves as other People did, and, which she took to be the utmost Rudeness, yet had more Manners when they talked to their Masters and Mistresses; that then they laid it aside, and ordering themselves with Decency and Respect, received their Commands by the Fingers Ends, and made return in the same Manner; and this was all the Way of Speech that she could entertain any Notion of, or that she had any Desire to understand.[42]

Defoe portrays this rejection of spoken language as less desirable than the immediacy, delicacy and grace of the body's gestural signs as a 'fatal mistake'.[43] However, the force of the passage demonstrates that the child's preference follows 'Native Reasoning' – after all, what's so wrong with a language of gestures – and through this inversion of the accepted system of speech also hints at the arbitrariness of all modes of communication. The girl's rejection of speech renders language momentarily strange to us, as we glimpse it through other eyes. The girl inverts our usual values: language collapses into noise, while silent gestures are elevated to beauty. However, the concepts of meaning and beauty remain intact: they are simply repositioned in the system of values. This manifests Peter's distance from the silence of the deaf and dumb. His silence is not a simple inversion, an entrance into a contrary scheme of things; rather Peter presents the notion of the absence of value as such, an existence outside all schemes of communication. The girl lives in her own miniature society; Peter is outside all societies. His wordlessness would be as incomprehensible to the deaf girl as it is to Defoe.

So Defoe worries over Peter, frets at the uncertain meanings of his tale. Yet while Defoe cannot envy Peter's solitude, he begins to envy his silence. He wonders if such silence doesn't bring Peter nearer to God, while our words remove us from direct contact with the divine. In language, we become self-conscious, always talking to ourselves in the endless dialogue of thought. On the other hand, in silence Peter communicates directly with God. Suddenly Defoe re-imagines the Peter he previously described as having no soul at all. Now Defoe's Peter lives in a pre-Adamic world, in which none of the animals has yet been named. His mind thinks in images that are not reproductions of the world, but an unmediated intercourse with it. For a moment, at least, Defoe finds in Peter the sense of wonder that none of his contemporaries could discover.

Yet Peter is the most invisible and indeterminate of all the children talked about in this book. So little of him remains: a plaything for a while, a source of jest or speculation, an exemplar of fashion and folly, a pathway to the animals, a mysterious mute – and that is all. We know so little of him, and more truly than in any other case we might say that all we know is what others thought about him. Defoe ends his book on Peter by asking the boy's forgiveness: 'It may be true, that in order to make this wild Youth a just Parallel to the Wisdom of our Brains, who have been taught better, and from whom there was more Reason to expect better Things, I have sometimes been free with his Character . . . '[44] The thought is one that will gather increasing strength and pathos as this book goes on. Defoe had used the boy as a starting-point for speculations that might appear to go far beyond him. Not for the last time, the child himself had been lost in the higher thoughts that he inspired.

IV: Courts Removing

> And all our beauty, and our trimme, decayes,
> Like courts removing, or like ended playes.
>   John Donne, 'The Calme'

All that spring and early summer of 1726 Peter was still hot news, a source of diversion for a society obsessed with miracles, freaks and scandals; but soon other stories took over. From the time of his coming to London, Peter had shared public attention with a sensation in the opera world, to the extent that some fanciful comparisons had been made in the pamphlets between Peter's silence and the (to English ears) unmeaning sounds of Italian opera. The presence on London stages of two prima donnas, the startlingly ugly Francesca Cuzzoni and her old rival Faustina Bordoni, caused an uproar in opera-obsessed London as partisans of each singer booed and hissed the other. (Handel got round the problem by writing operas with arias for two lead female sopranos.)

In the last pamphlet to mention Peter, published in 1727, he is relegated to an unimportant news item, sixth on a list of seven, ousted by opera news, the scandalous love affairs of Quakers, the already-mentioned case of 'the rabbit woman', and the death of King George I. Rabbit women now outranked wild boys as the hot topic of conversation: public curiosity had moved on.

Swift too had other, newer concerns. In the early summer of 1726, while Peter's education continued, a private poem of Swift's, *Cadenus and Vanessa*, a flirtatious piece written for Esther Vanhomrigh, one of the two women in his life, had appeared in

Dublin without his consent, and was now the subject of the town's malicious gossip. The poem could no longer really wound the reputation of Esther Vanhomrigh, who was three years dead; but Swift must have been concerned for its effect upon 'Stella' (Esther Johnson), the other great emotional support of his life. Stella herself was now ill, perhaps dying, and Swift met the news of her sickness with characteristic bleakness, worrying for her, but more profoundly fearing for himself. As the summer wore on, he delayed his return to Ireland, lest he should have to suffer the terrible pain of watching Stella die.

However, on 15 August 1726 Swift nonetheless left for Dublin: he would return to London and the homes of his old friends only once more. Before he left, he arranged for the publication of *Gulliver's Travels*, indulging in cloak-and-dagger games of dealing with his publisher, Benjamin Motte, through an alias ('Richard Sympson'), depositing the manuscript with him unseen and at night. The book appeared in November to universal acclaim: Arbuthnot wrote to Swift: 'Gulliver is a happy man, that, at his age, can write such a merry book.'[45]

Early in 1727 George I unexpectedly died; this news may be thought to have made Swift merrier still. Swift, Arbuthnot and their gang grew excited in anticipation of the rewards coming to them and their fellow Tories from the new king; but they never materialized. George and Caroline ascended to the throne and Walpole, the Whig, continued in his position of power and influence. Nothing really had changed.

And what of Peter? After less than a year Arbuthnot abandoned his education, and with fashionable interest waning in the boy, Caroline passed him into the care of a Mrs Titchbourn, a member of the Queen's household. Mrs Titchbourn, being used to spending her summer holidays at the house of James Fenn, a yeoman farmer, entrusted the boy to the Fenns at Haxter's End Farm, Broadway, near Berkhamstead. A sizeable pension was awarded to the family to provide for Peter's upkeep. Since he was, at first, in the habit of wandering off and getting lost, he was fitted with a collar on which was written: 'Peter the Wild Man from Hanover. Whoever will bring him to Mr Fenn at Berkhamstead, Hertfordshire, shall be paid for their trouble.'

Peter lived at Haxter's End for thirty years, at the end of which time he was taken to Broadway Farm, about a mile from Berkhamstead, by John Fenn's brother, staying on there after this brother's death with his successor, Farmer Brill. Sometimes Peter would return to the headlines, much as one sometimes hears snatches of news about faded stars. In 1751, he briefly ran away from the farm with the following results:

> *October 27.* was a terrible fire in *Norwich*, which consumed part of the city bridewell [prison], and several other houses. Peter the wild youth, who had stray'd from his keeper in *Hertfordshire*, and was committed to this bridewell as a sturdy vagrant, was with difficulty got away, seeming more to wonder at the fire, than to apprehend any danger, and would probably have perished like a horse in the flames. By his behaviour, and want of speech, he seems to be more of the Ouran Outang species than of the human. Soon after the keeper coming to the knowledge of the advertisement where his elopement was mentioned, restored him back to the person to whose care he had been committed by the late queen.[46]

Little else is known. Peter died in February 1785 and was buried at Northchurch; he never properly acquired language.

However, in the midst of the blank of those final years, for one moment Peter again rises up into visibility. For a moment we see him more clearly than ever before: an observer with a passionate interest in Peter, and in all children like him, had arrived on the scene. At the beginning of June 1782, James Burnett, Lord Monboddo, the Scottish philosopher and judge, paid a visit to

Peter on the farm. Two years later Burnett wrote his account of the visit: it is our best snapshot of Peter, and the last trace of him before his death.

The Wild Boy was now an old man – about seventy years old, only a year or two older than Burnett himself. Yet he had a fresh, healthy complexion with a full beard, and a pleasant face marked by a sagacious and sensitive expression. The farmer's wife affirmed that he could understand what was said to him quite well, though he could only articulate the words 'Peter' and 'King George'. (His own name he pronounced as 'Pe-ter', always leaving a gap between the two syllables.) She encouraged Peter to sing for Burnett, which he did happily, chanting out a wordless version of 'Nancy Dawson' and another tune as well. Music delighted Peter, and he would clap his hands and sing all the better for the promise of some gin. He was quite short – only five feet three inches – though still robust and muscular, and was quite tame. He was a gentle man, fond of water; would eat an onion like an apple; enjoyed sitting by a fire; was indifferent to money; lived quietly, only growing disturbed at the coming of spring, which delighted him, or at the onset of bad weather, which set him growling, howling and showing great disorder; liked to stand in the warmth of the sun, or to be out in a starry night.[47] And that is the last we hear of Peter. However, it is not the last we shall hear of Burnett, for that philosopher's life had already been embroiled with the even stranger story of that other wild child mentioned on Linnæus's list, the savage girl of Champagne.

CHAPTER THREE

Lord Monboddo and the Savage Girl

I: The Savage Girl

Into the dangerous world I leapt . . .
   William Blake, 'Infant Sorrow', *Songs of Experience*

She came to the village in the late summer evening, as the September twilight fell. The first ones to see her took fright, crying out that the devil had come to Songi, and fled into their houses, securing their doors and windows against her.

She was armed with a small club, thicker at one end than the other. One of the villagers set a bulldog in an iron collar upon her, hoping to drive her away; but when she saw the enraged dog running at her, she calmly held her ground, gripping hold of the little club and stretching herself to one side so as to give more force to her blow. The dog snarled closer and closer, its teeth bared; but just as it was within range, with all her strength she brought the club down on to the beast's head. With that single blow the dog was dead and, ecstatic with victory, she jumped several times over the bloody carcass. She then tried the door of one of the houses, but it was locked fast. So she ran back eastwards into the countryside towards the River Marne, clambered up into a tree and fell asleep among the leafy branches.

She was perhaps nine or ten years old. Her feet were bare, but she wore a scanty dress of rags and skins, and on her hair a gourd leaf. Her face and hands were 'black as a Negroe's' the villagers said. Perhaps it was thirst that had made her abandon the refuge of the woods and risk this foray into Songi. It was the end of a long, burning summer and water was scarce in the arid countryside. It was not the first time she had been spotted near Songi: a shepherd had seen her some time before around the vineyards outside the village, skinning and eating frogs, and chewing leaves.

They quickly took word of the savage girl to the Viscount d'Epinoy who was honeymooning just then at his chateau at Songi with his new bride, the beautiful former Mademoiselle Lannoy. His curiosity aroused, he gave orders to the villagers to catch the child – particularly charging the shepherd who had discovered her those weeks before with responsibility for finding her.

One of the cannier villagers came up with a cunning plan for taking her. Guessing that the girl must be thirsty, he advised that they should place a pitcher of water at the foot of the tree in which she was still sleeping, tempting her to come down from her hiding place to drink. The villagers stole up to the tree, left the water there as advised, and retreated some distance so that they could watch the young savage unobserved. Sure enough, some little time later the girl crept down from her perch in the branches and went to drink from the pitcher, plunging her chin into the water and lapping at it like a cat. But something startled her, and before any of them could reach her, she darted up the trunk and into the branches right to the very top of the tree.

Once again the canny villager suggested a stratagem. He told them that they should place a woman and some children near the tree, as these would be less intimidating to the girl than the men, and that they should smile to her and placidly act out a show of great friendliness. The villagers did as he said: a woman with a child in her arms approached the tree, carrying root vegetables and two fishes in her hands. She held out the food to the savage, who, pressed by hunger, came down part of the way, before taking fright and scurrying back once more to safety. The woman calmly persisted in her gentle invitation, smiling and gesturing her friendship by laying her hand upon her breast 'as if to assure her that she loved her, and would do her no harm'.[1] Betrayed into trust, the girl slipped down from her place of refuge to receive the fishes and vegetables that were offered to her. The woman continued to entice her, but moved imperceptibly away, still smiling and acting out for the girl her generous love. The girl followed her further and further from the tree; and the men who had lain in wait seized their chance to spring out from hiding and take her by force.

They took her to the chateau. She was brought to the kitchen while the Viscount was told of her arrival. The cook was just then dressing some fowls for the Viscount's dinner. Before anyone knew what was happening the girl flew at the dead birds and had one of them held tight in her teeth, tearing at the raw meat. M d'Epinoy arrived and, seeing what and how she was eating, ordered that she should be given an unskinned rabbit: the little girl instantly stripped its skin and devoured it.

They examined her and questioned her, but she could not understand a word of French. At first they assumed she was black. However, once they had washed her several times, they found that she was white, her apparent blackness being the result of dirt and, possibly, paint. Her skin was a little dark-complexioned perhaps, but the flesh on her upper arms and on her breast was white. Her hands were oddly shaped, the palms being as small and neat as any little girl's, while the fingers and thumbs were curiously enlarged. Later they conjectured that this formation was the result of leaping from one tree to another, like a squirrel, her strong hands grabbing at the branches.

She wore a necklace, some pendants, and a pouch fixed to a large animal skin that was wrapped around her body and hung down round her knees. In the pouch were a club and a small knife, inscribed with strange characters, unfamiliar to everyone.

The Viscount d'Epinoy was the first among several dignitaries who took up the savage girl's cause. He gave her over to the care of the shepherd who had first seen her, being anxious that she should be well looked after, and offering the man handsome payment. In order to tame her, the shepherd kept her closely confined in his house, so that sometimes she was driven to make desperate attempts to escape, scouring out holes in the walls or in the tiles of the roof. Once outside, she would run upon the rooftop, unconcerned whether she fell or not, in that way evading capture; or sometimes she squeezed herself through holes and openings so narrow as to arouse the wonder of her guardians and pursuers. In this way, on one evening she escaped in the midst of a severe frost and snow storm. Fearing M d'Epinoy's anger, the shepherd's family was thrown into a panic of anxiety about the young savage and searched every corner of the house to find her, never supposing that in such freezing weather she would have dared to return to the snowbound countryside. At last they gave up their search in utter dejection, only then to spy the girl sheltering from the swirling snow in the leafless upper branches of a winter tree.

A great number of visitors came to M d'Epinoy in order to see the wild girl for themselves. They watched her digging for roots in the gardens, using only her thumb and forefinger to scour out rapidly a deep hole, or fishing in the ditches, or climbing to the very tops of the trees and there imitating the songs of birds. The quickness of her eyes was amazing too: 'Their movement was so extremely quick; and their sight so sharp, that they might be said to see in the same instant on every side . . . '[2]

The villagers began to call her 'the shepherd's beast'. However, either because M d'Epinoy began to fear for the education of his charge, or because the shepherd no longer felt able to support such a wayward child, on 30 October of that same year (1731) the girl was taken to the hospital general of St Maur in the nearby town of Chalons, one of the largest towns in that region of Champagne. (However, she appears to have continued to spend much of the next two years at Songi with the shepherd and his family, often staying with the Viscount d'Epinoy at his chateau.)

They began to fit her for the manners of social life, but there were many setbacks in her domestication. When M d'Epinoy received guests, he would send for the young savage, who increasingly proved of a happy and amiable disposition. On one occasion she was brought to the chateau for a great feast. Observing that there were no dishes fit for her to eat, everything being cooked, she ran outside to the Viscount's ponds and came back laden with frogs, which she distributed among the guests. When the other guests tried to throw away the frogs she'd brought them, she gathered them all up together and threw them back again on to the dinner plates and table.

At first, she had a horror of being touched. She still could not speak, and could only express herself through squeaking cries, brought on by the harsh treatment she sometimes underwent; but it was when someone made as if to touch her that she would shriek and her restless eyes would grow more wild.

Once, while she was staying briefly at the hospital of St Maur, a man attempted to touch her. She was in the house of M de Beaupré, the Intendant of the province of Champagne. The man – a visitor – had heard of her distress at being touched by a stranger, but resolved nonetheless that he would embrace her. He found her happily standing and eating raw beef in one of the upper rooms. Before approaching her he had some of her familiar attendants contrive to catch hold of her clothes; he then advanced towards her and laid hold of her arm. Enraged, she immediately struck him with the hand that clasped the chunk of meat with such violent force that he fell back stunned and momentarily blinded, hardly able to stand. Then, in an instant of intense fear, she fought her way free of their hands and sprang for the window, intending to jump down and make her escape to the trees and river beyond; but they caught her and held her fast, and kept her there.

By slow degrees, the girl grew more tame. The Viscount d'Epinoy grew increasingly fond of her: she was *his* girl, the one he protected and had rescued from the harsh life of the abandoned. A bond grew between them. Her mouth was strangely small and round and when she laughed, her upper lip trembled and she drew her breath inwards.[3] She began to learn to talk, acquiring French slowly but not with as much difficulty as might be expected. From this, some of her teachers wondered if she had not already been among French speakers. As to her original language, this was now completely lost.

At St Maur, they began the next step in her reclamation, first attempting to wean her off her savage diet. The Viscount d'Epinoy had taken great care to keep her fed with the root vegetables and raw meat that she so loved, but as she began to spend more time in the hospital of St Maur she was fed increasingly on cooked meats. At first they gave her wine to drink and food preserved with salt. The unforeseen result was the loss of her teeth and her nails – all of which were kept as treasures for the curious. Salted bread pained her; biscuits and cooked meat made her vomit, even cough up blood. A physician came and bled her severely, saying that it was necessary to get some French blood into her veins. She began to experience terrible pains in her stomach, bowels and throat, and soon her health was so bad that they hurried to receive her into the Roman Catholic Church, lest she should die unbaptized. So on 16 June 1732, in the parish church of St Sulpice in Chalons, they baptized her Marie-Angélique Memmie Le Blanc.

Viscount d'Epinoy was terrified lest she might die. He hurriedly sent for a doctor, who advised that she should be allowed to eat raw meat from time to time. However, she was now too ill to eat even her accustomed food, and could only chew at the pieces of flesh, sucking what juice she could from the meat. At other times she was brought a live chicken or pigeon from which she sucked the warm blood, which revivifying 'licquor' aided her slow recovery; though the illness she went through at this time permanently weakened her health.

The Viscount loved his little savage, but he died within a year or so of her capture. If he had lived, how differently might Memmie's later life have gone; but it was her fate always to lose or be dropped by her protectors. On his death the savage girl was put in the care of the Convent des régentes at Chalons. For a while, the girl's fate hung in the balance: the Viscount's widow had a whim that the girl should live with her, and be brought up to a life of fashion and elegance; but the superior at the convent fought for Memmie to remain in the holy seclusion of the cloister. Mme Epinoy was persuaded and Memmie stayed where she was.

There she learned to sew and to do Dresden work and be weaned from her wild pursuits. The curates at Songi told her that it was not fitting for girls to swim or to climb trees; she began to abstain from doing both.

Her next encounter with a possible champion in the nobility came in 1737. The Queen of Poland, the mother of Maria, the Queen of France, was travelling through Champagne to take possession of the Duchy of Lorraine. Having heard of the savage girl still living in the convent at Chalons, the Queen ordered that she should be brought before her.

Marie-Angélique, familiarly known as 'Memmie' (after either her godfather or the first bishop of Chalons), was now about fifteen years old, but her voice and behaviour were like those of a child of four or five. Her voice was weak though shrill and piercing; she could speak very few words, and those confused and brokenly expressed, so that often she was at a loss to convey her meaning. Her disposition was childlike and fawning, her attention directed to those who caressed her most. Struck by her childish softness, the Queen caressed her extremely, and Memmie dutifully and wonderingly watched her.

They told the Queen how Memmie ran as swiftly as the wind. It may be true that her running was ungainly, but it was also inexpressibly agile. She did not so much run as gallop, not at all putting one foot down and then the other, but skipping, jumping, almost flying along, at such speed that it was hard for the eye to follow. To run beside her would be impossible. The Queen was intrigued and declared that she wished to take Memmie hunting with her. Out in the countryside again, Memmie was her old self and ran in pursuit of the hares and rabbits that the royal entourage started – chased them, caught up with them, took them and, running back at just the same pace, brought them, still warm and bloody, to the waiting Queen.

The Queen was impressed: she resolved to take the girl with her to Nancy, where she would leave her in the care of the convent there; but the nuns begged that the Queen should not disturb Memmie by taking her from her life at Chalons. The Queen listened to their pleas and acquiesced. However, she promised instead to write in Memmie's favour to her daugher, the Queen of France. With the let-ter she enclosed a strange plant made of artificial flowers that Memmie had made herself and presented to her – an art in which she had already acquired great skill.

We know little of what happened to Memmie over the next ten years. She learned how to speak French fluently; she willed herself to lose her savageness. The traces of her savage girlhood disap-peared; she grew into a young woman.

She almost became a nun. Only the consciousness that the others at the convent had seen her in her wild state kept her from making the final commitment. A complicated shame possessed her: she could not bear the insinuating glances of the nuns, reminding her always of what she had been. So, in September 1747, she left Chalons to go to the convent at St Menehold, where the people would be strangers.

However, she could not so easily escape her past. On her arrival at St Menehold, just as she entered the inn there, she met a M La Condamine, a fastidiously elegant and aristocratic middle-aged gentleman, his good looks marred slightly by smallpox scars. The meeting appeared fortuitous; he was friendly and courteous and dined with her and the hostess. What she did not know was that La Condamine had gone there simply in order to meet her.

As one of the most famous scientists of Europe, La Condamine was to prove a valuable ally for Memmie. Of particular importance for her cause was La Condamine's famous scepticism: he had especially impressed English readers by discrediting the miracle of the yearly liquefaction of the blood of St Januarius, and that despite being himself 'a Papist'.[4] For the sceptics of the time, to have such a rigorous empiricist on Memmie's side would prove sufficient gaurantee for the truth of her story.

La Condamine had returned only two years before from a gloriously successful expedition to the torrid zone of South America, where he had measured the circumference of the earth at the Equator. Having set out in 1735, La Condamine and his fellow scientists, Godin, the astronomer, and Bougeur, decided to head back to France by separate routes, thereby multiplying their opportunities for discovery. La Condamine, characteristically, took the longest and most difficult route home, deciding that he would map the River Amazon. Judging from his writings on the Indians he met there, we may assume that it was not romantic regard for the 'savage' that drew La Condamine to Memmie. He describes the natives he encountered in the rainforest as gluttonous, narrow-minded, cowardly (except when drunk), idle, incapable of foresight or reflection, sometimes joyful in an immoderate, childish way but generally stolidly insensible – in short, passing their lives without thought and growing old 'without having taken leave of infancy'.[5]

Through La Condamine's offices Memmie left St Menehold and went instead to the convent of the Nouvelles Catholiques in the Rue St Anne in Paris, where she was to be supported by the Duke of Orléans (who had met Memmie in 1744). She advanced in her religious education, received confirmation and for the first time attended mass. She then moved to another Parisian convent (of the Visitation, at Chaillot) and again made preparations for becoming a nun; but just then disaster fell. A window at the convent collapsed and struck her hard upon the head; she fell ill, and once again her life was in danger. Memmie was taken from the convent to the house of the Hospitalières in the suburb St Marceau where she could receive the best available medical help, the Duke of Orléans paying all her expenses. Once again, however, Memmie's luck with beneficiaries took its usual bad turn: just at the most crucial moment the Duke himself died. Memmie was left stranded: sick, friendless and penniless, her hopes thwarted and her health lost.

She spent the next years in destitution, ill health and poverty, until by another stroke of good fortune she met a benefactress in the shape of her biographer, Madame Hecquet, the woman whose account of Memmie Le Blanc's life has preserved her story for posterity – a work published in 1755 as *Histoire d'une jeune fille sauvage trouvée dans les bois à l'âge de dix ans*. Here is how Madame Hecquet describes their first meeting:

> It was in these disagreeable circumstances that I saw her for the first time, November 1752. They were hardly mended, when Le Blanc had recovered as much strength as to be able to come herself to tell me, that the Duke of Orléans, the inheritor of his father's virtues, had undertaken to pay the nine months board that had fallen due to her since his father's death, and that she had besides some reason to hope to be put on that Prince's list, for a yearly pension of 200 livres for life; adding, at the same time, that until this point should be settled, which could not happen till the beginning of the following year, she had accepted of a small apartment, which a person she mentioned had offered her. [This is probably a reference to La Condamine.] But how, says I, do you propose to subsist in this apartment for two months, and perhaps more, in your sickly situation? For what purpose, answered she, with a firmness and confidence that surprised me, has God brought me from among wild beasts and made me a Christian? not surely, afterwards to abandon, and suffer me to perish for hunger, that is impossible; I know no other father but him, nor no other mother but the blessed Virgin; their providence therefore will support me.[6]

The simplicity and piety of Mademoiselle Le Blanc's answer chastened Madame Hecquet; and yet there was something in Memmie that made her wonder. Her history since that September evening when she had arrived in Songi was clear enough; but what of those years before, that were empty, dark and speechless? Where had she come from? How had she lived? And, above all, there was the question of the inner identity of this woman before her – ill, sallow, near enough thirty years old. They had called her Mademoiselle Le Blanc, they had given her the name Memmie; but what did such names mean in face of the strange mystery of those nine missing years? Who was she really?

II: The Unhappiest One

The unhappiest one will always, therefore, be found among the unhappy rememberers . . .

    Søren Kierkegaard, 'The Unhappiest One', *Either, Or*

James Burnett, the future Lord Monboddo, had been in Paris for eight months when, on Friday 28 March 1765, he first saw and conversed with Mademoiselle Memmie Le Blanc. With his clerk, William Robertson, he had left their hotel, the Hôtel d'Espaine on the Rue Guénégaut, and crossed over the river from the Quartier de St Germain des Près to the Rue St Antoine, where Memmie now lived in an apartment. Of all the men introduced to Memmie, none could have been more excited in anticipation than Burnett.

La Condamine was to make the introduction and so took the short journey with them. La Condamine made a point of mentioning Mademoiselle Le Blanc to men of distinction, to some of whom he likewise introduced her. Among such men James Burnett was to prove crucially significant in Memmie's history.

La Condamine was now sixty-four years old and very different from the figure whom Memmie had first met some eighteen years before. His South American travels had wrecked his health: he was practically deaf and carried an ear trumpet everywhere he went. On his return from the Amazon his left leg had been partially lame, so that when he first met Memmie he was using a cane. Now he was completely paralysed, though no medical reason could be discovered for his incapacity.

Memmie herself was also unwell. Her apartment on the Rue St Antoine faced the old road to the Temple, between the back of the Hôtel de Ville and the church of St Gervais. It was potentially a good place to try to earn a living as a public curiosity, which is what Memmie was at this time attempting to do. The Rue St Antoine, running from Porte St Antoine in the east to Place Baudoyers in the west, was one of the largest and most beautiful streets in Paris, and one of the best known to travellers, as it was here that the ambassadors made their entrées and where public festivities took place. The district northwards was busy but austere – the respectable home of Parisian lawyers. Towards the Tuileries or at the city walls it was customary for 'freaks', showmen, rope-dancers, tumblers, mountebanks, purveyors of curiosities and sleight-of-hand people to call down from the windows of their houses to passers-by on the street, enticing them inside for their entertainment; but Memmie was mostly too ill and too retired for this, and her apartment faced away from the street, looking back on to the houses between herself and the river.

Unsuccessful in this way, she supported herself by making artificial flowers and by selling copies of Madame Hecquet's book of her life. On its publication the book had not done well and Memmie owned most of the copies, making a small profit by peddling them to the curious. She can't have sold many books in that room of hers. Her life must have been very hard; apart from Burnett, no other visitor to Paris makes any mention of her; she is not listed as a curiosity to be visited in English guidebooks or in contemporary descriptions of Paris. Her life was hidden.

However, for James Burnett, long fascinated by the study of the primitive origins of humanity, it seemed that he was now to have the chance to meet a living, breathing embodiment of such origins. She was, he already knew, the key to a mystery. Her body, her life, opened up for the philosophical observer the image of essential humanity. Who would not take a day off from his stressful and pressing legal work to view such a creature? He would have travelled to France in any case to seize such a marvellous and unrepeatable chance.

Considering La Condamine's mysterious paralysis, it must have been hard work to climb up to the third-floor apartment on that early spring day. Was what they then found a disappointment? She was ill, middle-aged, forgotten by the world at large. Her health had been permanently ruined at the time of her capture – by being forbidden to swim, Mademoiselle Memmie Le Blanc explained, and by the cooked foods they had charitably forced her to eat. All that was extraordinary about her appeared to have gone: she could neither run like the wind, nor sing like a nightingale, nor climb like a squirrel. By a conscious effort she had slowed the quickness in her eyes. She was merely herself. Perhaps only Burnett perceived how extraordinary this 'mere' self was, what miracles she represented. For the others there was just the distended belly of the savage and a trace of wildness in her look.

Burnett now sat, facing Memmie Le Blanc. How had she come to be in Songi? Where had she come from? And how had she managed to live in the woods of France? Surrounded by her visitors, Memmie talked and they listened; on his return to the Hôtel d'Espaine Burnett wrote down all that she had told him:

She supposed that she must have been only seven or eight years of age when she had been snatched away from her own country. She had been put aboard a great ship and carried off to a warm country. There they had sold her for a slave, but not before they had first painted her black all over. For there were many black slaves then, taken across the sea in great ships. In the hot country she had been put on board another ship and on that ship her master had put her to needlework, and if she would not work he had beaten her. But her mistress had been kind to her and would hide her away. Then the ship had been wrecked and the crew had all taken to the boat; but she and a negro girl had been left to live as they could. They had swum from the sinking ship, but because the negro girl could not swim so well as she, she had helped her, and the negro girl had kept herself from drowning by holding on to her foot.

So they had got to the shore. Then they had travelled a great way, moving only by night so that no one would see them and sleeping all through the day in the very tops of trees; and they had eaten roots, which they had dug out from the ground. When they could they had caught game and eaten it raw with the blood still warm, like beasts of prey; and once she had killed a fox, but the flesh had been bad to eat, so instead she had sucked the blood from it.

She had learned to imitate birdsong, for that was the only music known in her country; but she could not speak with the negro girl, for neither had known the other's language. For then she had known how to speak, though afterwards she had forgotten all the words she had known; and so they could only talk with each other by signs and by the wildest cries, such as had frightened the French people when she was caught.

Two or three days before she had been taken, they had passed across a great river; and there, unknown to the two girls, a man had been watching them from the woods, and seeing only the two black heads of the girls in the water he had mistaken them for two water cocks, and shot at them. But the man had missed them, and the sound of the gun had made them dive down and swim away out of reach of the danger.

When they had come out on the riverbank she had had a fish in each hand and an eel in her teeth; and she and the negro girl had eaten them up raw and gone on into the country away from the river. 'Soon after, she who is now become Mademoiselle Le Blanc, perceived the first a chaplet on the ground, which no doubt had been dropt by some passenger. Whether the novelty of the object delighted her, or whether it brought to her remembrance something of the same kind that she had seen before, is not known . . . '[7] And she immediately broke into dancing. As she was scared that her companion would take the chaplet, she reached to pick it up; but the negro girl, seeing her do so, struck her outstretched hand as hard as she could with the club she carried. And although her hand was hurt badly, she returned the blow, striking the negro girl on her brow. The negro girl fell to the ground and she was screaming; and the wound bled and she was touched with compassion about what she had done and ran in search of some frogs. When she found one she stripped off the skin and spread it upon the girl's brow to staunch the wound, binding the dressing in place with the thread from the bark of a tree.

With this the two companions wordlessly separated. The wounded girl took the way back to the river and the victorious one the path towards Songi; but she never said if she felt any loneliness then, nor anything of the pain and fear she felt on the day the French people trapped her.

Memmie gave this account on the first of many visits Burnett was to pay her. He was eager to have many more such conversations with her, for she was the greatest curiosity he had ever seen – a woman from the beginning of things, an atavism, a remembrance of all that we have lost. Steadily, determinedly, Burnett turned all his scepticism, shrewdness and philosophical fancy into two perhaps insoluble inquiries: who was Memmie Le Blanc? and where had she come from? And, more vitally, a greater question was forming in his mind: what could she tell him of the greatest mystery of all – the mystery of the origin of human nature?

III: A Paradoxical Man

He was much pleased with Lord Monboddo to-day. He said, he would
have pardoned him for a few paradoxes, when he had found so much that
was good. But that, from his appearance in London, he thought him all
paradox, which would not do . . .

Samuel Johnson on James Burnett, in James Boswell, *A Journal of a
Tour to the Hebrides*

James Burnett's obsession with Memmie Le Blanc began on that
spring day. For Burnett was pressed with a more than intellectual
hunger. He knew that the truth lay in Memmie, though concealed,
and he clung to her life in search of that answer.

There may have been other, more obviously personal reasons for
Burnett's fascination with Memmie. He was in France to secure
from hostile forces the inheritance of a remote relative of his, the
glamorous orphan, Lord Archibald Douglas. While he was in
France, Burnett's own mother died. He turned from his grief to his
investigations into the life of Memmie and to the writing of an essay
on Aristotle and intellectual elites. Burnett suffered from the abid-
ing fault of many overthoughtful men: his life too readily turned
into abstractions to shelter him from the blunt sufferings of experience. Yet in his captivation by Memmie Le Blanc we see a man
forcefully identifying himself with the bereft. In Memmie's abandonment there must have existed a dark comparison with his own
losses.

A satirical caricature by John Kay conveys Burnett's intense
thoughtfulness. He sits writing at a desk, dressed in a black tailcoat
with white cuffs and collar, wearing a grey powdered wig parted in
the middle with heavy bunches at each side. His elbow rests on the
table and he leans forward a little, a long finger pressed thoughtfully, rigidly, against his left cheek. A squashed, slightly crabbed face;
the nose jutting over a sceptical mouth and the eyes piercing and
rather sad, though the laugh-lines are strongly marked. His legs are

crossed, daintily stockinged, and his neat, small feet are pointed in black buckled shoes. Behind him there is a picture on a wall in which men with tails dance in a ring – a playful image for a man too eccentric to play.

All who met Burnett commented on his sprightliness and slim figure – the result of a philosophical abstemiousness. In imitation of the Ancients, he ate frugally and drank little: it was typical of his rigour that Burnett should live out his stoical principles in a manner that contemporaries found alternately laudable and ludicrous. In these habits he might be said to have lived out in actuality an otherwise intellectual pursuit of the primitive. For Burnett, there was little distance between thought and action: meeting Memmie was another way in which abstruse research would lead to actual, living involvement.

A clearer portrait of Burnett emerges in James Boswell's *Journal of a Tour to the Hebrides* (1785). Boswell himself stands at the edge of our story; some months after Burnett had met Memmie, Boswell arrived in Paris, where, like Burnett before him, he also heard of his mother's death. Where Burnett had studied, Boswell dissipated grief by heading straight for a brothel. The differences in the two men only added piquancy to their friendship: Boswell was great at remorse and, though inconsistent and promiscuous, attached himself limpet-like to moral, thoughtful, older men.

In his account of their tour of Scotland, Boswell described a visit paid in 1773 by himself and Samuel Johnson to Burnett (who had been made Lord Monboddo in 1767). Johnson and Burnett were old intellectual enemies, but Boswell guessed correctly that their surface antipathy masked a deeper affinity. Burnett met them at the gates of Monboddo castle, informally dressed in a rustic suit. The two great men spoke of Homer and of the uses of biography. Johnson tested Burnett's young son, Arthur, on his Latin knowledge, and was suitably impressed by the boy's learning. Burnett's black servant, Gory, also struck Johnson: Boswell 'observed how curious it was to see an African in the north of Scotland, with little or no difference of manners from those of the natives'.[8] Burnett himself comes across as affable, courteous, unaffected but nonetheless shrewd.

However, Burnett's home – the place called Monboddo – fares less well in Boswell's narrative. Lost in the bleakness of the Grampian Hills, as they rode on to Burnett's house, Johnson wonderingly and grumpily remarked how odd it was to be in a landscape quite so devoid of trees. Boswell lapsed into melancholy; they approached Monboddo in the falling rain across a wild and dreary moor. Monboddo itself seemed wretched, the house decrepit with age, despite the sad grandeur of its twin turrets.

This was the world in which Burnett grew up. He was born there on 25 October 1714 and spent his early years at the estate under the tutelage of Dr Francis Skeene. James Burnett, his father, was a large landowner, though not a fabulously wealthy one; his mother, Elizabeth, was, like his father, a Jacobite in politics and an Episcopalian in religion.

His education was typical of the intelligent Scottish landowners of his time: he followed his tutor to college at Aberdeen and from there went to Edinburgh University. He made the almost unavoidable choice of entering the legal profession and so went naturally to Gröningen, where he studied civil law for three years. Returning to Edinburgh, he passed his bar exams on 12 February 1737, and five days afterwards was admitted as a member of the Faculty of Advocates.

For the next twenty-six years he pursued an efficient if drab legal career. He practised the law; he studied; he established a fittingly intellectual outlet for his natural conviviality in the form of 'learned suppers' – fortnightly dinner parties at his house in Edinburgh, where he entertained his circle of legal and philosophical friends. It must have been an earnest, abstracted, bachelor life, though not one that could be called in any way 'retired'. In early middle age Burnett was a public figure: his career in the law was solidly successful and he moved as an equal among the best and brightest minds of his country.

Then, in 1758, at the age of forty-four, Burnett married. His bride was the 'beautiful and accomplished' Elizabeth Farquharson – stereotypical eighteenth-century adjectives that conceal more than they tell. In eight years she bore him three children: a daughter, a son, Arthur, and a second daughter.

In 1763, Burnett's legal life took a turn towards controversy and excitement. He found himself involved as a defence counsel in the legal case that made his name – the hotly contested Douglas Cause, one of the most rancorous and fiercely disputed legal actions of the eighteenth century. It was this that took Burnett to Paris, and without it he would never have met Mademoiselle Memmie Le Blanc.

It was during Burnett's third and longest trip to France to gather evidence for Douglas that he met Memmie. This third visit, which lasted well over a year, began in August 1764. He put up at the Hôtel d'Espaine in the Rue Guénégaut. (The pursuers, or prosecution, were staying at the Hôtel de Tours, one of the more expensive and exclusive hotels in Paris, just down the road from the defenders at Rue de Paon.) Paris must have seemed an alienating place to these visiting Scots. British visitors were struck by the lights of Paris at night: five thousand eight hundred glimmering lanterns of glass suspended from cords down the middle of the streets. There were other estrangements: the huge number of pet dogs, the lack of tea, the numerous convents and roadside Virgins, the arrogant trendiness of the French, the women's penchant for heavy white make-up, and the new and inexplicable fashion for rouge. Paris was the capital of amusement: 'Levity is the fifth element of the French . . . This is the Region of Pleasure. Lovers sigh not long, Jealousy torments no body.'[9]

Burnett was gathering evidence for Douglas, and there was plenty of evidence to be had. Rumours and stories circulated the city. But when he came to look for information regarding Memmie,

Burnett was not to be so fortunate. Memmie appears to us in her fullness: alive, quick of spirit, and – even after the long process of her taming – a vivid, unignorable presence. Yet, in comparison to what we might know, the background that surrounds Memmie is insubstantial and vague. It is typical of the way in which she was continually treated that the first few years of her life among the French are filled with detail and anecdote, whereas the years that stretch before and after are virtual blanks. Memmie was born to experience again and again the raising and dashing of her expectations, as champions appeared, turned their curiosity upon her, and then effectively discarded her.

Hadn't she been born into a life that did not have the depth to verify her identity? The meaning that would hold her in place was behind her and so lost as to seem irrecoverable. She was adrift in a Paris to which she did not belong: she had placed her secret, her self, in the hands of decent, curious James Burnett.

How mysterious to Burnett and how unknowable was the history of Memmie Le Blanc, cast adrift from solid fact and the provable; and if she was a mystery, how much greater was the mystery she herself embodied and lived: that drowned origin and pattern of the whole human race.

IV: On Eskimos

. . . no better authority than signs . . .
  Madame Hecquet, *An Account of a Savage Girl*

As we cast further back into Memmie's life, less and less is known for certain. So Burnett now engaged in an even harder process of detective work, reconstructing Memmie's lost past, just as Madame Hecquet, Memmie's biographer, had struggled to do before him.

A Mrs Cockburn had written to Hume that Burnett was, like himself, engaged in a quest for truth. Although Burnett knew that truth was necessarily relative and impure in this world of appearances, it was nonetheless his work and his passion to discover what could be known. With Douglas, he held fast to his faith; with Memmie Le Blanc, he would likewise set out to ascertain the truth about her.

In order to gather information for the Douglas Cause, Burnett travelled with Robertson, his clerk, to Rheims, in Champagne. The journey presented too good an opportunity to miss: Chalons, where Memmie had lived, was as near as it would ever be. So the two men took time off to journey on to the Convent des régentes at Chalons, and from there to Songi itself. At the convent, the abbess entertained Burnett with anecdotes of Memmie's girlhood, of how she could imitate birdsong, or run along the rooftops. At Songi, Burnett interviewed several of the villagers, confirming much of what he had already heard from Memmie's own lips; but Burnett was after more tangible evidence.

He had been immediately intrigued by what Memmie had told him of her club and knife. The strange characters carved on these weapons particularly had enticed him to Songi. If he could see them, copy them, even bring them back to Paris or Edinburgh, surely here would be the strongest possible clue for discovering Memmie's home and how she had been brought to France. The weapons were in the possession of the new Viscount d'Epinoy. So, following Memmie's footsteps, Burnett made the short journey from the village to the chateau. But he had no luck. Half an hour before Burnett and Robertson arrived, the Viscount left his residence at Songi. Not one of the household who remained behind could tell the Scotsmen anything concerning the bludgeon.

This dissolution of hard facts into doubtfulness seemed to occur at every point when Burnett, or anyone else, tried to really fathom out the identity of the savage girl. What, for instance, had happened to Memmie's companion, the negro girl she had lived with and left wounded by the banks of the Marne? There were vague reports that she had been found dead some leagues from Songi; Memmie remembered that she had been seen at Toul in Lorraine, though she did not say whether she was dead or alive. Was that likely? Could she really have swum back across the Marne, wounded as she was? Furthermore, Memmie had told Madame Hecquet that various letters had been found concerning this same girl; but where were these papers now? Only one letter existed saying that the lost black girl had been sighted near Cheppe, a village not far from Songi, but afterwards had disappeared, never to be seen again.

Then there was the question of the story circulated by 'M L–'. He had told Madame Hecquet of a report that he had once heard from M d'Epinoy's family. In this account, the two savages had been sold in the islands of America. They had become their mistress's favourites, but their master had disliked them and so had sold them both to slavers. The story was both convincing and likely; but there were doubts over its provenance. What could really guarantee its truthfulness?

> These circumstances agree pretty well with those set forth in the letter already mentioned, printed in the Mercury of France: But it is apparent, that these particulars arise altogether from conjectures more or less probable, formed upon the first signs and expressions that were obtained from the young girl, when she began to speak French, some months after being taken; and certainly so circumstantiate a relation, founded on no better authority than signs, is very little to be depended on.[10]

Soon after her arrival speculation began about where the girl had come from. She might be a Norwegian or a native of Guadeloupe or St Domingo or any other of France's possessions in the West Indies. After all, how else could she have learned her first words of French so easily? And hadn't a gentleman of Chalons not given her, out of curiosity, some manioc, a West Indian bread, which she had appeared to recognize instantly, exclaiming for joy and snatching it from him to eat?

This concern with Memmie's place of origin and hence with her racial identity marks out a new direction in the history of the feral child. In part, this is due to the particular nature of Memmie's case and the fact that she was effectively a castaway in populous France, a mirror-image of Robinson Crusoe, a savage shipwrecked in the midst of civilization.

Most of us are familiar with the experience of being abroad, confronted by strange customs and an alien language. Memmie is the ultimate exemplar of such alienation. There were other stories like hers current at the time – as, for instance, Voltaire's *L'Ingénu* re-imagines France through the eyes of a visiting 'savage'. Like Voltaire's Huron, or Shakespeare's Miranda, Memmie comes upon a Europe that appears to her as a brave new world.

Moreover, Memmie's discovery of Europe parodies and inverts the European discovery of the New World. Like Peter the Wild Boy, she presents to us the possibility of seeing *ourselves* as strange and new. For in Memmie's story, we find a curious inversion of the tourist's dilemma. This was not a case in which the outsider alone felt the shock of strangeness. The French – those who were at home – were themselves perplexed and disturbed by Memmie. The inexplicable fact of her arrival might begin to endanger the security and certainty of the known. Without setting one foot outside the familiar streets of Paris, here could be had an experience just then being repeated across the Americas, Africa and the South Seas: the complex fear, shame, disgust and enticement that European colonists felt on their first contact with 'savages'.

While Madame Hecquet was printing her biography of Memmie, Jean-Jacques Rousseau published his seminal work, *Discourse on the Origins of Inequality*. Rousseau looked back with regret to the primitive origins of humankind, seeing in our simple beginnings a dignity, grace and vitality lost in sophisticated society. Therefore Memmie appeared in France just at that moment in which Rousseau revolutionized our understanding of the 'savage'. Just as had happened with Peter, the rapid colonial expansion into America and Africa meant that the European public was fascinated by the diversity of human beings. The experience of this diversity could for a while fit into a sense of the universality of human nature. However, the colonial enterprise and the economic necessities of the enormous Atlantic slave trade meant that Europeans increasingly saw in the 'savages' they met, not a counter-image of themselves, but a species of human so different as to make any possibility of connection painful.

The issue at stake in Memmie's case was, as was always to be the way with feral children, the definition of what it was to be human. For here was a creature human in appearance, but acting in such a way as to seem inhuman. How could the civilized claim kinship with such a creature – dumb, vicious, bloodthirsty, dirty, bestial?

In the responses to Memmie we find the first indications of a wholly new solution to this problem. What if Memmie represented not a different way of being human, but instead belonged to the savage and animalistic place from which we have emerged? Might not Memmie, and all others like her, be simply that which we needed to conquer in order to become the civilized people that we are? In this way observers could console themselves with the idea that they had rejected the life that she had led, and had grown beyond the nightmare loneliness of her dark heart.

In Memmie's story we catch the first strains of a motif to be played over and over again in the next two hundred years. Here are the first indications of a way of thinking that combines an interest in race with an evolutionary model of human development. If Memmie was to be understood, it seemed she must be known in terms of her racial origins. Once her home had been found, she could be finally known.

It was Madame Hecquet and Burnett who investigated Memmie's origins most rigorously. Yet when Madame Hecquet began to explore Memmie's past, she found herself brought up against a wall of things forgotten.

Memmie had told Madame Hecquet that she did not begin to reflect on her life until after her reclamation from the wilds.[11] Before then she existed purely in an immediate, continuous now, aware only of her animal wants. Casting her mind back into that state, she could find nothing: no father, nor mother; no sister, nor brother, nor playmate. There were dim, unbodied recollections: she some-how felt that there could not have been houses in the place where she was born, only holes in the ground, or long barracks covered in snow into which the people crept on their hands and knees.

The only particular memory she had was of seeing a huge animal in the sea, swimming with two feet like a dog, with a round head and large eyes. The black creature had swum towards her and she, fear-ing that she would be eaten, had darted back to the shore. Could this be a seal? Madame Hecquet wondered; and, if so, what might that say about Memmie's place of origin?

In fact, from all she learnt, Madame Hecquet was convinced that Memmie must be an Eskimo, brought hither to France from the frozen sea in the far north. Memmie's love for the water, her indif-ference to the cold and the frost, her white skin and her love of raw food all seemed to indicate that the Arctic was her natural home.

However, how she had come to France was still unclear. Madame Hecquet speculated that it must have happened like this: a slave ship from Holland or the north of Scotland went to Labrador with the intention of getting slaves to take to the West Indies. There the savage girl was captured, and painted black, either for 'a frolic' or with the intention of passing her off as an African or, more specifi-cally, a native of Guinea.[12] Having brought the little Eskimo to the West Indies, by boat from Labrador or Greenland, her owners dis-covered that she would not acclimatize to the Caribbean heat. So the young savage and her negro companion were brought to Europe by sea. Perhaps then they jumped ship at the Zuyder Zee and made their way, journeying for several months, across the forest of the Ardennes. Or maybe they were taken for house servants to some French landowner, who bought them in the West Indies on a caprice. Finding them too unmanageable, once they were in France, the landowner encouraged or allowed their escape.

Madame Hecquet's self-appointed task was to prove that Memmie was an Eskimo. She admitted that the 'facts' were all highly doubtful. Yet she sought a truth about Memmie that might circumvent the errors and misjudgements of language.

At one point in her biography of Memmie, Madame Hecquet decides to try a curious experiment with her subject. An old friend of Madame Hecquet's, Madame Duplessis, had sent to Paris a collection of dolls from Quebec in the likeness of the New World savages. Among them were an Eskimo and his wife carrying her baby.

With these dolls, Madame Hecquet resolved 'to try the force of nature' in the savage girl.[13] She sat with Memmie and produced the box full of 'savage puppets'. On opening the box, Madame Hecquet carefully observed her subject, hoping to catch in her some indication of who she was. Memmie instantly picked out the Eskimo couple, despite the fact that the other dolls were more colourful and more interestingly adorned. She gazed at both, without speaking. Observing her delight, Madame Hecquet smiled and asked, 'in order to make her speak', whether she had found some of her relatives. Memmie could not be certain; and yet they reminded her of something. She had seen something like them before. 'How! said I, men and women of that shape? Pretty much so, answered she; but they had not that, (pointing to a sort of glove which my figures have).'

As they spoke further, Memmie's connection to the figures grew weaker and weaker. Madame Hecquet picked out some other figures, wearing earrings; Memmie explained that her people had rings that reached from the bottom of the ear down their backs; but as this had nothing to do with the Eskimos, Madame Hecquet reluctantly dismissed this new evidence:

> As I could discover nothing about my figures, nor in the accounts sent me along with them, that could give me any idea of this difference [that is, between the dolls and Memmie's remembrance], or which might have suggested it to her, I imagined that it had only occurred to her from the remembrance of something she had seen in her younger days, and of which she had just a confused idea. And, indeed, she immediately added herself, these ideas are so remote, that they are little to be depended on.[14]

However, crucially, Madame Hecquet chose not to depend on Memmie's words at all. It was not what Memmie said in this scene that bore her authentic self; it was that instinct, that 'natural unaffected sentiment' that made her act by directing her hands and her gaze to the Eskimo puppets alone. Words deceive; nature does not: 'Such, at least, was my reasoning on the distinction she made between them, and her saying so naturally, '*We had nothing on our hands*;' which the truth alone, tho' without her knowledge, made her utter.'[15]

In this scene the sense that Memmie exists as the unconscious authenticator of her own identity reaches a point of climax. Prejudice blinds Madame Hecquet, making her disregard objections to her favoured belief about Memmie's origins. She allows a place to doubts that might arise from her troubled apprehension of the Eskimo figures, but only in order to class them as peripheral. Memmie becomes a cipher, a bearer of a truth she herself cannot understand.

It is crucial that the girl's natural self appears in a physical action, the taking up of the Eskimo dolls, and not in her later, more ambivalent discussion concerning them. Memmie acts from a responsiveness, a sensibility, deeper than that of the civilized self. It is because she is 'sensible' – in other words, open to spontaneous feeling – that her actions display an inner, indisputable truth. The speaking presence of Memmie felt by the reader is immaterial to the writer's own conscious concerns.

Burnett's methods were somewhat different from Madame Hecquet's, yet both of Memmie's investigators shared a faith in the idea that beneath the confusion of signs an inner, essential truth is there to be discovered. Like Madame Hecquet, Burnett came to the disappointing – and, to us, irrelevant – conclusion that Memmie's secret was one that could be solved in racial terms. However, as we shall see, he was also reaching towards a further solution for Memmie's identity that moved beyond the barriers of race.

Burnett likewise found out as much as he could from Memmie in their meetings together in her apartment on the Rue St Antoine. She told him that the country she came from was very cold and covered with snow the greater part of the year; that the children there swam as soon as they could walk; that when she came to France she could not live if she could not swim and that she swam as well as any otter; that a child of a year old there could climb a tree; that there were fly-ing squirrels there; that the people lived in little huts over the water, like the beavers did; that they ate mostly fish; that their clothes were skins; that they had no fires there, and that when she came to France she could not bear a fire in a room, nor even the close air; that there were another people there, bigger than her own people, and stronger; that they fought together, and if their enemies caught them they would eat them.[16]

Some idioms of her lost language she could still remember: to wound was 'to make him red' and to kill was 'to make him sleep long'. For their greeting they said, 'I see you'. She remembered too how they buried their dead. The dead one was put into a case, some-thing like an armchair. His nearest relative then addressed the dead one, telling how they had eyes, but could not see; ears, but could not hear; legs, yet could not walk; a mouth, yet could not eat. What has become of you? And whither have you gone? And the burial was concluded with a cry of mourning and loss and utter despair, which she had used often to the terror of all those who heard her when she had been first caught.[17]

About one thing Burnett was certain: Memmie was anything but an Eskimo. He considered Madame Hecquet's knowledge of Eskimos to be rather sketchy. She seems to have relied chiefly on the travel writings of Baron La Hontan and a letter sent to her by Madame Duplessis. This letter describes how the Eskimos are sunk in the deepest barbarism: 'They are a nation of Anthropophagi, who devour men whenever they can lay their hands upon them. They are of a low stature, white, and very fat.' Madame Duplessis believed them to worship fire, to eat their food raw and to dress themselves in the skins of seals. Eskimo girls were much valued as servants, and were often captured and civilized; but although they seemed happy in the houses of their masters, they very soon died, like all the savages who lived among the French.[18]

Burnett effectively discredits Hecquet's Eskimo thesis. Most importantly, Memmie just did not look like an Eskimo: she was fair-complexioned, smooth-skinned, her features as soft as a European: 'Whereas the people of the Esquimaux nation, are, by the accounts of all travellers, the ugliest of men, of the harshest and most disagreeable features, and all covered with hair.'[19] (As we can see, Burnett's information on Eskimos was as flawed as Madame Hecquet's.)

However, Burnett was more convinced by Madame Hecquet's theory that Memmie's origin should be placed in the wildernesses of northern America. Memmie, Burnett declared, was a Huron. The evidence was plain enough: her language with its tell-tale lack of labial consonants (such as 'b', or 'p', or 'm') or lingual consonants (such as 'g'); her weapons, which were typical of the Huron tribe; her looks; her 'whiteness'.

So, what of Memmie's own reports of her history? Madame Hecquet felt that the whole narrative was founded on the most insubstantial of facts:

> Le Blanc acknowledges that in the various relations she has made
> to me on different occasions, there are several particulars of
> which she retains but a confused and indistinct remembrance,
> and which she suspects to be blended with circumstances that
> she may have imagined after she began to reflect on the questions
> asked her at first, and constantly repeated to her afterwards.[20]

Words were not enough. Furthermore, there was the question of
how much of Memmie's story had been suggested to her by her first
questioners. How far might her guardians' commentary on her
adventures have formed her own idea of her life?

Like Madame Hecquet, Burnett knew the protean nature of language. His work as a lawyer on the Douglas Cause was daily showing him the erratic and puzzling nature of the reconstruction of the
past. Yet like Madame Hecquet he saw in Memmie a clue, an indication, of something real, universal and innate – something that lay
just beyond the arbitrary culture of language.

Burnett was an odd mixture of the sceptical and the stubbornly
opinionated. He knew that the truth was difficult to find, confused,
melting, insubstantial; and yet he also trusted wholeheartedly to the
certainty of his beliefs. He saw in the Douglas Cause a maze of
contradictory facts and yet never appeared to really doubt the
authenticity of Archibald Douglas. In Memmie, he saw a puzzle, yet
one that never ceased to entice him on to the settling of the greatest
questions of all.

V: On Orang-Outangs

Man, the Prince of animated beings, who is a miracle of Nature, and for
whom all things on this earth were created, is a mimic animal . . .
  Carl von Linnæus, *The System of Nature*

We know of one further expedition that Burnett made during this
final stay in Paris. Le Jardin Royal des Plantes was in the 16th

Quarter of the city, a botanic garden of exotic trees and curious plants, looking out on to the countryside towards the Château de Vincennes. In the summer months students came to attend the morning lectures on botany and chemistry; there were also anatomy lectures given all year long in the great ampitheatre. The superintendent of the Jardin Du Roi was Georges-Louis Leclerc, otherwise known as Comte de Buffon, the most famous natural historian of the day and, as we shall soon see, a strong influence on Burnett's ideas about Memmie.

At the botanic gardens, Burnett had come to see the King's *cabinet des curiosités*, made internationally famous by Buffon's *Histoire Naturelle*. The collection was divided into three rooms. In the first there was a set of skeletons, a complete set of foetuses from the minutest embryo to a full-term baby, a fine collection of shells and coral, and all the newest inventions in machinery. In the second room you could find precious stones and rare geological samples; and in the third were more antique stones – agate, onyx, emerald, topaz – a collection of insects, fishes in spirits, serpents from the smallest to one six yards in length, skeletons of birds, a newly invented brazen sphere, and animals 'anatomically prepared'.

It was one of these animals that had drawn Burnett to the King's gardens: the orang-outang. The creature was stuffed and standing on a shelf. Burnett was struck by its exact resemblance to the shape and features of a man. He then found out from his guide that it also possessed all the necessary organs of pronunciation. The orang-outang had once lived for several years at Versailles, but had eventually died from drinking spirits. With a slight sexual and probably unintentional innuendo, Burnett notes of the dead beast: 'He had as much of the understanding of a man as could be expected from his education, and performed many little offices to the lady with whom he lived; but never learned to speak.'[21] Burnett's guide described another orang-outang – likewise mute – who lived in India with his French master, and would accompany him to the market.

Later Burnett was to have the luck of seeing two living orang-outangs in London. He was strongly tempted to buy one, poor as he was, for the asking price of £50. Then he might have had him educated, raising him perhaps even to the level of an ordinary, civilized man.

Burnett's curiosity about the orang-outang finally led him to the unshakeable belief that this creature was a kind of human that could be taught to speak. In popular understanding Burnett became famous for a series of such obsessions and cranky beliefs. The others were: that language was a social acquisition; that men had once had tails; that human beings had degenerated since ancient times; and his fascination with feral children. He pursued these ideas in two monumental works: the six-volume *Of the Origin and Progress of Language*, published between 1773 and 1792, and the equally enormous *Antient Metaphysics*, also published in six volumes, the last of which was printed in 1799, the year of his death, when he was eighty-five years old. These interests were generally condemned as eccentric – so much so that Burnett became in later years a figure of fun.

The most notable image of Burnett as visionary crank occurs in Peacock's satirical novel of 1818, *Melincourt*. Here Burnett is recast as Forester, a dreamy and melancholy man who educates and befriends a great ape, Lord Oran-Hutan. Lord Oran is a courteous if completely silent companion whose unusual airs soon mark him out for a glittering social career, culminating in his election to Parliament.

However, Burnett's fascination with the orang-outang was not as strange or as eccentric in his own time as may at first appear. Burnett took his place among a growing number of naturalists and natural philosophers becoming fascinated by apes and monkeys. For, as with the child of nature, here was something that dramatized the distinction between animals and humans, a living creature that challenged and so defined the limits and essence of humanity.

Burnett had come to the end of what could be known of the external facts of Memmie's history. If he was to think about her interior identity, he must now look elsewhere, turning to the writings of the natural historians. Maybe, in the work of Buffon and Linnæus, Burnett would find a clue that would solve the mystery that surrounded Memmie Le Blanc.

It was Linnæus and Buffon, the two giants of eighteenth-century natural history, who fixed the central importance of the orang-outang for Burnett. The great project of these natural historians was to establish and codify the essences, elements and distinctions that separate species. They approached this enterprise from radically different standpoints.

Buffon is often seen as a precursor of evolutionary thought. He places a potential for instability into his description of the natural world. His enormous forty-four-volume natural history is a surprisingly lively read, filled with eloquent anecdotes and improbable tales. His animals act like creatures in stories and possess an almost human capacity for changefulness.

Contrariwise, Linnæus depicts the static nature of animals and plants, the austere regularity of his work showing a creature removed from the flow of time and held up to an examining eye. Yet this should not imply merely the dry work of classification. In Linnæus we find the discipline of order raised to the level of vision, a hymn to the plenitude of existence:

'Awakened, as if from a dream of ignorance, I have seen darkly, as he passed, the Eternal, Infinite, Omniscient, Almighty God, and am amazed! I have read of him in some traces of his wondrous works, the smallest of which, though comparatively insignificant, even to a degree of nothingness, evinces the most incomprehensible perfection of Power and Wisdom.'[22]

It is not too far a leap from this to William Blake seeing heaven in a grain of sand.

In the classification of primates, Linnæus places the orang-outang among the order of 'Simia'. Yet in this division the orang-outang continues to play an ambiguous and destabilizing role:

2. Orang-outang. – 2. Simia Satyrus. I

Has no tail. Is of a rusty brown colour; the hair on the fore-arms is reversed, or stands upwards; and the buttocks are covered with hair. Amoen. acad. vi. 68. tab. lxxvi. f. 4.

Homo sylvestris, or wild man of the woods. Edwards, av. v. 6. tab. 213. – Orang-outang. Camper kort beright, &c. Amsterdam 1788, p. 8.

Inhabits the island of Borneo. – Is about two feet high, and walks mostly erect. The body and limbs are universally covered with brown hair, about an inch long, which is thinly interspersed with reddish hairs; the hair on the fore-arms, towards the wrists, is reversed, or lies with its points turned towards the elbow; the buttocks are covered with hair: The head is round, having a naked forehead; the margin of the mouth is hairy, the eye-lashes are black, the upper being longer and thicker than those below, and a range of transversely placed hairs occupies the place of eye-brows: The nose is very short, and is covered with down: The palms of the hands are smooth, and the thumb is shorter than the palm; the feet resemble those of man, except that the great toes are considerably shorter than the others, which are very long.

Much as this species resembles mankind, even possessing the os hyoides, it must still be referred to the genus of Ape, with which it agrees in wanting the flat round nail of the great toes, and in the structure of the larynx; besides those circumstances, it is evident, from the direction of the muscles, and from the whole figure of the skeleton, that the animal is not designed by nature for an erect posture.[23]

It is clear from this that Linnæus had no doubt that the orang-outang was not human. Yet confusion remains. Through the semantic and scientific identification of the orang-outang with the *Homo sylvestris*, or wild man of the woods, the orang-outang could be placed on both sides of the human–animal divide. Linnaeus's 'Four-footed, mute, hairy' '*Wild Man*'[24] could wrongly be felt to include the orang-outang in the context of the human species.

Confusions could likewise arise from a study of Buffon on the orang-outang. Buffon bases his analysis of the orang-outang on an account left by Andrew Battell, a sixteenth-century English sailor shipwrecked on the coast of Africa. Battell describes the Pongo and the Engecko, two species of 'Monsters' that he specifically separates from ordinary apes and monkeys:

> The greatest of these two Monsters is called, Pongo, in their language; and the lesser is called, Engeco. This Pongo is in all proportion like a man, but that he is more like a Giant in stature, than a man; for he is very tall, and hath a man's face, hollow-eyed, with long haire upon his browes . . . They feed upon Fruit that they find in the Woods and upon Nuts, for they eate no kind of flesh. They cannot speak and have no understanding more than a beast.[25]

In his *Natural History*, Buffon equates the 'Pongo' with the orang-outang and the 'Jocko' with the chimpanzee. Buffon describes the activities of one orang-outang as he himself witnessed it:

> The orang-outang which I saw, walked always upright, even when it carried heavy burthens. Its air was melancholy, its deportment grave, its nature more gentle and very different from that of other apes. I have seen it sit at table, unfold its napkin, wipe its lips, make use of the spoon and the fork to carry the victuals to its mouth, pour out its drink into a glass, touch glasses when invited, take a cup and saucer and lay them on the table, put in sugar, pour out its tea, leave it to cool before drinking, and all

this without any other instigation than the signs of the command of its master, and often of its own accord. It was gentle and inoffensive; it even approached strangers with respect, and came rather to receive caresses than to offer injuries . . . [26]

Here is a litany of politeness in which, through Buffon's rapt precision, the familiar becomes enchanted and strange. The ape performs the everyday etiquette of drinking tea; he both reduces that etiquette to a bestial charade and reveals it as a miraculous wonder. In this mirror of ourselves we are not just impressed by the accomplishment of a human task, but also forcefully grasp the fact that this experience is truly a convention in which we too are hapless mimics.

Like Linnæus, Buffon is clear that the orang-outang is simply an ape. Yet his descriptions of it reveal to us an animal capable of politeness, sensitivity and the most delicate tact. We see an orang-outang who covers her genitalia ('those parts . . . which modesty forbids the sight of'); even one ape that dies of a broken heart, pining away from grief after his 'wife' has died.

Likewise the captain, named Begg, of a Liverpool ship related the following story to Burnett:

In a voyage to Old Callabar in Africa, I purchased a female Ourang Outang from one of the natives. She was, as I was informed, about eight months old, four foot six inches high, of a dark brown colour, but white about the breasts; of a gentle disposition, walked generally upright on her hind feet, sometimes on all four; but the latter seemed to me not to be her natural motion . . . She would often drink a tumbler glass of wine and water, and always put the glass fairly down on its bottom, and never broke one. She was very fond of the girls and boys, but more particularly of the latter, and would weep and cry like a child when she was vexed; but never shewed any signs of great ferocity, and was easily appeased. I gave her a blanket for a bed, which she would take great pains to spread in such a manner as to make it smooth and easy, and then would lie down. She always slept with her hands (if I may use the expression) under her head, and would snore when asleep, resembling the human species. She lived three months, and died of the dysentery.[27]

It was primed with these images that Burnett made the short journey across Paris to the Royal Gardens to take his first look at a orang-outang; but what did this journey have to do with Memmie Le Blanc? In short, everything: Burnett's impassioned, obsessive defence of our own kinship to the orang-outang is the key for understanding all that he saw in Memmie Le Blanc. Burnett was famous for establishing a theory of evolutionary continuity; it was only when he brought together Memmie and the orang-outang in his mature philosophy that he found the answer to his questions concerning human life.

Burnett's philosophy is now little read, even in the universities. If he is remembered at all, it is as an Enlightenment precursor of Darwin, another signpost on a journey towards our own post-Darwinian, DNA-based image of ourselves. Paradoxically (and Samuel Johnson had declared Burnett all paradox),[28] it is where Burnett's philosophy looks most modern that it is most traditional. People have thought his work prophetic of evolution when it is an echo of scholasticism, pre-Darwinian when it is post-Aristotelian. Yet it is precisely this 'old-fashioned' quality in Burnett's writings that make him of continuing and lasting interest. His problems are our problems; his immersion in a tradition we have lost offers us the surprise of a possible solution.

Throughout his philosophical writings, Burnett returns over and over to the figures of the orang-outang and the child of nature. In these figures, Burnett could see that an answer might be found regarding the most important question of all: what makes us 'human'?

Burnett imagines a world continually in motion driven onwards
and upwards by the power of 'mind'. He rejects the Newtonian universe of mechanical bodies, placing in its stead a world of actual
striving and desire, in which the energy of 'mind' actively seeks to
realize itself in time. This principle of mind in human beings
embarks them on a journey from a life purely physical to one spiritual, absorbed in the contemplation of the highest of all minds, God.
The story of human life tells of a transition, a history of changes.

In this ascent of human nature, a moment comes in which the
tendency of humans to gather together socially leads to the invention of speech. Growing out of the impersonal, necessary messages
that we see in the animal kingdom there emerges in human terms a
mode of communication founded upon the personal and the gratu-
itous. The artifice of human society allows human beings to change
from a pre-linguistic to a language-using creature. With the
moment of language the human gives itself up to the fabrication of
its own world. For language brings the equivocal gift of self-consciousness, an apprehension that humans share only with the highest primates.

An immense series of imperceptible and minute changes draws
the human being away from its animal origins. Burnett links this
process to our development from infancy to adulthood, in which an
individual likewise passes through a continuous series of changes.
Burnett imagines a model of life in which humanity is not given, but
is instead something acquired at some indefinable point in a series
of subtle gradations.

This is what drew Burnett to Memmie Le Blanc, what took him on
that visit to Peter the Wild Boy, and what fascinated him in travellers'
accounts of the orang-outang. The child of nature and the orang-
outang are living records of an evolutionary process that all humanity has passed through. The orang-outang exists in the infinitesimal
gap that separates the human being from the animal. Possessing
humanity itself, it is an interval, a bridge between us and the beasts.

Burnett believed that the finite system of the chain of being abhors a vacuum: it wishes to fill every space with things that look backwards to that which they emerged from, and forwards to that which they will become.

Burnett describes the three prior conditions of humanity: the most primitive is that represented by Peter the Wild Boy – silent, bestial, solitary; then the orang-outang, still silent but possessing the possibility of speech and sociability; and finally the last hesitation before the full realization of the human embodied in Memmie Le Blanc, both social and language-using, yet separated from full humanity by the minutest of discrepancies. Human and yet different, she lives in the state of nature that we have left behind.

When Burnett arrived in Edinburgh, he suggested that Robertson, his clerk, might translate Madame Hecquet's work into English. Burnett himself provided a preface for the book. Here he indicated that for the 'philosophical reader' there are things in Memmie's story that those who read it purely for the Robinson Crusoe-like romance would miss. What would this ideal 'philosophical reader' find in Memmie Le Blanc?

He will observe with amazement the progression of our species from an animal to wild, to men such as we. He will see evidently, by this example, that though man is by his natural bent and inclination disposed to society, like many other animals, yet he is not by natural *necessity* social, nor obliged to live upon a joint stock, like ants or bees; but is enabled, by his natural powers, to provide for his own subsistence, as much as any other animal, and more than most, as his means of subsistence are more various. In tracing back the long line of man's progression, he will discover another state of our nature even beyond that in which this girl was, however near it may seem to the original, I mean the state before language was invented, that is, the communication of general ideas, by the articulation of the voice, when men were literally, as the poet describes them, *mutum et turpe pecus* [mute and disgraced by sin]: For it is impossible to suppose, that language, the most wonderful art among men, should have been born with us, and practised by us from mere instinct, unless we could at the same time suppose, that other arts came into the world with us in the same manner; nor can we believe that it was sooner invented than other arts much less difficult, and more obvious.

In this manner, the philosopher will discover a state of nature, very different from what is commonly known by that name: And from this point of view, he will see, – That these superior faculties of mind, which distinguish our nature from that of any other animal on this earth, are not *congenial* with it, as to the exercise of energy, but *adventitious* and *acquired*, being only at first *latent powers* in our nature, which have been evolved and brought into exertion by degrees, in the course of our progression above mentioned, from one state to another – That the *rational* man has grown out of the mere *animal*, and that *reason* and *animal sensation*, however distinct we may imagine them, run into one another by such insensible degrees, that it is as difficult, or perhaps more difficult, to draw the line betwixt these two, than betwixt the *animal* and the *vegetable*.[29]

Here is Memmie's significance for Burnett and for ourselves: in her we find a mirror of what we essentially were. Memmie's life is the world from which we have grown. In meeting her, in reading of her, we see in reflection the deepest origins of our selves; and isn't the orang-outang also a kind of mirror, a mimic of those actions we assume to be most natural to us: drinking our tea, wiping our lips with our napkins, turning on our side to sleep, neatly arranging our beds, acting out our modesty, crying, missing someone, dying from grief?

Imitation fascinated Burnett – that process by which we 'become another man'.[30] Perhaps language also emerged from mimicry.

Burnett saw that humans develop through imitation, through acquiring the process of analogy; and this principle of resemblance – of analogy – is at the heart of Burnett's understanding of Memmie Le Blanc.

The question Burnett asked himself was this: when, in the woods of Champagne, Memmie was silent, when all her own words had left her and she had not yet been stranded on the other shore of speaking French, what then made her human?

His answer was simple and surprising. It was the observable likeness of her behaviour, of her appearance, to our own, that made him certain she was human. Hadn't Linnæus declared man to be a mimic animal? Memmie was human in so far as she was caught in the web of resemblances.

Alongside Burnett's investigations into the origins of humanity, we find other, more divisive explorations of the human. Lord Kames, Burnett's fellow judge on the Douglas Cause and great philosophical rival, was similarly intensely interested in delineating the origins of the human. However, whereas Burnett extends the definition of the human to include, for instance, the orang-outang, Kames tends to limit humanity by multiplying distinctions between races, so that he ends by declaring a separate origin for the native Americans. What might particularly disturb us is that both Kames and Burnett place our ability to distinguish human from animal in a natural faculty that relies on external marks: human identity resides in a surface that can be read. The fact that this same innate sense leads Burnett to incorporate the diverse and Kames to reject the different indicates its weakness.

Burnett states the classical idea of the universally human, but in such a way as to indicate the later racialized direction of writing on feral children. In 1799 Charles White likewise used the orang-outang as a basis for defining human beings:

All those who have had opportunities of making observations on the orang-outangs, agree in ascribing to them, not only a remark-

able docility of disposition, but also actions and affections similar
to those observable in the human kind . . . They discover signs of
modesty: and instances are related of the strongest attachments
of the male to the female. When sick, these animals have been
known to suffer themselves to be blooded, and even to invite the
operation; and to submit to other necessary treatment, like rational creatures . . . They have been taught to play upon musical
instruments, as the pipe and harp. They have been known to
carry off negro-boys, girls, and even women, with a view of making them subservient to their wants as slaves, or as objects of brutal passion: and it has been asserted by some, that women have
had offspring from such connections.[31]

White also repeats Burnett's model of an evolutionary chain of
being. However, White lays more stress on the boundaries within
the genus 'Homo'. He places the 'lower' races such as the African at
the bottom of a hierarchical scale that ascends to the European
races at the summit.

This was a model that was to be transcribed on to Burnett's other
models of human development. A four-fold development emerged:
from ape to human; from 'savage' tribes to European; from infant to
adult; from feral child to civilized man. The wild child could therefore embody the condition of beast, savage and infant. The child of
nature was now placed firmly at the bottom of every possible scale
of development. By the middle of the nineteenth century, these
hierarchical models would be played against each other as analogies – and as more than analogies. As we shall see, these models of
development would grow to constitute a ubiquitous method for
understanding the world. The seeds of our own thought are there to
see in Burnett.

In his own view, Burnett had satisfactorily answered the questions that Memmie had raised. Almost despite himself, he had
reduced living, breathing Memmie Le Blanc to an image, a neces-

sary stage in an argument. In philosophizing her life, Burnett had unwittingly played his part in her subtle vanishing from her own story.

VI: On Aristocrats and Orphans

They named it. But my poor island's still
un-rediscovered, un-renamable.
None of the books has ever got it right . . .
   Elizabeth Bishop, 'Crusoe in England'

In the autumn of 1765, Burnett went home. His task in Paris was done. Back in Edinburgh, he began work on organizing the evidence gathered in France into the Defender's Memorial for Lord Douglas. (A 'memorial' was a compendium in prose form of all the evidence gathered by defence or prosecution in a Scottish legal case.) He relaxed by continuing his study on the lives of savages, reading John Byron's account of the Patagonians. His wife fell pregnant; they looked forward to the birth of their third child. But on 28 October 1766, Elizabeth Burnett died giving birth to a daughter. As had happened following the death of his mother, Burnett came to terms with his grief through the study of philosophy; but he was properly sentimental and moved enough to name his newest child after his wife.

For the next few years his interest in Memmie Le Blanc continued unabated. He supervised Robertson's translation of Madame Hecquet's biography of the savage girl, and wrote an introduction to the translation, in which he set out his first ideas on Memmie; but Memmie's influence did not end there: years later he was still recounting the way in which he had met her and using his conversations with her as the basis for his philosophical speculations.

Burnett lived on in Edinburgh for another thirty-two years, outlasting two of his children – his son, Arthur, the boy who had been tested in Latin by Johnson in 1773, had died only a year later at the age of eleven. Eliza Burnett, immortalized in verse by Robert Burns as a great beauty (without mentioning her rotten teeth), died of a respiratory seizure caused by consumption. In a letter Burns had said of her: 'There has not been any thing nearly like her, in all the combinations of Beauty, Grace and Goodness the great Creator has formed, since Milton's Eve on the first day of her existence.'[32] Now she was dead. There is a story that, on returning from her funeral, her brother-in-law covered her portrait while Burnett watched. 'Quite right,' he said, 'and now let us turn to Herodotus.'[33] A heartless comment? Those who knew Burnett would doubt it. Death was the one thing not mysterious for James Burnett. His views on death were firm: he did not doubt for an instant the Christian immortality of the soul, or the stoical consolations of philosophy.

It might have been hoped that he would settle into the old age of a respected and renowned philosopher. However, while well regarded on the continent, in his own nation it was Burnett's fate to become a kind of joke, a stock character to represent the wildest reaches of the abstract and over-excited brain. He died in Edinburgh in the spring of 1799. Before he died he told Dr Gregory, his doctor and his friend: 'I know it is not in the power of Art to cure me: all I wish is euthanasia – a happy death.'[34]

There is no record in Burnett's later writing – or, indeed, in anyone's writing – of what happened to Memmie Le Blanc. By 1779 La Condamine was dead, the mysterious Madame Hecquet vanished, and Burnett was a world away in the bleak Grampian Hills. So Memmie fades from our sight. Did she carry on, sick and impoverished, selling what few copies remained of her tale, reliant on the visits of the curious? Could we predict another rescue for her, an answer from the providence to which she held fast?

For Burnett she had been the solution to a mystery; and now, after over two hundred years, could we still find such a solution in poor Memmie Le Blanc? For La Condamine, Madame Hecquet, James Burnett and for ourselves it is the fantastic surprise of her story, her self, that amazes. A small child cast adrift on the shores of an unknown continent; a Robinson Crusoe in reverse; a 'savage' alone and isolated in the midst of civilized Europe; a philosopher's conundrum; a wonder to royalty; an inspiration to the pious – Memmie had been all these.

For us, the additional amazement is Memmie's presence here at all, an alien child connected by the faintest attachments to the lives of philosophers, monarchs and aristocrats – all those whose names habitually survive the erasure of time. Knowing what we do of the continental upheavals of the colonization of the New World and the vast Atlantic slave trade, what may strike us now is the very ordinariness of Memmie's suffering – a refugee, an exile, one of millions of human lives caught up in a slave trade that transformed all those countries facing the Atlantic Ocean, a world in which it was not unusual to be painted black so as to ease your sale, or to die in captivity, pining, disorientated and lost. This additional strangeness in Memmie Le Blanc is the fabulous fact of her fleeting visibility: among the countless dead, among the orphans and foundlings of Paris, somehow she found a way into the crowded interstices of history.

To think of the abandoned child of legend is to move to the safety of a fairy-tale story of abandonment and restitution, a family romance in which kings and queens are the real parents; but if we continue to think of Memmie? Perhaps it is only in a story that does not end fittingly, in which no judgement is reversed, in which nothing is confirmed – a story outside the fumbling, parodic certainty of the law – that a real semblance of the truth is ever found.

The brief miracle of Memmie's visibility ends, as all brief miracles end, with the unanswerable question mark of silence.

CHAPTER FOUR

Radical Innocence

I: The Wretched of the Earth

> In saluage forrest I him lost of late,
> Where I had surely long ere this bene dead,
> Or else remained in most wretched state,
> Had not this wylde man in that wofull stead
> Kept, and deliuered me from deadly dread.
> In such a saluage wight, of brutish kynd,
> Amongst wilde beastes in desert forrests bred,
> It is most straunge and wonderfull to fynd
> So milde humanity, and perfect gentle mynd.
>   Edmund Spenser, from *The Færie Queene*

The boy crouched in the room, rocking to and fro – like a beast in the Paris menagerie, the young doctor thought. He could not return his gaze, and his eyes wandered from one thing to the next, restlessly, insensibly. Sometimes a sudden spasm ran through the boy, a convulsive twitch that shook his whole body; but soon afterwards he would subside back into his habitual ceaseless motion. Locked in indifference, he submitted without affection to anyone who cared for him; he had bites and fierce scratches for those who thwarted his will.

Jean Marc Gaspard Itard was meeting a savage child – only for Itard the meeting was taking place on home soil, with a French boy, within the familiar confines of Paris: no border had been passed. However, the boy's own otherness, his disconnected place at the very limits of the human was border enough, a frontier within his life, his body, making him odd, remote and irredeemably strange. The meeting was irrevocably to change both of their lives.

The boy had first been seen, some three years before in 1797, a naked child, running free in the woods near Lacaune. They had caught him then, but he had escaped, before being trapped again, by hunters, some fifteen months later in July 1798. Once more the boy had escaped, but in early 1800 he had sought shelter in a house in St Sernin, in the department of Aveyron, and so was recaptured and finally held.

They moved the boy to the hospital at St Afrique, and from there he went to Rhodez, where he remained for several months. Here he was inspected by a man called Bonaterre, Professor of Natural History at the École Centrale at Aveyron and a friend of Linnæus's. After long study of the boy, Bonaterre came to the conclusion that here, at last, was another wild child, an astonishing individual, close study of whom might yet reveal much about our essential nature.

Bonaterre found numerous scars on the boy's hairless body and face; but most disturbingly of all, he detected a scar just over one and a half inches long on his neck. Could the boy have had his throat cut and then been left to die alone in the woods? Dark-complexioned when first taken, the boy's skin was now fair, after much washing, just as his teeth, once dark and dull, were now yellowish-white. His face was round and pleasant to look at, with an amiable smile, brown hair and deep-set eyes.

Four and a half feet tall, the boy walked with an uneven, rocking gait, much as runners use to improve their speed; there was no sign that he had ever gone on all fours, the knees being ordinarily uncalloused. Like Memmie before him, he was a dazzlingly fast runner, going straight on, with his head down; but unlike her, the boy could not swim. Most often, he would just sit and rock himself, from side to side, or backwards and forwards, his head held up and his eyes fixed ahead of him. His primary interest was in food. On being given a mirror, the boy could make nothing of it, looking at once behind it, to try to find the child that he had seen within its surface.

He would not go to sleep until it was late at night. Perhaps boredom kept him awake. He would stand by the window long into the night, looking out into the countryside from where he had come.

'When the wind of the Midi blows, his bursts of laughter can be heard during the night and, from time to time, other vocal sounds that express neither pain nor pleasure.'[1] Once asleep, he would slumber until ten or eleven o'clock in the morning; yet his sleep was light: the quietest knock might awaken him.

Now the boy seemed to Bonaterre more like an animal than a man, confined to bestial instinct and purely animal functions, his lower senses of smell and taste being overdeveloped at the expense of the higher, more humane sense of hearing – that sense which emerges from our magnificent invention of language. At first mistakenly thought to be deaf, the boy himself was completely without speech. Sometimes he might let out some cry of anger, murmuring grunt of contentment, or laugh of hilarity.[2]

Through the intervention of a local priest, the boy was sent to Paris for medical inspection. From the first report of the boy's capture, the post-revolutionary government displayed an official and paternal interest in his fate. He arrived in Paris on 18 Thermidor, and became an object of huge interest to those Parisians who had remained in the city during the August heat. France had lived through a revolution conducted for the sake of the oppressed poor, the *misérables*, and this boy was clearly the most unfortunate of all, the living symbol of an ultimate destitution and abandonment. Moreover, the revolutionaries had placed the 'rights of man' in the idea of an abstract and universal human nature, and the figure of 'the child of nature' exemplified this abstracted essentiality, being both an embodiment of human misery and also of original 'savagery'.

So it was that the curious and the fashionable came in their crowds to view him, eager to see what might prove to be a native 'noble savage', a representative of a vanished Eden, perhaps even the symbol of political renovation. Instead they found just what Itard was later to find: a dumb, slovenly, incurious and unresponding boy.

On arrival in Paris, the boy was taken to the Institution Nationale des Sourds et Muets de Naissance (National Institution for Deaf-Mutes), at 115, Rue de l'Observatoire. Founded by the celebrated teacher of the deaf, Abbé de L'Epée, control of the institute had passed over on his death to Abbé Sicard, his former student. At the time when the wild boy was admitted there were one hundred and twenty deaf children resident, each kept on a pension of 500 francs a year. The institute was a public one, being open to visitors once a week from eleven until one o'clock, except in the months of Fructidor and Vendémiaire (that is, from 19 August to 22 October).

The boy was sent for medical inspection to Phillipe Pinel, the foremost physician of his day. This was the innovative and humane teacher of the mad, the man who had struck the irons from the legs of the lunatics in the asylum of Bicêtre. Pinel examined the boy, and found him wanting. He simply saw an abandoned, mentally defective creature, and not Bonaterre's wild child, let alone the Rousseauist 'child of nature' that his contemporaries in Paris had eagerly awaited. The boy was an 'idiot' – at that time not a word of abuse but a precise medical term. Pinel saw in the boy an example of someone so mentally damaged as to be beyond help, his intellectual faculties effectively obliterated. As far as the professor was concerned, the boy was destitute of affection, unable to feel gratitude, kindness or any attachment to others. Insensible in the extreme, unmoved by anything, the boy could only live a kind of vegetative life, sunk in inaccessible torpor, capable only of detached and half-articulate sounds, or silent from an absence of ideas. At best, he might feel transient gusts of passion, but these would be brief, empty and without emotional significance. He was to be understood by reference to the mentally defective inhabitants of the asylum, and not to those long-past and once famous cases of wild children.

Now the boy might have been lost, pinned down by Pinel's diagnosis, taken and imprisoned in some institution until death; but it was just then that Itard paid his own visit to the boy, and perceived something more than the boy's other visitors. He had seen the boy and sensed a possibility.

Always there is an air of large and undaunted excitement about Itard. He approached the savage boy as someone reasonably taking on unreasonable danger, like a younger son in a fairy tale setting out to make his fortune; and, like such sons, Itard's triumph would depend upon finding the deep value in that which his elders could casually despise. He was just twenty-five years old when he first met the boy, a promising student (the pupil of Larrey) at the military hospital Val-de-Grâce on the Rue St Jacques, working on his unfinished thesis on pneumothorax. By day he supported himself by working at Val-de-Grâce, while each evening, after a long day's labour, he diligently went to work once more as a consultant at the Institute for Deaf-Mutes. In his dealings with the boy, Itard's own youthfulness inevitably entailed a serious opportunism; even now one senses the ardent enthusiasm he felt. He was pugnaciously handsome, with his curled hair, his prominent nose and jutting chin. Like a true Stendhalian hero, Itard was a provincial (he was born at Oraison in Basses-Alpes), the son of a carpenter, yearning to make good in the great metropolis. Here, in the boy, was a sure way to attain renown, to raise himself at one bound from the obscurity of the medical grind to a respected and secure fame.

Pinel's diagnosis was exact and final. To him, the boy was an idiot, deprived of that faculty of reason that alone distinguished men from beasts, and left only with his human form as the symbol of his lost inheritance. The boy had probably been abandoned a year or two previously, by desperate and long-suffering parents at the end of their tether. He had survived for a couple of years, reduced still further to his animal instincts. Pinel asserted that it was his idiocy that separated him from others, and not his supposed 'wildness'. But what of the boy's laughter? Pinel knew the answer to that: the sound meant nothing; it was just the clatter of a hollow and meaningless stupefaction. Incapable of attention, he was therefore

necessarily 'destitute of memory, of judgement, even of a disposition to imitation'.[3] His life had annihilated his humanity.

Itard revered Professor Pinel. The older man had, after all, first
introduced into France 'that sublime art' of moral medicine, the scientific and humane treatment of mental damage, begun in England
by Sir Alexander Crichton and Francis Willis (who had healed
George III in his wildest madness). Professionally speaking, Itard
was Pinel's disciple; he knew that he owed the old man a debt. Yet
he felt that the boy was indeed a wild child like Memmie Le Blanc
before him, and that his apparent backwardness could not be the
result of innate idiocy, as Pinel had suggested, but the inevitable
result of his abandoned life. On consideration, Itard thought the
boy must have been living rough in the forests around Aveyron for
seven years, from his fifth year to his twelfth. In any case, how could
the old man give up on the boy so easily? He felt that a proper faith
in the methods that Pinel himself had championed could transform
even so enormously maltreated a person as the Savage of Aveyron.
Young Itard knew that he had the conviction to go to the end of the
path that Citizen Pinel had merely started upon.

Moreover, Itard felt that society, in taking hold of the boy, had
become beholden to him. In catching the wild child, society had
created an obligation. All rights begin in weakness, all duties in
power, said Tracy, the contemporary French philosopher. Here in
the savage boy was absolute weakness, a dependence that was complete despite his obvious and formidable ability to survive. A social
contract had been struck, which could only end with the boy's
death. They could not return him to the wilds; they could not pun-
ish him for his misery with endless incarceration. An indissoluble
link was formed. Itard must take on the task that the very nation of
France had made indispensable: he must save the boy.

Itard must already have begun his work with the young savage
when, on New Year's Eve 1800, Abbé Sicard appointed Itard resident
physician at the Institute for Deaf-Mutes, with official responsibil-

ity for the education of the boy. To make life easier for the young doctor, as well as for his wild charge, Itard was also presented with an apartment in the Institute for the duration of the appointment.

The naturalist Virey, a colleague of Itard's at the hospital Val-de-Grâce, himself studied and wrote on the boy in the months following his arrival in Paris. He noted that, like any other child, sometimes he liked to be tickled, and when the tickler stopped, he would grasp their hand to get them to continue: 'He has a very pleasant laugh,' Virey thought.[4]

Yet Virey saw just how selfish and indifferent to others the boy really was. He could not detect in him any sign of an interest in other human beings. He showed no affection and formed no attachments, beyond that of mere necessity. He was neither wicked nor good, being unaware of both. His animal life and his world without language had imprisoned him in an awful and imperturbable isolation. Experimenting, Virey put the boy with another person and gave each an equal portion of food in order to see if he would respect the notion of fairness. Of course he didn't, taking all the food for himself, since he himself was all that he thought of. He stole habitually and without consideration. Itard told Virey how the boy seemed to be quite incapable of pity or compassion, since he only lived for and within himself, having no more thought for others than as if they were simply useful or unnecessary objects.

Virey thought the boy's case must be a hopeless one. He was so ignorant, so empty; a mere animal, confined within the constricting bounds of his own sensations. He could see in prospect the tragedy that Itard himself would soon enough perceive. Virey imagined how the boy's life had once been lived in an innocent world, in harmony with nature, his thirst satisfied by crystal springs, his hunger by simple food. Now he was dependent, powerless, at the mercy of others' compassion. His Rousseauist independent freedom had fled. The boy must learn how to be human and, in doing so, gather into himself a thousand petty desires that would trammel his soul. 'The path of your education will be sprinkled with your tears; and when your pristine soul turns again toward the azure vaults of the sky, when you discern the order and the beauty of this vast universe, what new ideas will germinate in your young head! When love at last opens to you the gates to a new way of life, oh how many new and delicious sensations, how many unknown passions will trouble your young heart!'[5]

I: Of Savages and Statues

> Shy as a leveret, swift as he,
> Straight and alight as a young larch tree,
> Sweet as the first wild violet, she,
> To her wild self. But what to me?
>   Charlotte Mew, 'The Farmer's Bride'

The boy had come from a wild loneliness, a blanked-out space, an invisible world from which nothing would ever be discerned. Ensconced in the Institute, he lived on, alternately vivacious and dull; sleeping late, a shallow sleep and agitated by dreams; his head and body bare, wrapped up in a sheet, lying on straw. He defecated wherever he wanted, but never wet his own bed. He would stand to shit, and squat to urinate. Having arrived in Paris painfully thin, the boy began to put on weight and to grow a few inches in height also.

The wild boy continued to live quietly in a Paris returning, after years of violence, to its usual way of life: vivacious, impetuous, fickle, but fundamentally tranquil and law-abiding – you would hardly have known it to be a city so recently traumatized by the horrors of the Revolution. Unrest had ended, though the authorities still sometimes feared riots in the more heavily populated areas of town, such as the Faubourgs St Antoine, St Jacques and St Marceau.

Republican modes of speech and dress had died a natural death: only officials were still addressed as 'Citizen'; to use the

term in private speech almost amounted to an insult. The streets,
re-baptized in the Revolution, town names replacing saints' names,
returned slowly to their ancient and sacred titles. A comfortable and
pompous ostentation returned to dress and to official life.
Fashionable women began to dress *à la grec* – like fanciful Greeks –
or (until the attentions of the mob made such exposure dangerous)
à la sauvage – that is, clad in light flesh-coloured drapery.

Fun had returned to the city: you might visit the area around the
Palais Royal – a world in itself where all tastes could be gratified: in
shops, restaurants, coffee-houses, drink, gambling, whores – or go to
the swimming academy where the French learnt to swim in the Seine,
the men clad in short breeches or in large wrappers tied about the
waist; or learn the newly fashionable and curious dance, the waltz.

It was in this frivolous, Napoleonic Paris that expectations had
grown so high around the arrival of the wild boy. Those high hopes
primarily owed their existence to the ideas of Jean-Jacques
Rousseau (1712–78). Rousseau had seen in the child of nature an
image of our unfettered origins, and an implicit rejection of the
hypocrisy and injustice of social life. He pictured the wild child's
original state as one of solitary bliss, like that in which our savage
ancestors lived purely within themselves, indifferent to the opin-
ions or desires of others. Once all lives were like that of the feral
child: untramelled by the trivial demands of society, wild, untameable and free.

Yet there is something nightmarish in Rousseau's lost ideal: his children of nature inhabit a world without beauty, art, love or friendship,
where mutual need instantly becomes ownership and oppression. As
all our wants in that state are simple and therefore easily supplied, an
age-long indolence becomes the stagnated pace of human history.
There imagination pictures nothing; the heart yearns for nothing.
Rousseau was reaching back to 'an age at which the individual would
like to stand still', to a moment of history when we might again enjoy
something of the imagined omnipotence of the child.

In separating the 'original' and 'natural' roots of humanity from the corrupt trappings of the artificial, Rousseau instinctively marked his preference for 'simple' emotion and feeling. The child of nature lived at ease within that self-sufficing simplicity. With these models, Rousseau created a cult of sensibility that fed the revolution in France that was to follow him:

> Some time before the revolution, the people of *bon ton* had adopted a certain *sentimental philosophy*, which was the act of excusing themselves from being virtuous. This philosophy had its jargon, its sensibility, its accent, its gestures; it even assimilated passion, tender modulations, affectionate expressions . . . persons of good company at the recital of an immoral action, or the misfortunes of virtue, have affixed to this feigned and barren sensibility the name of *sensiblerie*.[6]

The arrival of the young savage of Aveyron therefore fed these fanciful ideas of original perfection. The wild boy could fit neatly into an already existing culture of simplicity, operating both in France and across the English Channel in Britain. Primitivism was in vogue, the subject of fictions by radical novelists such as Robert Bage (1720–1801), whose book *Hermsprong* (1796) depicted a hero who had been brought up among American Indians before returning to the drawing rooms of England. William Wordsworth (1770–1850) and Samuel Taylor Coleridge (1772–1834) had only just published their *Lyrical Ballads* (1798) in which the insights of children, savages and idiots were treated with revolutionary interest and respect. Voyages to far-flung places by explorers such as Cook (1728–79) and Bougainville (1729–1811) provoked new interest in the savage; and fables such as Bernardin Saint-Pierre's (1737–1814) recent *Paul et Virginie* (1788) fostered an idealized and delightful image of primitive life.

However, in educating the wild boy, Itard's guide was not Rousseau, for whose ideas he felt a profound ambivalence. There were other philosophers equally well placed to explain the nature of this savage child; but none was to prove more influential on Itard than Etienne Bonnot De Condillac (1715–80). Little read now, in the Paris of the 1790s Condillac was a sage, an ultimate authority. In the last thirty years, Jacques Derrida has written of this now marginalized philosopher as a master of the frivolous. This would have been unthinkable for Itard, for whom Condillac represented all authority. An inheritor from John Locke, Condillac drew this authority from the methodical rigour of his thought. Where Rousseau appears to reason in flashes – to reach truth by way of fiction – Condillac offers a path of rational direction; though, as we shall see, in imagining the wild child Condillac too can fall back on the resources of invented myth.

Itard could use Condillac, for the philosopher had worked out a history of human development that followed the path of life from a state strikingly similar to the wild child to that of the civilized man. Imagining the original man as a statue waiting to be called to life, Condillac had unwittingly provided a template for Itard: the young doctor now would be that Pygmalion, putting words and thoughts into the blank space that was the Aveyron savage.[7]

There were other reasons why Itard's thoughts turned so naturally to the example of Condillac. For, like Rousseau, Condillac had also found a place in his philosophy for the wild child. To discover the source of language, he had turned to the abandoned and animalistic child as a symbol for an essential humanity deprived of all inherited knowledge. He conjured up the image of a child lost in a perpetual present, adrift in a world without past or future, invoking as an example Bernard Connor's Lithuanian bear-boy – wordless, bestial, without world. How could such a boy remember his past state? Only words preserve our sense of continuing identity. Without them, Condillac argued, we would be lost, like the unfortunate bear-boy; imagining our lives to be a continuous moment; lacking history or progression, animals living in a perpetual and unchanging present tense.

Condillac asserted that language was a self-sufficient system.

Feral children were useful tools to prove his argument, for the wild child of necessity exists outside that system of language. Looking at the wild child, Condillac raises the following question: when does identity begin to exist? Can we exist outside language, and then simply enter, finding expression for ourselves in the artifice of words? Or can the self only come into being in the medium of language, being only a blank until reaching the fulfilment of speech?

Condillac knew his answer. For this philosopher, there can be no identity outside the coherency and order of language. Yet what of the wild child? Does he then have no sense of self? Condillac's answer was simple: there is no self and no identity outside the system of signs. For the wild child only an animal awareness exists, an awareness that never arrives at the coherence of identity. However, Condillac's answer begs another question: how then does this silent, storyless subject attain the status of a reflective, language-using self?

For Itard, sharing Condillac's beliefs, this question was more than a philosophical conundrum. For on the strength of its answer lay his best hope for educating the wild child from the ever new sensations of animality into the world of the historical self. Yet Condillac's solution to the puzzle of how a sense of self might begin was far from being the practical answer that Itard required. It is here at this crucial point that Condillac forsakes his rigorous reasoning. To solve the problem, Condillac invents a myth, a fable of human origins.

His myth begins with a terrible catastrophe – a second flood, perhaps. Only two children survive the universal destruction. There have to be two in Condillac's fable: for him selfhood requires the presence of an 'other' in order to come into being. Yet for now the children are apart. Lost and alone, they live in the following way:

So long as the abovementioned children lived asunder, the operations of their minds were confined to perception and consciousness which never cease to act while we are awake; to attention which must have taken place whenever any perception affected them in a particular manner; to reminiscence, which was when they recollected some circumstances that had struck them, before they had lost the connexions formed by those circumstances; and to a very limited exercise of the imagination.[8]

Everything changes when the two children finally meet. Companionship develops in them the faculty of sympathy, a sympathy that is founded in need. They acquire the habit of trying to read each other's sounds and gestures, and learn to use such signs to express themselves to one another. The sounds they naturally make, those 'arbitrary signs', begin to be repeated as agreed signals.

Years pass and the couple have a child. This infant, out of its own need, and possessing a pliant tongue denied to its parents, *invents a word*:

> Let us suppose this young couple to have had a child, who being pressed by wants which he could not without some difficulty make known, put every part of his body into motion. His tongue being extremely pliant, made an extraordinary motion, and pronounced a new expression. As those wants continued to press the child, this occasioned a repetition of the same efforts; again he moved his tongue in the same manner as at first, and articulated the same sound. The parents surprized, having at length guessed his meaning, gave him what he wanted, but tried as they gave it him, to repeat the same word. The difficulty they had to pronounce it, showed that they were not of themselves capable of inventing it.[9]

As a practical solution to the problem of how to educate the wild boy of Aveyron, this myth does not resolve doubts; it multiplies them. However, there was a clue here for Itard to follow. The elaborate conceit of creating silent parents must be gone through in order to create a child born into a world without language, but in which its cries could be heard. Yet, in the end, it is simply the child's needs or wants (*besoins*) which create in it the spontaneous invention of a word. It speaks to gain sympathy, which is itself a *besoin*. This sudden and unprecedented institution of spoken signs really brings us no nearer to the commencement of human language. Condillac senses this, and exaggerates the slowness and false starts required to institute language in this manner: the adults not being able to use sounds themselves discourage the infant, who is co-opted into a language of gestures. For this reason, language progresses with extreme slowness, as each generation builds up the stack of words. However, even then Condillac imagines a second, more effective origin for language, which begins again purely with proper names. The impact of this wild child fable is rather to concentrate our minds upon the strangeness of such a figure, rather than to successfully incorporate it into a convincing model of the origin of language. Yet in the process of elaborating his myth, Condillac let slip the clue that Itard wanted: the key to civilizing the wild child potentially lay in innate need and, above all, the need for sympathy. It is from these primal drives that Itard's own very practical education of his real wild child would draw.

III: Sad Music

The sounding cataract
Haunted me like a passion: the tall rock,
The mountain, and the deep and gloomy wood,
Their colours and their forms, were then to me
An appetite; a feeling and a love,
That had no need of a remoter charm,
By thought supplied, nor any interest
Unborrowed from the eye.
> William Wordsworth, from 'Lines composed a few miles above
> Tintern Abbey'

Itard knew that he was faced with an apparently impossible task. The most famous physician of the day, Pinel, had given up the case as a hopeless one. It was one thing to leap into the breach, and quite another to patiently, painstakingly draw this almost animal boy back into the fold of the human.

He recorded the methods of his education in a little book entitled, *An Historical Account of the Discovery and Education of A Savage Man, or of The First Developments of the Young Savage Caught In The Woods Near Aveyron, In The Year 1798*. Published in France in 1801, this remains one of the masterpieces of scientific literature, and a remarkable account of a unique human relationship.

The condition of the boy at the beginning of his education meant that he was more like a ten-month infant than a twelve-year-old boy, 'and an infant who should have against him anti-social habits, an obstinate inattention, organs scarcely flexible, and a very blunted sensibility'.[10]

How was Itard to surmount these difficulties? His entire method for educating the savage boy depended upon a radical understanding of Condillac. Itard inherited from the philosopher a model of human development as the reception of a myriad sensations, each one building up over time into the ideas that establish an individual human life. Moulding those sensations, Itard felt that he might redirect the boy's development. In doing so, he had five methods: 'to attach him to social life'; to awaken his nervous sensibility; to extend the sphere of his ideas; to lead him to the use of speech; and to unite mind and body by exercising the simple operations of the mind upon the objects of his phsyical needs.[11]

In doing so, Itard was as anxious to disprove Rousseau as he was to validate his new educational methods. Itard knew that Rousseau had lied. He had woven a beautiful and enchanted spell around our vision of the natural human. He had, as a kind of injustice, painted a pernicious illusion. The state of nature was not magical, attractive or beautiful: it was a state of vacuity and barbarism, an empty, ugly and unmeaning condition of entrapment.

Itard sought to prove that Rousseau was wrong. He knew that a human life can only be realized within society. Yet something in the young doctor pined for that same vision of savage freedom that his reason consciously rejected. Itard despised Rousseau, but could not, even in antagonism, escape his influence. He learnt from Rousseau that there is an innate human instinct for sympathy. Our nature leads us inevitably into relation with others. Similarly, the French Revolution had drawn such human feelings into the web of the political. Pity, that once could only operate between individuals, became the very basis of social life. The social contract now originated not in an action, but in an emotion.

For Itard to help the boy he had to establish his ability to give and return sympathy, the emotional connection between one human being and another. That was the only route out of the boy's isolation. So each day, as they worked with each other, Itard watched the boy moving apart in his stolid indifference. If only he could for a moment gain the boy's emotional attention. For the boy was capable of intense feeling; Itard often glimpsed the most passionate and rapt responses in him. Yet all those fleeting passions were too distant from the humanizing need for others. They came and went, and still the boy did not get better.

There is a strange secret in the work of Rousseau – a secret that Itard seems to have intuitively guessed, knowing it from his own solitude. Like Defoe before him, Rousseau celebrated and feared being alone. His savages wander in superb isolation, extricating themselves always from the contact of others, mating briefly, leaving their children as soon as they can. That Rousseau's life should itself be the sorrowing record of failing to find a friend should not distract us from the dismal clarity of his vision. So Itard found in Rousseau the enemy of his own beliefs and the embodiment of his loneliness. Rousseau's savage lives in clarity, because he lives alone. Itard sensed the longing for isolation that was Rousseau's deepest desire, and recoiled from it as from something unclean. Each day he worked late, his constant companion a boy who could never truly respond to him. Itard drew back and rested within the vision of himself as citizen. He told himself that he wanted only one thing: to draw the boy out of his savage and asocial world, and to create in him a need for an 'other'. And that other was Itard himself.

Sometimes the boy could be observed, balancing himself with a tiresome uniformity, gazing through his chamber window. When the wind sprang up, or the sun flashed out, he would laugh uproariously, pulsing with delight, looking as if he might leap at any moment out through the window and down into the garden. At other times, it was as though he were mad, wringing his hands and gnashing his teeth. One morning, after a heavy snowfall, he awoke and, with a cry of joy, leapt out of bed and dashed to the window, and then to the door, then back to the window, then back to the door – on and on until, set free from the room, he fled, still only half-dressed, out into the snowy garden, where he ran, rolled, threw himself down, jumped up, scooped snow in rich handfuls and greedily ate it up.[12]

Yet the boy was not always simply boisterous. Sometimes nature aroused in him a sorrowing and melancholy mood. Here Itard himself describes just such an occasion:

> When the severity of the season drove every other person out of the garden, he delighted in taking a great many turns about it; after which he used to seat himself on the edge of a bason of water. I have often stopped for whole hours together, and with unspeakable pleasure, to examine him in this situation; to observe how all his convulsive motions, and that continual balancing of his whole body diminished, and by degrees subsided, to give place to a more tranquil attitude; and how insensibly his face, insignificant or distorted as it might be, took the well-defined character of sorrow, or melancholy reverie, in proportion as his eyes were steadily fixed on the surface of the water, and when he threw into it, from time to time, some remains of withered leaves. When in a moon-light night, the rays of that luminary

penetrated into his room, he seldom failed to awake out of his sleep, and to place himself before the window. There he remained, during a part of the night, staring motionless, his neck extended, his eyes fixed towards the country illuminated by the moon, and, carried away in a sort of contemplative extacy, the silence of which was interrupted only by deep-drawn inspirations, after considerable intervals, and which were always accompanied with a feeble and plaintive sound.'[13]

Here Itard composes the elegy for an experience that he must himself kill. Yet as he watches, the young doctor shares the child's wordless melancholy. The tone is elegiac and wistful; the boy's boisterous pleasures quieten; things slow down into an almost motionless attentiveness. Previously, we have seen the boy as constrained by those around him, the object of imprisonment and coercion; here, he stills himself. Yet the boy's melancholy is experienced as ecstasy – his delight in witnessing the world is that intense. In wonder and self-reproach Itard regards the intensity of the boy's sad pleasure in the natural world, his wholly being given up to his experience. Yet he himself stands outside, recording the boy's wordless experience with scientific objectivity, raptly attentive to all external appearances and actions.

The sense of exclusion heightens when we realize, as Itard himself had, that in the process of civilization the boy's immediacy of passion must be forgone, and must be distanced and understood through the medium of language. Itard wants the boy to achieve an intellectual understanding of his sensations; it is not enough that they should exist as pure sources of unmeaning delight or sorrow.

The boy is like Condillac's wild child – a creature imprisoned within the limits of each moment as the philosopher here describes:

Supposing in order to try every hypothesis, that he had likewise remembered the time when he lived in the forest, it would have been impossible for him to represent it to himself but by the perceptions which he would have recalled to mind. These perceptions could be very few; and as he had not remembrance of those which had preceded, followed, or interrupted them, he would never have recollected the succession of the parts of this time. The consequence of this must have been, that he would have never suspected it to have had any beginning, and yet he would only have considered it as an instant. In a word, the confused remembrance of his former state would have reduced him to the absurdity of imagining himself to have always existed, though he was as yet incapable of representing his pretended eternity to himself but as a moment. I do not question but he would have been greatly surprized, as soon as he had been told that he had begun to exist; and still more so when he had been also told that he had passed through different degrees of growth.[14]

From this Itard reasoned that his own wild boy could have no history, only a continual sensual present, a materialist parody of the mystical *nunc stans*. In such a world, the notion of others cannot exist, as the self is not even an 'other' to itself, having no notion of itself as a thing existing in time.

In such a condition, how could Itard enter into a relationship with the young 'savage'? The moment at the basin expresses just how complex Itard's relation to the boy is. The water acts as a failed mirror, in which the wild boy fails to recognize himself. The boy stares into the water, while Itard echoes his attentive gesture, staring likewise, for long hours, at the boy. The child's pleasure does not require an other to be present. However, Itard's watchfulness is voyeuristic, an intrusion into a privacy. He both yearns for the boy's recognition of himself, since such a moment would prove the success of his education, and also depends upon his indifference, that as he watches, the boy should be looking away.

It is a moment in which connections form: between Itard and the boy, and between the boy and the natural world. Yet the connection between the adult and child is flawed and uncertain, while that between the boy and his world is intense and fulfilled. Itard's entire aim is to establish a social link between himself and the wild child, but instead he finds himself envying the boy's absorption in nature. This envy is also an imaginative identification, a moment of sympathy, in which Itard's words attempt, and fail, to share the abundance and melancholy of the boy's experience.

The boy's solitary moment of melancholy proves him to be human even though his life remains beyond the reach of others. The boy destroys Itard's thesis of the necessity of society for a fully realized human life; for here are powerful and identifiably human emotions enchanting a boy living only to himself.

The child's moment of rapture survives; and its fragile tenderness holds the whole meaning of this book. We are at once present in the abandoned, hurt boy, the one without speech or power; and there, too, in the place of the rescuer, the one who nurtures and controls, and preserves the relationship in articulate speech.

IV: Educations from Nature

> The will to neither strive nor cry,
> The power to feel with others give.
> Calm, calm me more; nor let me die
> Before I have begun to live.
> > Matthew Arnold, 'Lines Written in Kensington Gardens'

The boy's taste for wild places remained strong. Itard and he went into the country again, to the estate of Citizen Lachabeaussière, in the vale of Montmorence. The sight of real countryside inflamed the boy again with a desire to escape, had him running again and again to the window of the house, to look out once more on to the park. Itard knew he must mortify this taste, while still restrainedly indulging his enjoyment of outdoors. So, on their return to Paris, they began to take regular walks amidst the more orderly and regular beauties of the gardens local to the Institute.

Similarly the housekeeper, Madame Guérin, began to take him almost daily to the Luxembourg Gardens. On each visit they would go to see Citizen Lemeri at the Observatory. There the young savage, having brought out a wooden bowl, in dumbshow would ask for and be given a breakfast drink of milk. Sometimes he would be taken out for his walk in an old wheelbarrow, or otherwise just wheeled about the garden in the Institute. During these walks the boy began to develop a lively liking for Madame Guérin. He would want to be near her, and parting would make him uneasy and anxious. Once, having lost her on the streets during their daily journey, he burst into floods of tears on finally finding her again; these were the first tears he ever shed out of need for another. His feelings for Itard himself were unmistakably weaker, perhaps as a result of the young doctor's attentions being inevitably connected to the process of his education, and not to his pleasure.

Yet Itard describes with great pathos the tenderness that slowly grew between himself and the boy. At bedtime, he would go to visit the boy in his room, and the child, having prepared himself for a hug, would draw Itard to him by the arm and make him sit next to him on the bed. 'Then in general he seizes my hand, draws it over his eyes, his forehead, and the back part of his head, and detains it with his own, a long time, applied to these parts.'[15] Here the boy both submits to affection and engineers how that affection will be applied. He uses Itard to give to himself the softest caresses; and Itard, concerning these moments, notes how much a *mother's* affection gains an educational result. By becoming like a mother to the boy, Itard replaces the mother the boy has lost (both the real woman and a symbolically maternal Nature) and allows for himself a fantasy of motherhood, in which, as a man, he gives birth to the boy's earliest joys. In Itard's relationship with the boy lies the template of all parental relationships: he nurtures the one who will leave him.

Itard had already worked wonders with the boy, bringing him on in ways that Pinel had at the beginning considered to be impossible.

Yet a barrier had been reached – the process of his education had hit an impasse – and the boy was still only half civilized. The key was to give him language.

Yet here Itard failed. At the Institute, they discovered early on that the boy was certainly not deaf. Itard saw that his indifference to some noises was compensated for by an impressive ability to pick out the very slightest sounds: the plucking of a walnut, or the touch of the key in the door. However, if the boy could hear sounds, there was no certainty that he would be able to articulate them for himself. Speech, Itard thought, is a kind of music to which certain ears may be insensible.[16] Was the boy one such person? And how was he to teach him to speak?

The boy already possessed what Itard was to name a 'language of action', a 'pantomimic language' of expressive gesture. Itard was far from dismissing this mode of communication. He could see that it clearly reproduced the most primitive form of human intercourse. The young savage could make his wishes clear enough. If the time for his walk had come with Madame Guérin, he would simply lay her clothes out before her, ready for her to dress in, and even, if impatient enough, would start dressing her himself. Yet Itard also felt that this system of gestures was essentially limited. Only words – only a system of speech – could embark the individual human on the process of development, as Condillac had described it, by affording him access to a medium capable of indefinite improvement. Without such a system we would fall back into being like the wild boy himself.[17]

In the month of Frimaire (November), as the nights drew in and the autumn turned to winter, for the first time the boy began to listen specifically to the sound of the human voice. Sometimes he would go to the door of his chamber and listen to arguments in the gallery down below, and then make sure that the door was secured and the latch pulled down tight. Around Christmas time, in the month of Nivose, he was busy boiling potatoes for himself in the kitchen, while Itard watched. (He had since his captivity acquired a taste for cooked potatoes.) People were talking heatedly behind him and, at first, he appeared to be taking no interest in their words, until Itard suddenly noticed that the young savage's attention was drawn by one of the talkers who was using over and over the word 'Oh!'. Itard watched; there could be no mistake: each time the word was used, the boy would quickly turn his head.

That evening, Itard consciously repeated the experiment with the same results. He ran through the other vowel sounds, but to these the young savage made no particular response. Out of this preference, Itard chose a name for the boy: he would be called Victor, since the sound of that name would play upon his peculiar attentiveness to the sound 'o'.

To name someone is an act of communication as well as appropriation, the calling of that person into relation with the namer. We are a 'you' to our parents, before we are an 'I' to ourselves. The name has its brutal irony: in what sense can this boy have found victory? Yet there *is* victory here of a sort. Once named, Victor becomes recognizably a person to Itard, not just an exemplar of that human type, 'the young savage', 'the wild child'.

Victor had acquired a name; could he now acquire speech? Examination of his tongue and vocal chords showed no phsyical reason why not, despite the damage that might have been inflicted by that old cruel knife wound to his throat. Yet was it fair to expect words from Victor? An infant doesn't speak its first syllables until it is nearly eighteen months old and Victor, moreover, had to combat the deep effects of his long isolation in the forests of France. His starting point was infinitely worse than that of an ordinarily neglected child, growing up in the midst of others.

Itard seized upon the coincidence that the one sound Victor had shown a preference for was the very sound used to convey one of his chief wants: *eau*, or water. Itard habitually exclaimed the word '*eau*' as he gave a glass to the demanding boy, trying to instil in Victor's mind the connection between the sound and the thing. The experiment failed: Victor begged for water by gesture after gesture, or by hissing, but could produce no articulate sound.

Itard tried again with another word: *lait*, or milk. The experiment was repeated and then, on the fourth day, it appeared that the desired breakthrough had finally come. Hesitantly at first, and then incessantly, he repeated in a harsh and piping voice the sound – '*lait, lait, lait*'. Victor had mastered a human word! But instantly Itard knew that his triumph was a hollow one. He fetched Victor a glass, poured in the milk and handed it to him; and once again, Victor repeated '*lait*' with evident satisfaction. But Itard's heart fell. The boy had not joined the word to the thing, establishing the arbitrary connection of sound and object; he had merely exclaimed in his pleasure, and Itard supposed the insignificant sound he uttered was no better than an inarticulate cry or sigh.

V: The Proper Order of Words

Victor's linguistic progress did not end with his misuse of the word '*lait*'. Victor himself was awakening to teenage desire: Itard noticed his ability to pronounce the 'liquid *l*', attributing this difficult triumph to his pubertal inclination towards Julia, Madame Guérin's twelve-year-old daughter, and his romantic attachment to her very name. He learned also to repeat the words, '*Oh Dieu!*', probably as a result of hearing Madame Guérin repeat them so often.

Itard pressed on with Victor's education, seeking to develop his intellectual faculties by placing obstacles between the boy and his wants. Itard made up games to teach him, drawing shapes of everyday objects on a blackboard and then having Victor fetch, one by one, the object required to match each individual drawing. The game failed when Victor simply brought all the objects back at once and deposited them in a heap before the waiting Itard.

Itard tried to get round the obstacle of Victor's laziness by playing upon the boy's love of order. He placed the household objects in order, and suspended them beneath drawings that represented them. They were left like that for some time, each hanging below the relevant drawing by a hook, so that Victor could get used to them. Then the objects were taken away. Victor duly put them all back on their hooks, in order. It was unclear if Victor was really linking the object to the drawing, or merely displaying a feat of memory in reproducing the right order. So Itard rearranged the drawings and repeated the test. Victor put them back in their first order, simply ignoring the placing of the drawings. However, by perseverance and by wearying Victor's memory by enlarging the number of objects and so on, Itard did finally succeed in establishing for the boy the right connection between object and drawing. Flushed with success, he went on to the next stage: adding the written name to the drawing, with the aim of eventually replacing the drawing with the written word. Here Itard once again drew a blank. Victor just could not take in the written word.

The education continued. Itard tried various experiments with shapes and colours. There was progress, but Victor was growing tired and angry. A stand-off was approaching between teacher and pupil, pseudo-parent and surrogate child. Itard knew that he must enforce discipline. Victor resisted, grew sullen, and sometimes exploded into fits of rage. However, unlike when first captured, now his anger was no longer directed against people, but against things: he smashed, broke, tore. Events had reached a terrible stop: Victor was too upset and recalcitrant to learn anything more. But Itard had to keep things moving. Discovering that the boy was terrified of heights, Itard began to use his fear as an educational tool, threatening him by taking him close to high windows in order to enforce his will. Yet Itard began to wonder, as Virey had done before him, what they were gaining for the boy by making him suffer so.

Yet the torment worked and Victor's will softened. The education could now continue. Great strides were made. With the use of cut-out letters, Itard taught Victor how to arrange the alphabet, then how to recognize the word '*lait*', and finally what its use was as a written sign, though he still could not see the connection between the written word and the sound that he had mastered. Nonetheless, one morning on his walk with Madame Guérin, he arrived at Citizen Lemeri's, and, rather than holding out his wooden bowl to gain his milk in dumbshow, he took out the cut-out letters and wrote out on the table before him, the single word '*lait*'.

VI: Radical Innocence

As yet ungolden in the dense, hot night
The spikes enter his feet: he seeks the moon,
Which, with the touch of its infertile light,
Shall loose desires hoarded against his will
By the long urging of the afternoon.
Slowly the hard rim shifts above the hill.
    Thom Gunn, from 'The Allegory of the Wolf Boy'

Itard's account of Victor's education was published under the auspices of Napoleon's Imperial Government in Paris, in the first month of the new year, Vendémiaire, Year 10 of the Republic (that is, between 23 September and 22 October 1801). Both Victor and Itard became internationally famous: Itard was able to begin his own private medical practice; Madame De Staël, the great woman of letters, visited; the Tsar of Russia sent Itard a ring; within six months the work had been translated into English (during the Peace of Amiens, when for the first time for several years travellers could cross from England to France).

In England, the case fascinated Coleridge. Only a few months after the book appeared in translation, in February–March 1803, he was wondering about a man who, out of hypochondria, 'fancied himself to have been a lonely Savage; & poisoned by Civilization/-Savage of Aveyron'.[18] Six years later, in the summer of 1809, he was still pondering Victor's story, and musing on its suitability for

Wordsworth's magnificent projected, unfinished, unfinishable poem, *The Recluse*:

> A fine subject to be introduced in William's great poem is the Savage Boy of Aveyron in Itard's account – viz – his restless joy and blind conjunction of his Being with natural Scenery; and the manifest influence of Mountain, Rocks, Waterfalls, Torrents, & Thunderstorms – Moonlight Beams quivering on Water, &c on his whole frame – as instanced in his Behaviour in the Vale of Montmorency – his eager desires to escape, &c. How deserving this whole account of a profound psychological examination/ & comparison with wild animals in confinement/The savage seems clearly a *man*/ & his conduct nearer derangement than absolute Imbrutement.[19]

In these words, we witness the way in which one of the great Romantic intellects absorbs Victor into his own passionate concerns.

The peace with Britain quickly ended. Napoléon continued his conquest of Europe; and unnoticed again in Paris, Itard's work with Victor quietly continued. Six years after the first publication, a second report was published, again by the government and under the auspices of Champigny, the Minister of the Interior. This later text is really a grant application – the greatest ever written – and an immediate means of requesting more government funds to enable Itard to continue his education of Victor.

Puberty had come to Victor, bringing with it not love, but an agonizing, restless sexual urgency. Itard did his best to cool his charge's lust, giving him cold baths, a soothing diet and violent exercise; but it was no good. He would grow sad at times, then anxious, then stimulated to a kind of fury of desire – sighing, shedding tears, crying out, tearing his clothes, working himself to such a pitch of frenzy that blood would flow from his nose and ears.

But Victor was growing up: the emotional delicacy that one might have suspected was there from the beginning began to show itself.

Madame Guérin's husband died. Victor, as usual, laid his place at table, and Madame Guérin wept to see the cutlery lying there forlorn and never any more to be needed. Slowly, Victor took up the knife and fork, and put the cutlery away. He would never again lay that place.

The work went on, but after Itard's early success, Victor's education once again stalled: he was never to master any more spoken language than his first words, '*lait*' and '*Oh Dieu*', though Itard did succeed in getting him meaningfully to write other words. Yet there was to be one further moment of triumph for Itard, and it was to come through a moment when his own control of Victor was wonderfully refuted.

Like Peter the Wild Boy before him, Victor was a natural thief. In order to repress this greed in him, Itard diligently punished Victor by depriving him of those foods that he stole. The system worked, and he stopped stealing. Then, in order to test if Victor had learnt the nature of justice, or merely stood in fear of punishment, Itard decided to try out an experiment. One day Itard, instead of rewarding Victor for success in his lessons, arbitrarily feigned stern dissatisfaction and anger. Without warning he scattered their papers and toys, and dragged Victor to the little dark room that had served as a prison on his arrival in Paris. For the first time ever Victor resisted a punishment. Instead of going limp and submitting himself to his fate, he braced his legs with all his strength against the edges of the door to the dark room, and fought back. Itard, secretly greatly pleased, tried to pick him up and throw him into the room. Victor struggled manically, until he realized that he could not defeat the grown man's strength and so did the only thing left for him: he seized his teacher's hand and bit him hard.

Itard could never hope to tell the boy how that bite filled him with the finest satisfaction. What this moment showed to him, more forcibly than any before, was that Victor possessed an innate human sense, a fiery and courageous desire for justice. In an instant, he had shown to Itard an unquenchable human heart. The very ideal for which France had fought some few years before was endorsed and celebrated in the child's instinctive action. The boy shared in that marvellous and noble assumption upon which all justice is founded. The wild boy had become a moral man.

Yet doubts tormented Itard. Had he done wrong in trying to educate the boy at all? Once, he sat at one end of the room with the boy, thinking through the stark alternatives. Either the boy must end in an asylum, a hopeless case; or, after enormous and relentless work, he might just procure a little education, though hardly enough to secure any happiness for him. '"Unhappy creature," I cried as if he could hear me, and with real anguish of heart, "since my labors are wasted and your efforts fruitless, take again the road to your forests and the taste for your primitive life. Or if your new needs make you dependent on a society in which you have no place, go, expiate your misfortune, die of misery and boredom at Bicêtre [the asylum]."'[20] Just then a strange thing happened. As though he had understood every word (as Itard knew he could not), Victor's chest began to heave, his eyes shut, and bitter tears streamed from his closed eyelids.

Itard could persuade himself that he had watched Victor follow the Enlightenment's favoured path from solitary savagery to civilized life, moving from the feeling of need produced by self-preservation, to less purely selfish feelings, to the heart's expansion in sympathy, to the birth of the civilized and generous feelings of the human heart. Yet did he ever free himself from the certainty that he had also failed with Victor – that he could never have done anything else but fail?

How much in reality had Itard unwittingly destroyed? Perhaps, the boy's solitary soul was left more intact than Itard himself had imagined. The boy remained at a standing point between civilized manners and his primitive life. Even now, when his social affections had lessened his wild pleasures, he only needed the noise of a stormy wind, the stillness of a beautiful summer evening, or a glimpse of the deep woods to restore his ecstasy in an instant.

On the presentation of his second report, on 3 May 1806, Itard received an official letter from the Ministry of the Interior, letting him know that the government would pay a yearly sum of 150 francs for Victor's upkeep and education.[21] But Itard spent less and less time with his charge. In 1810, Victor moved in with his beloved nurse, Madame Guérin, in an annexe of the Institute at 4 Impasse des Feuilliantines, the home where he was to live until his death.

Itard died, unmarried, on 5 July 1838, at the age of sixty-four. His success with Victor had gained him the European reputation that he had once desired. Victor had died ten years previously in 1828, when he was about forty years old.

It is hard not to feel as sorry for Itard as one feels for the wild child. For Victor's story catches hold of a vivid and tactful tenderness: its subject is ultimately that of yearning for and missing love. Unwittingly, perhaps, Itard left us a story not just of the education of a young savage, but of his own inability to be close or intimate. A scientific detachment operates in Itard, and he watches with surprise and regret as the emotions he obviously feels for Victor are hardly reciprocated, while, like a rival in a love affair, the simpler affection of Madame Guérin finds a place in the boy's heart. Like a stern father who alienates a son and makes him turn to his mother's quiet simplicity, Itard seems doomed to detach himself from those he tried to get too close to. Pupil and teacher, father and son, adult and child, doctor and patient, scientist and subject – in each case the relationship is skewed and fundamentally unequal. Itard clearly dreamed of rescue for the young and abandoned boy. Some lost part of himself must have seemed contained in poor Victor, something that he might retrieve, look after and make better. Yet the imbalance of power between the two of them, the unbridgeable distance between their several worlds, doomed the attempt; and in the end, it is Victor, the named one, who haunts us as he haunted Itard – biting back; lost and impenetrably different in the moonlight, as he throws into the pool clutches of withered leaves.

CHAPTER FIVE

The Child of Europe

I: His Half Murdered Life

Suis-je né trop tôt ou trop tard?
Qu'est-ce que je fais en ce monde?
O vous tous, ma peine est profonde:
Priez pour le pauvre Gaspard!
    Paul Verlaine, 'Gaspard Hauser Chante'[1]

The story of Kaspar Hauser is both curious and instructive. It shows on how commonplace and unpromising a foundation a myth of European celebrity may rest.
    The Duchess of Cleveland, from *The True Story of Kaspar Hauser*

These children are exceptions: their stories have survived. Even a cursory study of the records of modern Europe will show just how painfully frequent the abandonment of children has been. So many lives were marred, so many histories lost. Yet these very few cases became talismanic, brief icons of the times in which they lived. Why was it that only these dozen or so children found such passing fame? And why of those have only half a dozen actually been granted the permanence of extensive written record?

I am reminded in each case of those anamorphic portraits that delighted the morbidities of the Renaissance: look at them one way, you see a beautiful face in the height of its glory; look at them from the other side, and you find only the excoriating sarcasm of a grinning skull. Likewise, with each of these children we can glimpse the wonder and mystery that the most perceptive observers of those times once bore witness to; while from another angle we see merely a child, exceptional perhaps only in suffering.

In no case is this puzzling dual quality so striking as in that of Kaspar Hauser. Discovered in a Germany of Romantic ferment, Hauser, like Victor before him, seemed to the people of the time the embodied fulfilment of fantastic narratives they were telling about themselves. Hauser must have seemed a personification of the fevered imaginations of Kleist or Büchner, or to have strayed from the pages of one of Hoffmann's tales. Like a figure from an old fable, Hauser stumbled into the modern lives of medieval Nuremberg and found there a fame that spread his story across the whole of Europe.

Yet the very fittingness of Hauser's discovered singularity might awake in us the germ of a dark surmise. For in Hauser's tale we find the first instance of a suspicion that may be thought to occur quite naturally in thinking of these wild children. Was Hauser a liar? Sceptics might think these earlier cases to be the result of mistaken fantasy in those who found them, while it may actually be that Hauser was a conscious impostor. Perhaps Hauser is the first person, otherwise insignificant and beyond notice, to actively assume the guise of a child of nature precisely in order to lift himself into the starred category of the exceptional? To enter his story is to find ourselves back in the frame of an old romance; and the tale begins appropriately enough with a mysterious arrival in the quiet precincts of a German town.

Whit Monday, 26 May 1828, was a public holiday in Nuremberg, so that afternoon the city was quiet, the majority of its scant population having left to spend the holiday in the countryside beyond the city walls.[2] In the Unschlittplatz, just after four o'clock, Herr Weichmann was lingering outside his front door, talking to his fellow shoemaker, Jacob Beck, before setting out for the New Gate, when he saw, struggling down the Bärleinhuter hill, some little distance from him, a full-lipped young man about sixteen years old, dressed like a stable boy or a travelling tailor in outlandish peasant clothes: grey trousers that were far too wide for him, a shirt, a short grey jacket, a black silk handkerchief tied around his throat, and a low-browed, wide felt hat.

Something odd in the boy's manner, as if he were drunk, led Weichmann to approach him to see if the stranger was well. The boy muttered the words '*Neue Thor Strasse*', and Weichmann, thinking that he wanted to see someone on that street, began to lead him there. While they were walking, Hauser drew a letter from his pocket and held it out to Weichmann. The letter was addressed 'To His Honour the Captain of the 4th Squadron of the Shwolishay regiment, Nuremberg'.[3] Not knowing where this captain lived, Weichmann conducted the stranger the short distance to the guard house by the New Gate. There the boy presented his letter to the servant who answered the door, saying to him: '*Ae sechtene möcht ih waehn, wie mei Votta waehn is*' ('I would like to be such a one as my father is').[4] The boy's accent was that of a peasant.[5] Nothing more could be drawn from him, except for the repetition of two further phrases: '*woas nit*' ('dunno'), and '*Reuta wähn, wie mei Votta wähn is*' ('I want to be a rider like my father is'). The servant explained that the Captain was away at the consecration of the church at nearby Erlangen. As the servant talked, he thought how tired the strange boy looked, and wondered why he reeled as he walked. The boy really did seem all-in and kept pointing to his feet to show how they hurt. Suddenly the stranger collapsed in a state of distress and wept. Despite their offers, he vehemently refused all food except bread and water. The townspeople took him for some kind of savage, and led him out to the stable, where he stretched himself out on the straw and promptly fell asleep.[6]

On the Captain's return, it was discovered that he knew nothing of the boy and had never seen him before. They questioned the stranger further, but nothing more could be learnt from him, so he was taken to the police station, where he was interrogated. They guessed that he must be about sixteen years old, for though he was quite short (only four feet nine inches tall), the first signs of a beard and moustache were just showing.[7] They found stuffed in his pockets (left there perhaps as a mocking joke) a religious pamphlet on 'The art of regaining lost time and years misspent'. At first, the focus of dispute among the townspeople was whether this stranger might be a madman, an idiot, or a 'wild man'. However, these guesses were silenced when Christopher Wüst, one of the policemen on duty, presented the boy with a pen and paper. Seeming greatly pleased, the boy wrote out clearly the name, 'Kaspar Hauser'. However, no further revelations were forthcoming and the boy fell back into apparently meaningless reiterations of his stock phrases. He also repeated the word '*Ross*' (horse) over and over, pleadingly. Finally, the boy was taken to the Vestner Tower, which was used as a prison for down-and-outs and vagabonds, where he climbed the ninety-two steps to his cell, and there was left to sleep.

The following events are best described in Hauser's own narrative of his arrival at Nuremberg, written long after the event. Here Hauser sits, waiting in his cell, tended to by Hiltel, the prison-keeper; listening to the striking of the hours by the church clock:

I heard the same thing as I had heard at first, but I mean, however, that it was somewhat different, as I heard it much louder; it was not the same, but (instead) that the clock struck, it was become sounding. This I listened to a very long while; but when from time to time I heard it continually less and less, and when my attention was at an end, I said these words, *Dahi weis wo Brief highört,* by which I meant to say, he might also give me such a beautiful thing, and not always teaze me . . . I began to weep again, and said the words which I had learned, by which I meant, Why are the horses so long without coming, and let me suffer so much? I wept a very long time, and the man came no more. I heard the clock strike; this always took away half of my pain, and on which the thought comforted me, that now the horses will soon come. And during this time, as I listened, a man came to me, and asked me all manner of things; perhaps I gave him no answer, as my attention was turned towards what I heard. He seized me by the chin, and lifted up my head, by which means I felt a frightful pain in my eyes from the day-light. The man of whom I now speak, was he that was shut up with me, therefore I did not know that I was shut up. He began to speak to me; I listened to him a very long time, and constantly heard other words; then I said to him my words already mentioned, *Dahi weis wo*, &c.; by which I meant, What is that which has given me so much pain in my eyes when thou hast held up my head? But he had not understood me in what I said; he had well understood what the words signified, but not what I meant. He let my head go, seated himself near me, and continually asked me questions. In the meanwhile, the clock began to strike . . . I said to him, *I möcht ah*, &c., by which I meant, that he should give me such a beautiful thing; but he understood me not, as to what I meant to say; he continued to speak, however: I began to weep, and said, *Ross ham*; by which I meant to say, he shall not always plague me so with speaking, all this gives me very great pain. He stood up, went away to where he lay, and left me to sit alone. I wept a very long while; I felt a great pain in my eyes, so that I could not weep any longer. I sat alone a very long time, then I heard something quite different, upon which I listened with such an attention as I cannot tell. What I heard was the trumpet in the Emperor's stable; but I heard not this long, and when I heard it no longer, I said, *Ross ham* – he shall also give me something so beautiful. Then the man came to me here, and said several times the words which he had spoken before, very slowly at first, and I said after him; he said, Dost thou not know what this is? I said these words to him several times, by which I meant to say, he shall give me the horses soon, and must not always plague me so. The man now stretched out his hand towards the water pitcher, which stood under my bed, and wanted to drink, but I stretched out my hand towards it, and said, *Ross ham*. The man gave me the pitcher forthwith, and let me drink; when I had drank the water, I became so lively as cannot be described; I asked him for the horses. I said, *Ross ham*; upon which he said several times, I know not what thou wantest. I said also the same words after him, but I could not immediately speak after him so clearly, and I said, *I wös net*, and by *Ross ham*, I meant to say, that he should also give me my horses. He understood not what I had desired, and stood up, went to the place where his bed was, and left me to sit alone . . . Just then, *Hiltel*, the keeper of the prison, came, and brought the bread and water, which I knew again immediately, and said to it, *I möcht ah*, &c., by which I said to the bread, Now go not away again, and let me not be plagued any more. He laid the bread down by me; I also took it up in my hand immediately; he poured the water into the pitcher, and set it down upon the floor. Just then he began to ask me questions. He questioned me with so harsh a voice, that it caused me much pain in my head, upon which I began to cry, and said, *I möcht ah*, &c. *I wös net. In gross Dorfs da is die Voter*. These words I made use of without distinction to get what I wanted. The keeper of the prison went out, as he had not understood me; he knew the words well, as to what they meant, but not what I had wished to express by them, and I also understood not what he had said to me.[8]

This passage offers us a strange insight into Hauser's mind in those first hours in his cell in the tower. For the first time since Memmie's reported words we hear the original accents of one of our children of nature. More than that, never before have we heard first-hand their actual words. The effect is one of improbable strangeness: Hauser writing in a German that is curiously off-beam, dislocated, odd and idiosyncratic in expression. Repetition of phrases throws us into a state of mind in which difference struggles to overcome a deadening sameness. Things happen as in a dream; consequences appear arbitrary and uncertain; and the barrier between the animate and the inanimate seems no more than a prejudged convention: Hauser's address to the loaf of bread is a masterpiece of pathos. There he sits in his little cell, bound within himself by mutual incomprehension: he speaks, but no one understands him; he wants for things, but nobody comes. Only the desire to possess beauty is coherently there, repeated over and over, wishing for something – horses, the stable-boy's bugle, the striking of the clock – to steady his continually dissolving self.

Over the next few days spent in the Vestner Tower, Hauser remained bewildered, though peaceable enough. Moved by his constant desire to see horses, one of the soldiers on guard made him the gift of a little wooden horse – probably fetched from one of the marvellous toy shops for which Nuremberg was then so famous. The boy's joy was so rapturous, and then his misery so excessive at being parted from his toy at bedtime, that several others were given to him the next day. From then on, Hauser played with his wooden horses endlessly, absorbedly, hardly noticing what else happened around him.

The letter borne by Hauser was examined and quickly revealed to be, if not a forgery, at least duplicitous. They found that there were in fact two letters. The first was written in a mock Bavarian dialect, and the second in Latin script, perhaps in a disguised version of the same hand. The anonymous author of the first letter declared that Kaspar Hauser had been living with him since October 1812, during which time he had never been permitted to leave the house. The author of the letter asked for the boy to be looked after and allowed to become a soldier. The second letter was apparently from one of Hauser's parents, giving the date and circumstance of his birth. Looking for more information, Hauser's questioners demanded that he write out his name for them, which he did, writing afterwards of the moment that he wrote it down, 'and this was my name, but I have not known what I have written'. The investigations appeared to be leading nowhere, and, realizing that in all likelihood Hauser was an abandoned and neglected child, he was therefore released from his prison cell to be taken into lodging for the next six weeks in the tower with Hiltel, the prison-keeper, his cross-eyed wife and the rest of his family. Julius Hiltel, the prison-keeper's eleven-year-old son began the task of tutoring the strange arrival.[9]

Herr Binder, the Burgomaster of Nuremberg, took over the investigation of Hauser's case. His sensitive and kindly questioning gradually uncovered an extraordinary story, revealed to the world in an official proclamation published on 7 July 1828. For thirteen years, Hauser had been locked away in a hole, or so he termed the low room or barely lit dungeon where he had been imprisoned. There he had sat, day after day, completely alone – hearing nothing; meeting no one; seeing neither the sun nor the night-time sky. Clothed in a shirt and a pair of breeches, he was always barefoot. Daily a man visited him to give him food and water; but Hauser had never seen the man, who came in the darkness, approaching the boy from behind and ensuring that his back remained turned. His only companions had been wooden horses.[10]

Hauser himself was to write of how life had gone in his hole:

I will write the story of Kaspar Hauser myself! I will tell how I lived in the prison, and describe what it looked like, and everything that was there. The length of the prison was 6 to 7 feet, and 4 feet in width. There were two small windows which were 8 to 9 inches in height and were [the same] width; there were in the ceiling as in a cellar. But there was nothing in it but the straw where I lay and sat, and the two horses, a dog, and a woollen blanket. And in the ground next to me was a round hole where I could relieve myself, and a pitcher of water; other than that there was nothing, not even a stove. I will tell you what I always did, and I always had to eat, and how I spent the long period, and what I did. I had two toy horses, and a [toy] dog, and such red ribbons with which I decorated the horses. And the clothes that I wore it was short pants, and black suspenders, and a shirt, but the pants and suspenders were on my bare body, and the shirt was worn on top, and the pants were torn open in back, so I could relieve myself. I could not take off the pants, because nobody showed me how. I will give a picture of how I spent the day, and how my day went.

When I woke up I found water and bread next to me. The first thing I did, I drank the water, then ate a little bread until I was no longer hungry, then I gave bread and water to the horses, and the dog, then I drank it all up. Now I start to play, I remove the ribbons. It took me a long time until I had decorated a horse, and when one was decorated, then I again ate a little bread, and then there was still a little water left; this I finished . . . So I picked up the pitcher probably ten times, wanting to drink, but never found any water in it because I assumed the water came by itself . . . When the thirst was too terrible, I always went to sleep because I was too thirsty to play. I can imagine I must have slept a long time, because whenever I awakened, there was water, and bread. But I always ate the bread from one sleep to another. I always had enough bread but not enough water, because the pitcher was not large . . . And how long I had been playing I cannot describe because I did not know what was an hour, or a day, or a week. I was always in a good mood and content, because nothing ever hurt me. And this is how I spent the entire period of my life until the man came, and taught me to draw. But I did not know what I was writing.[11]

'Because nothing ever hurt me.' Poor Hauser – unable even to express proper anger or articulate the hurt of his own abuse. No wonder the idealistic men and women who championed his cause could see in him an almost Christlike figure – the rage, the fear, the pain with which he could not connect, that threatened to engulf him, could be conveniently forgotten or denied when his own words were so full of a delighted acceptance of everything. Thus Hauser had spent thirteen years of his life.

Then, a few weeks before his appearance in Nuremberg, a change had come. The man who had visited him, unseen, for so many years, now showed himself to Hauser and began to teach the boy to write, guiding his hand across the page, encouraging, cajoling, playing with him sometimes, beating him on occasion too. Then one night the man came and dressed Hauser in long trousers, boots and a jacket. He then picked Hauser up and carried him out of the prison. It was the first time that the boy had left his hole. Assaulted by the strange smells of the outside world, Hauser fainted, overwhelmed by the strangeness of all things. The man revived him and tried to teach the boy to walk. The next hours, or days, were confused in Hauser's mind: a nightmare journey of walking and pain, weeping and waking, and sleeping, and promises of new horses, and that he might too be a rider as his father once had been. A village at night; strangers bring food to him; the unquenchable longing to be back in the hole. And then, Nuremberg. Standing there waiting, the letter in his hand; lost, forlornly alone – and staggering down to Herr Beck, the shoemaker, standing talking outside his door in the Unschlittplatz, about to be the first person to see Hauser on his coming into the world.

Nothing could be discovered of the first three years of Hauser's life before he first entered his hole. Hauser himself could tell little else of his marvellous history. He did not know who he was, or where he had come from. He had been brought to Nuremberg by an 'other', and left there to fend for himself with his two letters. It was only then that Hauser learnt of the existence of other people beside himself and his gaoler. Why had he been released after so many years? What did his captor hope to achieve by passing him on to the captain of cavalry? Hauser could not say. It was as if he had only just then been born, and had come into the wide world for the first time, innocent and full-grown.

Hauser's innocence required protectors. Inevitably he found them. In fact, over the few short years of his life on the outside, Hauser would benefit from the attentions of three mentors: Georg Friedrich Daumer; Anselm von Feuerbach; and the Earl of Stanhope.

The young Professor Daumer (1800–1875) was the first to attach himself to the fate of the boy. A fortnight after his arrival in Nuremberg, he visited Kaspar. A young teacher and amateur psychologist, Daumer was broad-browed, sensitive and thoughtful in expression, long curled hair falling on each side of his strong-featured face. He was a passionate convert to the pseudo-science that proliferated in Germany at that time: galvanism, mesmerism, animal magnetism, vegetarianism, and the new craze of homeopathy. His investigation of Hauser was to depend upon these faddish beliefs in the more fugitive and obscure areas of human consciousness. Daumer quickly secured a place for himself as the boy's teacher, and from this position of intimacy became the author of a series of books on Hauser.

Daumer appears to us now a youthful combination of zealous ambition and naive kindliness. As had happened with Itard and Victor, Hauser's arrival presented Daumer with an unmissable opportunity to make his name. This is not to taint the young academic with mercenary motives. Rather Daumer needed a Hauser; his whole life seems now a process of ensuring his readiness for just such a bizarre event. The prospect of an early retirement from his work at the *Gymnasium* (at the age of twenty-eight), due to poor eyesight, had left him looking for a new aim in life.[12] As we shall see, Daumer brought his sense of human consciousness, as in any case mysterious and strange, to his involvement with the mysterious arrival. Like one of the fervent adepts in Nathaniel Hawthorne's uncanny tales, Daumer sought to know hidden secrets. Hauser must have seemed a gift to him, a key into the dark realm of the mind. A few months after their first meeting, Hauser left the Vestner Tower to move in with this young academic. Twenty-eight years old and unmarried, Daumer lived with his mother and sister in a house by the banks of the Pegnitz river, a quiet and secluded area of Nuremberg. There he undertook to teach the boy, to educate him from his state of new-born ignorance. The *Gymnasium* where Daumer worked granted him leave of absence; now he could devote himself to Hauser.

If we put down Daumer's enthusiasm for the boy to a youthfully romantic opportunism, it is more surprising perhaps that Hauser should also engage the impressive support of one of the greatest lawyers in Germany. Here there could be no trace of adolescent idealism. Paul Johann Anselm Ritter von Feuerbach (1775–1833) had the reputation of a rational and sober man, though one who certainly shared something of Daumer's passion for the obscure and occult in human nature. His status in Germany was assured: he had campaigned successfully for the abolition of torture in legal investigations, and written the Bavarian legal code, a document that served as a template for German nineteenth-century law. Feuerbach visited Hauser on 11 July 1828. The meeting sealed Hauser's international fame: it was Feuerbach's work on Hauser, published in 1832, that was to prove the single most influential book on the strange case.

Feuerbach was fifty-two years old when he met Hauser, and was no impractical dreamer. A jurist, and for ten years President of one of the Bavarian Courts of Appeal, he was an unlikely man to fall for an imposture. The impression one gains of him is of a worldly-wise and ironically knowing middle-aged lawyer, though one with an imagination strongly tinged by the Romantic. In portraits, Feuerbach looks incisive, sharp-eyed, high-cheekboned, quizzical, daring the viewer to answer his gaze. The ageing lawyer was not one to discount a tale purely on account of its oddity. He knew of regions in Germany where such stories as Hauser's would not appear strange: 'Dr Horn for instance, saw in the infirmary at Salzburg, but a few years ago, a girl of twenty-two years of age and by no means ugly, who had been brought up in a hog-stye among the hogs, and who had sat there for many years with her legs crossed. One of her legs was quite crooked, she grunted like a hog, and her gestures were brutishly unseemly in a human dress.'[13] Nuremberg itself could anyway seem a city lost in some vanished past, a town of ghosts, the repository of an archaic Germany – it too was a region where strange things might happen.

Those portraits of Feuerbach reveal a stark-featured, shrewd and rather canny man: inevitably one is reminded of James Burnett, though Feuerbach has little of his Scottish counterpart's eccentric whimsy. If Burnett pursued his passions, Feuerbach characteristically tempered his. Following an early marriage in 1796 he had been forced to abandon his youthful enthusiasm for philosophy and history in favour of the more practical and lucrative study of the law. Yet, as with Burnett, a yearning remained to return to the philosophical bent of his youthful studies. Similarly, these philosophical leanings expressed themselves in an interest in the bizarre and unusual. Lacking the restraints of Burnett's Scottish pragmatism and Enlightenment hankering for order, these leanings express themselves in Feuerbach's evident search for literary renown, and a penchant for the oddities of human psychology. His *Narratives of Remarkable Criminal Trials* still makes entertaining reading, with its tales of homicidal wives and entranced axe-murderers. More pragmatically, as has been said, his early writings argued against the use of torture in the investigation of a crime, while his later works disputed the value of vindictive punishment; indeed, it could be said that his writing on Hauser forms part of a broader, sustained argument against the effects of imprisonment as such. Feuerbach rapidly befriended Hauser and began to act as his unofficial but widely respected mentor, protector and advocate.

We shall hear more of the Earl of Stanhope, Hauser's third benefactor – and, some would say, his murderer – later.

II: Soul Murder

> This world to me is as a lasting storm,
> Whirring me from my friends.
>   William Shakespeare, from *Pericles*.

As word spread of the boy's strange arrival in Nuremberg, Hauser became a source of fascination across the Western world, known and written about in the newspapers and journals of every European country. They named him 'the child of Europe', partly in fitting tribute to his fame, and perhaps from a sense that a child who has no parents becomes the son, not of an individual, but of a whole culture. Something akin to this process occurs with Hauser: the weight of images and narratives that Europe had used to explain its origins came to aid the construction of Hauser's fragile identity.

Daumer educated Hauser carefully, introducing the boy to new tastes and sensations, teaching him to read, write and draw. In August 1828, he showed him for the first time the sight of the stars at night. Hauser, as always when presented with something new, fell into a stunned reverie. On coming to from this absorbed stillness, Hauser wept that for so long he had been kept from the sight of such beauty.

During his first months in Nuremberg, Daumer and the others conducted many experiments on Hauser. They discovered that while some of his senses were exceptionally acute (his night-vision, hearing and sense of smell), in other regards his ability to perceive the world was seriously damaged. He could not distinguish foreground from background in looking at a landscape; he thought of animals as having fully human intelligence; and he had no notion of the distinction between animate and inanimate. For this reason, he would grow anxious at the sight of crucifixes and plead that the suffering man might be taken down. His only skill was in riding horses, which he mastered easily and with enough success to astound his military instructors.

In appearance Hauser seemed an unlikely amalgamation of child and adolescent:

> His face, in which the soft traits of childhood are mingled with the harsher features of manhood, and a heart-winning friendliness with thoughtful seriousness, tinctured with a slight tinge of melancholy; his naïveté, his confidential openness, and his often

more than childish inexperience, combined with a kind of sage-
ness, and (though without affectation,) with something of the
gravity of a man of rank in his speech and demeanour; then, the
awkwardness of his language, sometimes at a loss for words and
sometimes using such as have a harsh and foreign sound, as well
as the stiffness of his deportment and his unpliant movements, –
all these, make him appear to every observant eye, as mingled
compound of child, youth, and man, while it seems impossible at
the first glance, to determine to which compartment of life, this
prepossessing combination of them all properly belongs.[14]

Hauser's face and demeanour embodied the terrible confusion produced by his disrupted history. While other people live through and
grow out of the stages of their lives, in Hauser all the broken parts of
his development were simultaneously present and visible.

Meanwhile, Hauser's education progressed slowly. However, he
showed definite improvements, and very soon mastered language,
learning to communicate verbally, and to read and write. During his
first few weeks in Nuremberg, Hauser responded to people and
objects with a blank incuriosity, masking perhaps some inner
implacable anxiety. This torpor soon gave way to an intense and
delighted interest in the world. Starved of sensation or novelty for
thirteen years, he now briefly gloried in a world of innumerable
pleasures and new experiences. Barred for so long from the use of
his senses, Hauser was drunk with plenitude. Mingled with this
intoxication with the world, Hauser also experienced fits of over-
excited panic or disgust. He felt too intensely the beauty and variety
of things, and yet at times appeared burdened by the oppressive-
ness of their very existence.

New things overwhelmed him, pushing him into a bewildered
stupor:

Whenever anything was told him that he did not understand, or
when anything attracted his admiration or aroused his curiosity,

a spasm passed over his face, his features twitched convulsively, and the whole left side of his body (especially the arm and hand) was affected. The convulsive movement was usually followed by a kind of numbness: he stood perfectly still, his eyes fixed, apparently neither seeing nor hearing, his mind turned in upon itself until the idea was seized and mastered.[15]

This confusion and numbness on being presented with the new suggests one of two things: either that these states were his means of defence against the psychical shock experienced in taking in the external world, or that his only possible response was this chaotic or anaesthetic demeanour. Existing in a state of vulnerability before the pressure of objective things, Hauser could soon slip from its balance into a condition of fear and trembling. What is crucial in Hauser's response is that delight as much as pain evoked this self-induced (though no doubt unconscious) flight into stillness.

Such flight may have been the result of Hauser's lack of knowledge about the repertoire of appropriate responses. If Hauser's story was true, it would be surprising not to find such effects caused by his solitary past. Babies learn ways of responding to external stimuli by imitating the responses that parents show them to be apt. In the absence of others who might help him mediate and comprehend the world, Hauser remained trapped in the overwhelming comprehension of the presence of things. In Robert Graves' phrase there was for him no 'cool web of language' to wish the hurt of things away.

Taking this knowledge of Hauser's unsurpassed sensitivity, Daumer set out to prove to the world that Hauser was a kind of sleepwalker or what was called an 'automatist'. He believed that Hauser, loosened from ordinary consciousness by the strange violence of his past, had fallen into the somnambulistic world of fleeting and liminal states. Hauser excited Daumer chiefly because he seemed to him a wonderful 'example of the "sensitive", and a noble proof of the powers of "animal magnetism"'.[16] There was great enthusiasm in the Germany of that time for such ideas as the somnambulistic or hypnotic state, and for mesmerism – the belief that magnetic forces pass between persons, or between people and certain objects, such as magnets, metals, or stars.

Hauser's curious life, which had been, as Feuerbach suggested, 'slept away', was perhaps bound to intimate conditions derived from the state of magnetic somnambulism. In his *The Discovery of the Unconscious* (1970), Henri Ellenberger describes the symptoms of somnambulism:

> Kluge, in his textbook on animal magnetism, distinguished six degrees of the magnetic state: (1) Waking state, with a sensation of increased warmth; (2) Half-sleep; (3) 'Inner darkness,' that is, sleep proper and insensitivity; (4) 'Inner clarity,' that is, consciousness within one's own body, extrasensory perception, vision through the epigastrium, and so forth; (5) 'Self-contemplation': the subject's ability to perceive with great clarity the interior of his body and that of the person with whom he is put into rapport; (6) 'Universal clarity': the removal of veils of time and space and the subject perceives things hidden in the past, future, or at remote distances.[17]

Kluge's set of distinctions depends upon an idea of the external self and the visible world as mere veils of illusion spread over another deeper and invisible reality. That was certainly the purport of most mesmerist thinking – though not in fact of Kluge's, who was a rigorous materialist. However, in Ellenberger's words, the mesmerists' passion for magnetism and somnambulism was an 'audacious attempt at experimental metaphysics'. The metaphysical here was the mysterious inner self, one in which '"the bestial in man borders on the angelic"'.[18] Somnambulist writings portray human beings as liable to fall into one of two alternative magnetic states: we either rise to a heightened self-contemplation or lapse to a state of exag-

Mishukov, the Moscow boy who chose to live with a pack of wild photographed for the world's press in the summer of 1998.

He was overjoyed to find that it sucked as naturally as if it had really found a mother. The Goat too seemed to receive pleasure from the efforts of the Child, & submitted without opposition to discharge the duties of a Nurse.

Published as the Act directs Dec.r 8.th 1787, by John Stockdale, Piccadilly.

2 'Little Jack', Thomas Day's children's
book character from the 1780s,
shows his heroic status by suckling from
a goat.

3 John Ssabunnya, a Ugandan orphan,
in 1991, just after being found living
in the bush among a family of
monkeys.

ng Peter the Wild Boy, who, in 1726, was brought from living wild in
ods of Hanover to the court of George I in London.
r as an old man, as Lord Monboddo saw him in a Hertfordshire
ouse at the close of the eighteenth century.

Arbuthnot, writer, friend of Swift and Pope, physician to the
amily, and Peter's guardian on his first arrival in London.

THE SAVAGE GIRL.

The Manner in which the Savage Girl was taken   *Vide Page 4*

7 An image of the capture of Memmie Le Blanc, the Savage Girl of Champagne, from a book on her life published in the 1820s.

8 A caricature of James Burnett, Lord Monboddo, the Scottish laywer and philosopher who travelled to France to investigate the life of the Savage Girl of Champagne.

9 Victor, the savage boy, discovered in the woods of Aveyron and brought to post-revolutionary Paris in the summer of 1800.

Jean Marc Gaspard Itard in middle-age: once the young, ambitious physician who undertook to reclaim the wild boy of Aveyron from his savage state.

Kaspar Hauser, the child of Europe, in the peasant clothes he wore when he first left his dungeon and entered into the deserted streets of Nuremberg in the spring of 1828.

Philip Henry, 4th Earl Stanhope, the English aristocrat who became Hauser's guardian, and may also have been his killer.

13 Kamala and Amala, two Indian girls brought up by wolves, sleeping overlapping each other at the orphanage where their saviour, Rev. Singh, had brought them.

14 Kamala, after her sister's death, taking food from Mrs Singh's hand.

15 The romantic image of Rudyard Kipling's Mowgli, the hero of 'The Jungle Book'

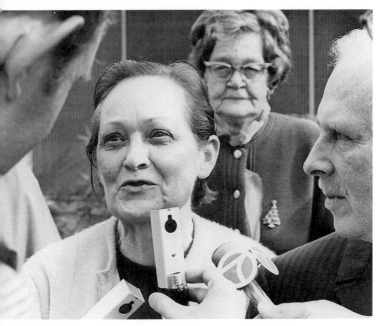

...rk, with his son John, stands outside the suburban house where for ...n years he confined his daughter, Genie, to a single room. ...ie, Genie's mother, faces the press outside the Los Angeles ...oom after being cleared of charges of abuse.

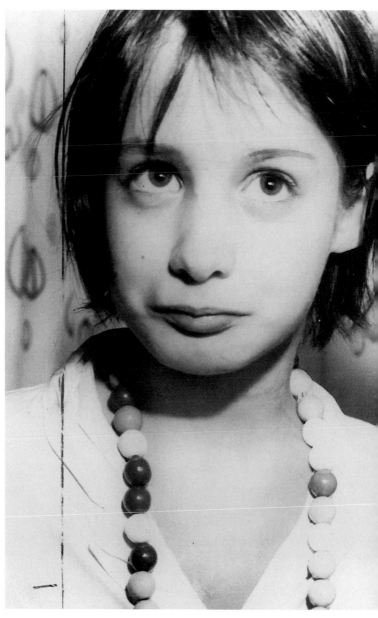

18 The only photograph of Genie to appear in the press on her discovery in 1970; the wide-eyed, undernourished, tiny ghost of the girl she might have been.

gerated self-ignorance ('inner clarity' or 'inner darkness'). Hauser possessed each of these opposites at once. His intense sensitivity to the outside world, the result of 'magnetic' properties, both created an inner self and annihilated it, returning Hauser through an over-load of experience into the condition of a waking sleep.

Daumer was not the only one of Hauser's protectors to be fasci-nated by such obscure mental states. Curiously, in his *Narratives of Remarkable Criminal Trials* (*Merkwürdige Criminal-Rechtsfälle*), Feuerbach himself writes the case history of another automatist. John George Sörgel, the 'idiot murderer', confessed to killing a man, chopping off his hands and feet, and drinking his blood. However, both murder and confession were undertaken in a trance. Coming out of this 'hypnotic' state, Sörgel was unable to remember any-thing of these horrific events. For this reason, Feuerbach, as judge in his case, found him to be guilty but insane, and sent him to an asylum, where he died shortly afterwards. Wasn't Hauser another such automatist, losing his sense of identity through access to a hypnotic condition?

There were other such sensitives in the Germany of the time. Friederike Hauffer, the so-called 'Seeress of Prevorst', was famous throughout German-speaking Europe. The experiments performed on her by Justinus Kerner, a respectably eminent physician and lyric poet, became the template for Daumer's own investigation of Hauser.[19] As with Kerner and Hauffer, Daumer plied Hauser with a succession of substances, gauging each time his strong and hyper-sensitive reactions. Anything might throw the boy into a fit, cause cramps or convulsive shivers, or plunge him into sudden uncon-sciousness. Daumer wondered at the odd succession of Hauser's sensitivities. Thunderstorms, the full moon, brandy, loud noises, quiet noises, squeezed cheese, bright daylight, beer, cats, spiders, snakes, flowers and grape juice – all these things powerfully moved him. He was also found to dislike beards, the colour black and comedy.

Daumer took Hauser to see a visiting female somnambulist. Here he describes in his own words what happened at their meeting:

Hauser, by the proximity of this person, was seized with the greatest aversion; in the same manner, on the other hand, she experienced a peculiarly abhorrent effect from Hauser. I ordered him to put on paper an account of the sensation which he felt, which he did as follows: 'As I came into the room, and the door of the diseased person was opened, which I did not know, I felt a sudden dragging on both sides of my breast, as if any one wished to pull me into the room; as I went in, and proceeded towards the sick person, a very strong breath blew on me, and as I had her at my back, it blew on me from behind, and the pulling which I felt before in my breast I now felt in my shoulders. As I went towards the window, the sick person followed me. At the time that I wished to ask a question of Mr. Von Tucher, I felt a trembling in my left foot, and it became unwell; she went back again, and that trembling left me; she seated herself under the canopy, and said, Will not the gentleman sit down? . . . Mr. Professor Hensler told her that I was the man who had been wounded; at the same time she noticed my scar, and pointed towards it; then came the air strong upon my forehead, and I felt pain in it; also my left foot again began to tremble greatly. The sick person seated herself under the canopy, and said, that she was ill, and I also said that I was so unwell, that I must sit down; I sat down in the other room: now the other foot began to twitter. Although Mr. Von Tucher held my knees, I could not keep them still. Now a violent beating of my heart came on me, and there was a heat in all my body; that beating of my heart left me afterwards, and I had a twittering in my left arm, which ceased after some minutes, and I was again something better. This condition lasted until the next morning; then I had a headache again, and a twittering in all my limbs; still not so violent. In the afternoon, about three o'clock, it came

again, something less, and left me earlier; my bowels were
opened, and again in half an hour after, then I was quite well
again.'[20]

Daumer transformed Hauser's story into a myth of sensitivity. Once
deprived of sensation by his mysterious imprisonment, Hauser had
come into the world and suddenly found himself released into the
world of the senses; but just as the blind are popularly supposed to
develop in finer form those senses left to them, Hauser discovered
that long disuse had actually refined his senses far beyond the
dulled limitations of ordinary people. He could perceive the mysterious mesmerist fluids supposed to emanate around each human
being, could feel the quick presence of a spider scuttling into the
room.

So Hauser's world was one of myriad sensations, 'stunning' him,
seizing him and whirling him about. In those first months of coming
into the world, Hauser lived in a curious mixture of intoxicated nau-
sea and mingled fascination and disgust. It is the beauty of things
that Hauser now sees – a perception of beauty that contains both
wonder and an endlessly perplexing anxiety. The corporeal world is
enough: the surfaces of things satisfy him.

In his vanity Daumer believed that he too shared something of
Hauser's exceptional acuteness. He portrayed himself as another
such 'sensitive', vicariously experiencing the effects that Hauser
himself feels. Teacher and pupil belong to an elite of feeling, distinct
from the leaden sensibilities of ordinary citizens: 'Somnambulists
say, "I feel – I behold;" never, "I understand – I trace – I discover."
Their communications are not like knowledge acquired, *a posteri-
ori*, by the understanding; but like direct intuitions.'[21] On finding his
freedom, Hauser rose up and opened himself to the wealth of the
world. He was soon to find that such richness could not last, that the
ecstasy of vision was not something that could be sustained – and
that the world to which he lay open continued to be dark and

threatening. For an event was about to take place that would immediately blunt Hauser's amazing receptivity, and plunge him once
more into an apathy that cruelly repeated the long years of his
incarceration. Fallen into a gap within himself, he reached out to a
world that at all points would overwhelm him with its power and
strangeness.

Newly able to write, Hauser began to keep a journal. Rumours circulated in Nuremberg that the mysterious boy was engaged in writing
his memoirs; a newspaper reported news of Hauser's literary
endeavours.[22] Perhaps the fear of what such a document might
reveal is responsible for the next turn in Hauser's story. On Saturday
17 October 1829, he was taken ill and so stayed in bed that day, missing his lessons. Professor Daumer left him at home while he took his
habitual walk before dinner; Daumer's mother and sister were occupied with cleaning the house. Hauser, feeling sick, went to the privy,
which was masked by a screen in one corner of the courtyard. There
he heard sounds of someone coming into the house and, peering
behind the screen, saw a man covered with black in the corridor. He
thought: The chimney-sweeper has arrived. Hauser had an unrea-
soning terror of all black things, and this fear extended to the sweep.
So the boy decided to wait there in the privy until he was gone.

After some little time, Hauser peeked once more from behind the
screen, found the man in black right by him, and then suddenly felt
a blow to his forehead. He fainted and fell to the ground. When he
recovered, he found that there was blood all over his face. He tried
to stagger to his room, but felt dizzy and then, fearing that his
attacker was perhaps still lurking somewhere in the building, he hid
in the cellar, where he lost his senses.

Nothing was ever discovered about the identity or whereabouts
of this unknown assailant. He had made his way into the house
unseen, and left likewise invisibly, unheard, unnoticed in the busy
streets of the medieval town.

Later Feuerbach would speculate that the would-be assassin had tried unsuccessfully to slit Hauser's throat; only the boy's low position seated on the privy had saved him. The knife had instead only wounded his forehead. (This was the wound that had ached in the presence of the magnetic lady.) The damage was slight and Hauser soon recovered physically from this murderous attempt. However, there were other forms of damage, less noticeable at first. From then on, Hauser's demeanour changed. The miraculous flood of sensations that had so exhilarated him in his new-found freedom dissolved and vanished. He lost his sense of wonder and hectic excitement, and instead grew brutishly dull and suspicious. His remarkable ability to learn left him; the rapid advances he had made in his education consequently slowed. Daumer and his family began to notice in him a new capacity for deceit.

For Feuerbach, the story of Hauser's stolen childhood was the record of a new and uniquely terrible crime. This new crime against the boy was only a repetition and an objectification of that greater, more insidious villainy. Those lapses of self in Hauser that Daumer described, his falling into trances and fits, seemed echoes of the silence and deadness of those long-lost years in the cell. Wasn't this propensity in himself the product of his imprisonment? These were symptoms of what Feuerbach named 'soul murder'. Locking Hauser in that gloomy hole had robbed him of an ordinary development, killed his soul and left the victim alive. In a Freudian reading of the Hauser story in *Halo in the Sky* (1988), the psychoanalyst Leonard Shengold argues that the concept of 'soul murder' means: 'killing the joy in life and interfering with the sense of identity of another human being. It is primarily a crime committed against children.'[23] Feuerbach's reflections on Hauser amount to an impassioned amplification of the meanings of this appalling and ineradicable crime.

The attempt on Hauser's life repeated that earlier crime of 'soul murder'. His essential fear and anxiety had been realized in the 'black man'. Attacked from outside, Hauser inevitably returned metaphorically to his state of life in his 'hole': indifferent, blank, incurious, empty. His innocent wonder could not sustain itself; he fell back into a kind of deadness. It is in this way that the crime of 'soul murder' concludes. Hauser becomes an accomplice in the murder of his own soul.

Hauser's identity was inevitably weak, vulnerable and fragile: he needed a world free of hostility or fear, lacking the resources acquired in a normal development to deal with these inescapable presences. Leonard Shengold remarks that for an individual whose development has not been disrupted like Hauser's, the renunciation of an imagined invulnerability can be at its best essentially renewing and creative, a recognition of the limitations of the self. But Hauser had nothing to fall back on and so collapsed into the condition of an automaton, abandoning feeling because he lacked the strength to absorb the hurt that accompanies it. Feuerbach watched in dismay as Hauser's incredible vitality and sense of wonder withered:

> The extraordinary, almost preternatural elevation of his senses, has also been diminished, and has almost sunk to the common level. He is indeed still able to see in the dark; so that, in respect to him, there exists no real night but only twilight; but he is no longer able to read in the dark nor to recognise the most minute objects in the dark at a great distance. Whereas he was formerly able to see much better and more distinctly in a dark night than by day-light, the contrary is now the case. Like other men, he is now able to bear, and he loves the light of the sun, which no longer distresses his eyes. Of the gigantic powers of his memory, and of other astonishing qualities, not a trace remains. He no longer retains anything that is extraordinary, but his extraordinary fate, his indescribable goodness, and the exceeding amiableness of his disposition.[24]

So it was that Hauser lived out the representative life of the Romantic sensitive failure. Like Chatterton and Keats, he seemed the archetypal adolescent orphan – rejected, abandoned, but passionate in the intensity of his sufferings. Like Wordsworth and Coleridge, he embodied the mourned-for loss of youthful vision, sinking back from the rapt pinnacle of childhood into the light of common day. For Feuerbach especially, Hauser came to stand for natural and heartfelt sensibility. The old lawyer was only too well aware of the inauthenticity of most people's feelings. In one of the cases in his *Narratives of Remarkable Criminal Trials*, Feuerbach describes the case of Maria Zwanziger, a murderous German Madame Bovary:

> Married to a man whom she feared and disliked, and who moreover was always engaged either in business or in drinking, leaving her to lead a life of solitude and monotony, which contrasted most disagreeably with the gaiety of her guardian's house, she endeavoured to divert her melancholy by reading novels. 'My first novel,' said she, 'was the "Sorrows of Werther", and it affected me so much that I read "Pamela" and "Emilia Galeotti".' Thus uncultivated and frigid natures excite their imaginations to represent as really felt emotions they are incapable of feeling. Such natures strive to deceive themselves as well as others by a mere grimace of sensibility, till at last it becomes so habitual to them, that they are really incapable of distinguishing truth from falsehood, and end by poisoning the very source of truth, the natural feelings. Hypocrisy, falsehood, and malice are fruits easily produced, and fearfully soon matured in a soul accustomed to disguise its real feelings under assumed ones; and thus it is that sentimentality is perfectly consistent with total hardness of heart, and even with cruelty.[25]

Maria's heart is empty; Hauser's once moved with genuine, spontaneous emotion. Literature shaped Maria's life; her sorrows were second-hand, and her joys were forgeries. Hauser lived for a time in the light of direct and unmediated experience. If natural feelings create truthfulness, then, for Feuerbach, Hauser existed absolutely truthfully: his unnatural life had made him completely natural. For Feuerbach, Hauser was no wild man; he was not a 'savage' to be civilized, but a natural man to be learnt from. Reversing what Itard had declared about Victor, both Feuerbach and Daumer assume that Hauser's hypersensitivities, his tastes and his emotions are an index of what it would be to be fully and naturally human. Hauser had lived in an unfallen world. Now, into this unfallen world the last of Hauser's protectors was coming – and a new epoch in Hauser's life would enter with him.

III: The Child of Europe

I am a mockery king of snow . . .
   William Shakespeare, from *Richard II*

Only five days after the first attempt on Hauser's life, Philip Henry, Fourth Earl of Stanhope, arrived in Nuremberg. An accident to his carriage was to detain him there for some days. He put up at the hotel 'Zum wilden Mann' or, as it was known in English guide-books, 'The Savage', apparently a cheap and shabby inn at the time, and therefore unlikely accommodation for a visiting English peer (though this was the one inn in Nuremberg where post-horses were to be had).[26] However, it would fit the later image of Stanhope as a villainous melodrama aristocrat, if we guess that he may have chosen the hotel in a spirit of irony prompted by its oddly appropriate name. It was while staying at the hotel that Stanhope first heard about Hauser, and decided to take the opportunity to visit him.[27]

All access to the boy was impossible, and so Stanhope left the city disappointed. Then, in May 1831, he returned to the city on business. He applied to meet Hauser, and this time his request was

successful. They met at the Burgomaster's house; Stanhope was
extraordinarily impressed.

Lord Stanhope was the nephew (through his father's first marriage) of William Pitt and the half-brother of the eccentric traveller
and orientalist Lady Hester Stanhope. Like Hauser, Stanhope had
difficulties with his parents. His father was Charles Stanhope, the
Third Earl, a politician, obsessive amateur scientist, indefatigable
inventor, and Rousseauist philanthropist who had supported the
French Revolution. Six months after his first wife's death, Charles
Stanhope married his dead wife's cousin, Louisa Grenville, a shallow, vain woman, 'stiff and frigid, with a chilling, conventional
manner'.[28] Charles was a stern, arrogantly intelligent man, difficult
to love and much driven. His fiercely democratic political principles
often wavered in their practical application and certainly did not
extend so far as to countenance one of his daughters marrying, as
she had wanted to, the family apothecary. Born in 1781, Philip
Henry, the son, grew up in the family home at Chevening Manor in
Kent, but spent some of his youth in Germany, where he published,
at the impressively precocious age of nineteen, a popular and pious
work entitled *Gebetbuch für Gläubige und Ungläubige, für Christen
and Nichtchristen* (*Prayer Book for Believers and Unbelievers, for
Christians and Non-Christians*). This precocious entry into the literary world was accomplished despite the potentially detrimental
effects of his own upbringing. Like many radicals of the late eighteenth
century, his father had *views* on education: he insisted that the
young Philip and his brother should be brought up as ordinary
working men and so had them apprenticed to a blacksmith. The situation between father and son worsened, the elderly Earl refusing
to educate his son – so as, Philip suspected, to keep him weak and
malleable. Philip eventually broke with his father and fled England
for Germany, under an assumed name, where he enrolled at the
University of Erlangen. There he grew severe in his tastes, foppish in
his appearance, and quick in his speech.[29]

The strained relationship between the old, irascible radical and the wayward son led eventually to a scandalous law suit against the father, caused by the old man's bitter decision to disinherit all his children. As we shall see, this was not the last time that Stanhope was to be involved in scandal. On his father's death in 1816, Philip Henry returned to England to take up his seat in the House of Lords. He was married to Catherine Lucy Smith, one of Lord Carrington's daughters; had two children with her, but chose to live away from home, travelling for much of the time in Germany as an agent for various Christian societies, distributing tracts, prayer books and hymnals.

Stanhope's role in Hauser's story is a puzzling one. As is so often the fate of those who hate their father's temperament, young Stanhope nonetheless inherited it. His writings reveal him to be a sensible, if rather tetchy character, with an awareness of beauty but little sense of humour, and abstemious by nature (he became a tee-totaller soon after he first met Hauser).[30] In portraits, we see a typical English aristocrat, with the customary look of hauteur and implacable condescension; a high forehead, a long nose, and rather cold, untroubled eyes. Altogether Lord Stanhope must at first appear an unlikely character to share Daumer and Feuerbach's obsession with Hauser. Yet Stanhope too was fascinated by the liminal edges of consciousness – some ten years later he involved himself with editing a book on somnambulism, hallucinations and dreams, and had been one of those present at the magnetizing of Jane O'Key, the 'Prophetess of St. Pancras', by Dr Elliotson, the infamous mesmerist.[31] Above all, he shared his father's philosophic interest in science, though without the older man's mechanical and fervently inhuman zeal. On one famous occasion, in order to test his hypothesis that combustion will not take place where there is no air, Stanhope's father invited his friends to a party in a wooden house that he had attempted to render fireproof. Then, to prove the effectiveness of his work, he started a fire outside while they were still drinking and talking on the upper floor. The flames poured around the building, to a height of over eighty feet, but the apprehensive party-goers remained mercifully unhurt.[32] Obsessive like his father, but without the old man's energy, before meeting Hauser Stanhope looked set to become an armchair enthusiast, an impractical and self-indulgent philosopher.

His relationship with the young man followed a sad trajectory. What began as infatuation would soon dwindle to indifference, and then lapse to hostile disenchantment. It is futile to look for consistency in the English aristocrat's reactions or motives. At first, Stanhope appeared almost shamefully enamoured of the mysterious young man. Soon this passionate attachment faded into boredom: within a few months, Stanhope was leaving Hauser for Britain – although admittedly on the pretext of preparing a home for him there. What Stanhope did next remains unclear, his actions from now on creating a scandal that would dog the family name for the rest of the century.

Some years after Hauser's death, Stanhope published his own volume on Hauser's life. In this book, he set out the case that Hauser was an impostor and a liar. Such a book from someone who had so famously championed Hauser was in itself startling. For some, the sudden shift in Stanhope's ideas seemed not so much surprising as sinister. Writers of the late nineteenth century suspected Stanhope of something worse than disillusionment. A writer called Von Artin in Germany, and a free-thinking biographer specializing in the exotic, named Elizabeth Evans in Britain, suggested that Stanhope was in fact the murderous agent of Hauser's enemies, coldly setting out to defame and destroy the young man. These claims led the Duchess of Cleveland, Stanhope's daughter, to write her own impassioned defence of her father's role in Hauser's life in order to clear his besmirched name. These accusations are still made today: the most recent (and best) book on Hauser in English, Jeffrey Masson's *The Wild Child*, repeats the claims and describes

Stanhope as acting with 'a guile, cunning and ruthlessness that was to lead to the undoing of Kaspar Hauser'.[33] We shall consider the question of Stanhope's guilt in detail later.

Following the first assault on Hauser, in order to protect the boy and to relieve the failing health of Professor Daumer, he was moved to the house of Herr Bieberbach, a merchant and city councillor. Hauser's stay there was not a success: he irritated his host family, particularly Frau Bieberbach, who accused him of deceit and boorishness. As a result, Hauser was very soon moved to the house of Herr von Tucher, who was appointed his guardian.

Hauser was now eighteen years old. Andrew Lang writes in the following dry tones of his character at this point: 'He was very vain, very agreeable as long as no one found fault with him, very lazy, and very sentimental.'[34] Yet Hauser was certainly still enough of an attractive character to ensnare the affections of an English lord: it was at Tucher's that Stanhope befriended Hauser. Tucher disapproved strongly of the relationship. He saw Stanhope as extravagantly affectionate towards the boy – even passionately so – showering his young protégé with expensive gifts and money in a way that Tucher thought could only damage the boy's character.

Hauser disagreed. Stanhope stayed past the day appointed for his departure; and the young man began to spend a great deal of his time at the inn with Stanhope. Each day the two men would walk arm in arm through the streets of Nuremberg. Stanhope, who we remember preferred not to live with his wife, is said by Elizabeth Evans to have shown towards Hauser 'an affection so excessive as to disgust right-minded persons and create suspicion as to the honesty of his intentions'.[35] In her book on the case published in the 1890s, Elizabeth Evans depicts the two men as 'unnaturally' close, hinting at a homosexual relationship forced upon a naive Hauser by the suave, older man, citing Tucher's suspicions of the Englishman as evidence.[36]

Were Stanhope and Hauser in love? Once we suppose this to be the case, much that might remain otherwise inexplicable in the story becomes as clear as a cliché. The progress of the older man's feelings might well be seen as the history of a failed love affair – unless, of course, we assume with Evans that Stanhope was simply leading the boy on in an attempt to get him into his power, and so destroy him.

Despite the disapproval of both Daumer and Tucher, Stanhope began to press for Hauser to go away with him back to England. Tucher was exasperated and outmanoeuvred; he could do nothing, it seemed, to keep hold of Hauser's affections. On 11 November 1831, Tucher wrote to Stanhope asking him either to assume responsibility as Hauser's guardian or else to cease communication with the boy completely for two years. As things stood, he argued, his own position with Hauser was being seriously weakened by the Englishman's profligate generosity. Stanhope refused. The next day, Tucher wrote to Feuerbach, asking to be relieved of his position as Hauser's guardian. So it was that on 26 November 1831, just over a year after moving to Herr Tucher's, Hauser was officially bound to the care of Earl Stanhope. The King of Bavaria wrote personally to Stanhope to thank him for his great benevolence.

The next month Hauser and Earl Stanhope left Nuremberg together for Ansbach, Feuerbach's charmingly small, pretty, but fully provincial home town. Lieutenant Hickel of the Royal Police was appointed as Hauser's guard, in readiness for any repetition of the attack that had occurred in Nuremberg. Away from Daumer, Hauser's education was to continue under the supervision of Herr Meyer, a schoolmaster and physician at Ansbach. Stanhope had succeeded in removing Hauser from the care of both Daumer and Tucher; and though he was now living in close proximity to Feuerbach in the town of Ansbach, in effect his chief protectors were now Stanhope and his two friends, Hickel, the police officer, and Meyer, the teacher. The boy had effectively been isolated from

his first friends. Yet at this time Hauser's future seemed bright. I
was expected that at any time he would move to England and a new
life:

> The continued inclination to brood over his destiny, of which
> Casper must be daily reminded at Nuremberg, being removed, he
> will begin a new life; as soon as the sails are spread to convey him
> to England, all melancholy reflections will be left behind him.
> New air, new modes of life, and new interests of life, will restore
> freshness and strength to his youth. Probably there is reserved for
> him in England a quiet, and therefore a more certain happiness
> than he (even if he belonged to a race of princes) might have
> found on the tempestuous sea of time, if the hand of wickedness
> had not made him such an *incognito*; therefore we will not pity
> his fate any longer.[37]

However, soon all three of Hauser's new guardians were to turn
against him. In time, each of them was to accuse him of imposture,
deceit and a desperate need to aggrandize himself with a false story
of his origins. Meyer, in particular, appears to have grown to despise
Hauser: his treatment of the boy was certainly bullying, if not sadistic. Under the relentless surveillance of his suspicious and needling
host, the decline into apathy initiated by the murder attempt continued. Emotionally, Hauser was back in the life he had led in his
hole.[38]

While Hauser's guardians of the time increasingly suspected and
disliked him, his old protectors continued to see in him a model of
simplicity and childish freedom from guile; but Hauser was no
longer a child. At Meyer's home, we see for the first time evidence of
heterosexual feelings in Hauser, as he began a flirtation with a servant girl. All those written narratives that celebrate Hauser -
whether written by eyewitnesses such as Daumer and Feuerbach
or by later nineteenth-century writers such as Elizabeth Evans – tend
to underplay Hauser's emerging sexuality, being more concerned to

show how unspotted innocence makes its way in a corrupt world. In the 1890s, Elizabeth Evans approached Hauser's innocence in terms of his 'saintly' qualities, his 'supernatural perfection of character' – a perfection that is tarnished by contact with the ordinary qualities of human beings. Her Hauser is neat, orderly, obedient to authority, refined, truthful and forgiving. Only once does she show him voicing any condemnation of the man who had locked him up for the greater part of his life. (It is clear from the sources that there was actually more than one occasion on which Hauser expressed such hostility.)

Just as Evans – and Feuerbach – praise Hauser for this apparent absence of anger, she also celebrates his absence of sexual desire. The representation of Hauser's 'innocence' clearly involved a need to deny both sexuality and passionate emotion. The image of Hauser's innocence is peculiarly neutered. Denied active and passionate responses, he appears instead as a passive perceiver – the recorder for others of a distinct mode of seeing the world. This passivity is integral to how Hauser's story was taken, as it fosters the view of him as a sufferer. Even Feuerbach's consistent praise of Hauser's obedience can seem to a contemporary reader to be an endorsement of a compliance that may strike us as simply a negation of life.

We now understand Evans's insistence on Hauser's chastity through our awareness of Freud's presentations of the sexuality of children, but even without Freud the reiteration of this point would strike a reader as curious. It is as if Evans's wish for Hauser's innocence involves a desire to place him outside his body (the body of an adolescent male) and to depict him as being as arrested physically as mentally. Evans equates Hauser's original goodness, his '"perfect innocence of soul"', with his 'dormant' sexual instincts. Furthermore, such interest as Hauser is allowed to have in women based itself on their capacities in non-sexual areas, such as cooking and cleaning. His views on women were frankly chauvinist: 'Whereas he at first

distinguished females from males only by their clothing, he now
seemed to judge between them by their respective capacity for
intellectual achievement and general usefulness, to the great
advantage of the masculine portion of the race [. . .] His idea of a
woman appeared to be a vain, lazy, useless creature, dressed up in
feminine apparel.'[39] Nonetheless Evans sees Hauser's condition as
an '"angelic purity"'. Von Tucher, Hauser's previous guardian
described him as a '"being such as we may imagine in Paradise
before the fall; a precious, unique, ever to be remembered embodiment, which shone like a ray of heaven's own light upon this
impure, degraded world of sinners"'.[40] Hauser's pre-lapsarian condition marks him out from other children, all of whom have been
tainted by the condition of society. Therefore Hauser's flirtation
with the servant girl at the Meyers' home merely calls forth from
Evans a reiteration of his unspotted innocence: 'Whatever other
faults might justly be laid to his charge, in sexual matters he
remained innocent to the last, unconscious, and therefore
untempted.'[41]

However, Hauser's new guardians were less likely to believe these
radiant images of an angelic youth. Increasingly they distrusted and
disliked the young man, seeing him as deceitful, changeful and
insincere. In the 1890s, writing to clear her father the Earl of
Stanhope from attack, the Duchess of Cleveland shows just what
was thought of Hauser's unstable character:

> In a report furnished to the police authorities in 1834, Meyer gives
> a curious picture of Kaspar's powers of dissimulation. He was so
> different at different times that no one could have believed him to
> be the same person; and Feuerbach well described his nature as
> 'chameleon like'. The every-day face, which he wore to those
> immediately about him, was neutral and commonplace enough,
> but instantly vanished if he was in company. Sometimes, when
> surprised sitting alone in his room, it was gloomy and morose,

and looked years older: then changed as if by magic when he saw himself observed. It could wear whatever expression seemed appropriate to the occasion: sometimes the bright intelligence of an appreciative listener; now it beamed with affection and sympathy, and then again, when he was reproved or angered, bore the unmistakable stamp of an evil and vindictive temper.[42]

This protean Hauser might seem a born deceiver, a person acting without the restraint even of a continuity in identity. His states of mind obliterate each other; rather than a succession of moods, we have here a succession of faces.

With the distrust of his guardians just beginning to grow, Hauser's position was increasingly beleaguered, and he was constantly threatened with the exposure of himself as the impostor he may or may not have been. Things worsened even further with the sudden death of Feuerbach, a few days after Hauser's confirmation. This blow fell in the Whitsun holidays of 1833, exactly four years after Hauser's first appearance in Nuremberg. Now Hauser's wisest guide was gone. The young man was left in the hands of men who increasingly doubted all of his claims. His only supporters now were Daumer and Tucher, both of whom were far away in Nuremberg.

Following Feuerbach's death, Stanhope left Hauser in Ansbach in order to continue his travels around Europe, prior to the move to England that he and Hauser were soon expected to make. While Stanhope travelled, Hauser began work as a copying clerk in a law office. In December 1833, his guardians began to notice a strange alteration in the young man's behaviour. He appeared distracted and preoccupied. On 9 December, Meyer and Hauser argued heatedly; the row ended with Meyer threatening to tell everything of Hauser's innumerable deceits to Stanhope when the English lord returned from his travels. Hauser became sullen and withdrawn, and for the next few days refused to shake his guardian's hand. On 11 December, he mentioned to Frau Hickel that he had an appointment with an acquaintance to watch the boring of the artesian well in the park, the gardens of the disused palace. Frau Hickel said that he should not go, but should instead visit a friend of his who was giving a ball. Hauser followed her advice and went to the ball, where he danced and greatly enjoyed himself.

On 14 December, Hauser left the law office at noon. After lunch he went to visit his spiritual director, Pastor Fuhrmann, to help with putting up the Christmas decorations. When they had finished, the two men left the house together, but Hauser excused himself, saying that he had made a date to meet a young woman friend of his. However, instead of going to see this friend, Hauser walked directly to the gardens of Ansbach's abandoned palace. It had snowed a few days previously and the snow was still lying, owing to the bitter cold. Hauser said later that he was there to meet a mysterious stranger who had promised to tell him the secret of his birth. This stranger was to wait for him at the artesian well. However, when he arrived at the well there was no one there, so in spite of the cold Hauser wandered across to the monument that commemorates the poet Johann Peter Uz. A man was waiting there for him, and they walked together through the snow to a quiet place, under the bare winter trees. Then the man, making as if to give him some letter or document, suddenly stabbed Hauser hard in the chest and quickly ran off.

Bleeding hard, Hauser managed to run home, where he found Meyer and excitedly told him how a stranger had stabbed him in the park. Perhaps not realizing the extent of Hauser's injury, Meyer doubted the young man's word, and so made the young man take him back to the gardens to show where the assault had taken place; but before they could reach the park, he collapsed and had to be taken back to the house. The killer was never found. Hauser took four days to die. For much of this time he was lucid and able to talk with those around him, but as death approached he grew increasingly weary and incoherent. The end came in this way:

Pastor Furhmann, seeing that the last moment was approaching, leaned over Kaspar and said: 'Father, not my will,' and Kaspar continued, 'but Thine be done.' 'Who said those words?' asked the clergyman. 'The Saviour,' was the reply. 'When?' 'When He was dying.' After a short silence, Kaspar murmured: 'I am tired, very tired, and I have a long way yet to go!' then turned his face to the wall and died.[43]

On 28 December 1833, Pastor Furhmann conducted Hauser's funeral service. Large crowds followed the body to its grave.

IV: The Family Romance

Me waiting until I was nearly fifty
To credit marvels. Like the tree-clock of tin cans
The tinkers made. So long for air to brighten,
Time to be dazzled and the heart to lighten.
   Seamus Heaney, from 'Fosterling'

There are two stories of Kaspar Hauser, two sides to him in that anamorphic portrait that represents his face to the world. In one, he is the swindler-hero of his own constructed romance, a pauper child reaching from his obscure poverty to the special fate of the exceptional ones. This Hauser is a liar, on impulse or by design. His very existence is a deception, his body and face a confusing and mystifying sign. But in the other story, the same young man becomes the lost prince of a marvellous tale. His fate and history are evidence of the unique suffering allotted to the royal son in exile, the imprisoned child in the tower.

For Hauser's sympathizers did not stop at accepting the young man's extraordinary account of his early life. They hunted for a reason why such a bafflingly unnecessary punishment should be visited on any one child; and the reason they found was that Hauser was special and exceptional even before he was first led, a small child with faltering steps, into the dark hole that was to be his dungeon and his home. They said that Hauser was no less than a child of royal blood, perhaps the missing heir to the throne of Baden, and so the innocent victim of court intrigues and aristocratic plots.

In this account of Hauser's history, Stanhope, and probably Meyer and Hickel as well, were privy to the machinations of the royal family and, as mercenary hirelings, set out to destroy the living evidence of the plot. Was Stanhope really this heartless villain of an old romance, falling in love deceitfully with the boy he had been contracted to kill?

However, Stanhope had his own theory about who Kaspar Hauser really was. In a book written about Hauser three years after the young man's death, Stanhope argued that the boy came to Nuremberg as a peasant on the make, with the intention of receiving charity from the captain of cavalry, and perhaps looking for support in beginning an army career.[44] However, when events grew strange, Hauser soon found himself complying with perceptions of himself as a special and unique child of nature. An attempt to gain sympathy rapidly led Hauser into being trapped in an imposture that he was then forced to maintain for years:

> He also became more and more involved in the story which had been suggested to him; and the longer he acted this part the more difficult must it have been to him to extricate himself from it; till at last he found satisfaction in it, and as Professor Daumer states (in an article in the Universal Gazette of the 6th of last month), 'lying and deceit were become to him a second nature'.[45]

Stanhope even had an alternative account of how Hauser had actually met his death. In this version, following a row with Meyer over an instance of deceitfulness, Hauser decided to injure himself in order to regain the sympathy and attention of those around him. He walked alone to the park, and there slowly pushed a knife through his thick padded coat. When the knife had pierced through to the skin, he accidentally used too much force. The knife penetrated much more deeply than he had intended, a full two inches into the flesh. Unwittingly, he had given himself his death wound.

To substantiate his case, Stanhope adopts in his book the mode of a legal inquiry – a form that carries an implicit critique of Feuerbach's role in Hauser's life. Stanhope implies that the respected judge had forsaken impartiality in order to become an advocate for Hauser. By this analogy Stanhope takes for himself the role both of prosecuting counsel and also of unimpassioned observer of events. In setting out to debunk Hauser's story, Stanhope does make some astute points, in particular concerning the absurdity of some of the experiments conducted on the boy; but his argument leads him in turn into his own absurdities. The problem with the imposture thesis is quite simply that it is as fantastic as Hauser's story itself. Did Stanhope really imagine that a barely educated peasant could deceive for years on end men as intelligent as Feuerbach and Daumer?

However, there were precedents for such a deception. Stanhope pointed to the strange case of Caraboo, the 'savage' persona of an impoverished English girl named Mary Baker:

In the year 1817 or 1818, there appeared upon the south-west coast of England a female impostor who was not born far from the place, who two years before, disguised in man's clothes, had been employed in a farm, and had afterwards made the acquaintance of some gypsies. She appeared under the name of *Caraboo*, as a native of India, and had an unknown language and writing. She seemed on her arrival very weary; her hands showed that she was not accustomed to hard labour; she ate no meat, drank only water, and had the greatest horror of wine and spiritous liquors. She was extremely neat in her dress, very modest in her behaviour, and her whole conduct made such a favourable impression as removed all suspicion of imposture. After this cheat was discovered by an English Physician, with whom I was acquainted, she related that she had played this part without any preparation, that she had learned it through the different observations which were made in her presence, and which were supposed to be unintelligible to her.[46]

What Caraboo had done, mightn't Hauser also have managed? Both Caraboo and Hauser might have played the part of the exotic stranger, the 'savage' in the homeland, to an audience only too ready to have their fantasies of the primitive played out before them. Both the impostor and the imposed upon had their investment in accepting the lie of strangeness: each needed contact with that elusive quality of the exceptional. For the urbane observers there was the chance to believe in wonders. For Hauser and Caraboo, the rewards of appearing exotic were more immediate. Caraboo's autobiography, a work dictated by the hapless Mary Baker, details a life marked by random suffering and extreme poverty. For Mary Baker, becoming Caraboo was an act of theatre, but one where the enticement was survival, notice and rescue. In her desperation it must have seemed the only escape route.

Stanhope's guilt or innocence in the Hauser case is now beyond proof, although he still has accusers among those experts who have written on Hauser's case – such as Mayer and Masson. They are persuasive arguers, yet neither image of Stanhope – as malevolent melodrama villain, or wronged, upright English lord – feels quite right. Whether they were fraudulent or honest, it is difficult now to comprehend Stanhope's actions. Perhaps Stanhope brought to his relationship with Hauser (as he had already brought to his marriage) a spirit of self-justifying inconsistency, inherited from a father given to abrupt shifts from immense kindness to implacable hatred for those closest to him. Given this damaged and damaging relationship to others, it was an unlucky day for Hauser when he was first introduced to Earl Stanhope.

Whatever the effects of Stanhope on Hauser, there are numerous weaknesses in the conspiracy theory of Hauser as benighted and threatened prince. Later, less romantically inclined observers were quick to make the accusation that the story of Hauser as abandoned prince was mere fable. For instance, when Andrew Lang, the Scottish anthropologist and folklorist, first wrote on Hauser in 1843, he displayed incredulity:

The Duchess of Cleveland's book, *Kaspar Hauser*, is written in defence of her father, Lord Stanhope. The charges against Lord Stanhope, that he aided in, or connived at, the slaying of Kaspar, because Kaspar was the true heir of the House of Baden – are as childish as they are wicked. But the Duchess hardly allows for the difficulties in which we find ourselves if we regard Kaspar as absolutely and throughout an impostor. This, however, is not the place to discuss an historical mystery; this 'true story' is told as a romance founded on fact; the hypothesis that Kaspar was a son and heir of the house of Baden seems, to the editor, to be absolutely devoid of evidence.[47]

When first writing on the boy, Lang combines disbelief and the willingness to tell the story as 'a romance'. By 1904 when he came to write on the Hauser case again, he indulged himself in an outright attack on the story's romantic propensities. Lang begins by setting out the case for the Baden theory: 'I state first the theory of the second party in the dispute, which believed that Kaspar was some great one: I employ language as romantic as my vocabulary affords.'[48] His vocabulary turns out to afford him language which is very romantic indeed: 'Darkness in Karlsruhe! 'Tis the high noon of night: October 5, 1812. Hark to the tread of the Twelve Hours as they pass on the palace clock, and join their comrades that have been!'[49] He continues in this vein for some pages. Naturally, the whole thing is a pastiche that both luxuriates in and ridicules the romance elements of Hauser's story. Lang particularly has fun with the 'White Lady of

Baden', a ghost who appeared in the palace at Baden whenever on
of the royal family was to die, and who was mixed up with the sup
posed disappearance of the infant heir to the throne in 1812.

This dual attitude of scorn and indulgence to the Hauser myth i
symptomatic of Andrew Lang's writings on Hauser. It is possibl
that the debunkers of the late nineteenth century are involved in
subtle anti-Germanism, in which (contrary to Rupert Brooke notin
that '*das Betreten ist verboten*') German high-flown Romanticism i
contrasted unfavourably with British good sense. Lang replace
romance with an appeal to the probabilities of the case:

> Thus briefly, and I trust, impressively, have I sketched the histor
> of Kaspar Hauser, 'the child of Europe', as it was printed by vari
> ous foreign pamphleteers, and, in 1892, by Miss Elizabeth I
> Evans. But, as for the 'authentic records' on which the partisan
> of Kaspar Hauser based their version, they are anonymous, unau
> thenticated, discredited by the results of a libel action in 188;
> and, in short, are worthless and impudent rubbish.[50]

Lang even goes so far as to directly criticize Feuerbach:

> In 1832, four years after his [i.e. Hauser's] appearance, a boo
> about him was published by Paul John Von Feuerbach. The ma
> was mortal, had been a professor, and though a legal reforme
> and a learned jurist, was 'a nervous invalid' when he wrote, an
> he soon after died of paralysis (or poison according t
> Kasparites). He was approaching a period of life in which Britis
> judges write books to prove that Bacon was Shakespeare, and hi
> arguments were like theirs.[51]

Lang disputes both Feuerbach's use of evidence and the consis
tency of his account. He has even harsher words for Evans. He firs
ridicules her, and then declares that she should consider herse
lucky that the libel laws in England (unlike those in Germany) can
not be invoked in slanders against the dead.

However, it is Stanhope that first teaches us to think of Hauser's story as a romance, when he attacks Hauser's veracity and Feuerbach's methods:

> But before I come to the consideration of these official documents, I must examine a little of Feuerbach's Romance. He himself, taught by his own experience, began, in the last period of his life, to doubt the truth of his narrative, as I have learned from a witness, in every way deserving of credit, said, 'Perhaps Feuerbach has written a romance in his old age.' He did not, however, allow the matter to be further investigated, and did nothing towards rectifying the errors which he himself had disseminated, and to throw light on a story which had received great weight from his authority.[52]

While obviously intended as an insult, Stanhope's description of Feuerbach's text as romance is also astute criticism. For his own part, Stanhope's work itself may be characterized as anti-romance, challenging the original fable with an appeal to the 'facts'. This attack upon the fabulous nature of Hauser's story may also mark out Stanhope as a bad reader of Feuerbach's text – in other words, as someone instinctively unsympathetic to the nature of such a narrative. However, what excuses Stanhope from this charge is that both he and Feuerbach have the same objective: that is, the elucidation of Hauser's origins and self. Stanhope attacks Feuerbach for attempting to make a romantic story of Hauser's life and condemns what he considers to be the culpable perversion of truth that results from such an attempt: 'Such a falsification of history, as is shewn in the points above mentioned, would have been conceivable if Feuerbach had been a writer of romance, or a poet. It is not, however, permitted or pardonable in a Judge, to whom truth should be sacred, to trample it under foot in order to defend his theory.'[53] Where Stanhope does a disservice to the facts is in not recognizing that sometimes reality may itself take on the nature of a fable –

something particularly likely to occur in a society fascinated by romance. Life's imitation of art may well shape real events.

Nearly sixty years later, writing to exonerate the Earl of Stanhope, her father, from blame for Hauser's murder, the Duchess of Cleveland repeats his arguments, writing: 'And yet, with all this, there can be no question as to the result. It is not the highly wrought romance, but the plain and simple truth, that eventually wins the day.'[54] From the nature of their argument Hauser's position on the fault line between the romantic and the hardheaded grows clear. What is at stake in the representation of Hauser is a view of the world that can include the marvellous, the strange and the numinous. In short, Hauser exists to prove the validity or the error of romance.

But why should those first protectors of Hauser have turned to the plotlines of old romance to explain him? Hauser's story as interpreted by Feuerbach takes us back to those narratives of the abandoned royal child with which this book began. We return here to the primal origin of such tales in the Oedipus or Romulus myths. In Hauser's case this plot is reworked into what has been termed 'The Baden Thesis'.

The story goes like this: Hauser, it was said, was in fact the legitimate heir of the throne of Baden, which in the 1820s and 1830s was still an independent kingdom. He was supposed to have been born in the royal palace at Karlsruhe, the child of Stéphanie de Beauharnais (the niece of Napoléon's wife, Josephine) and Karl, the intemperate Duke of Baden. Rival claimants to the throne kidnapped Hauser while he was only a few days old and replaced him with a dead or dying male infant. (All sides agree that the bereaved Stéphanie never saw her dead child.) Hauser, the rightful heir, was then kept for many years in complete isolation, and in complete ignorance of his rights, brought up, as is usually the case in such stories, by a humble peasant. This continued until it was thought expedient to get rid of the boy by releasing him once more into the world, where he was expected to make some kind of career as a soldier. Unfortunately this plot stumbled when, instead of quietly entering a military life, Hauser became a celebrity and an object of fascinated interest across Europe. This turn of events forced his previous captors to kill Hauser, lest his very visible existence should lead to the discovery of their plot.

The Duchess of Cleveland, as Stanhope's daughter perhaps not an impartial witness, remarks that Stéphanie herself knew of and believed the story of Hauser's imprisonment. She loved Feuerbach's book on the boy, and remarked to Stanhope that she wanted to translate it into French. 'But if the idea that this phenomenal being might be her own child even crossed her mind, it was promptly dismissed as an "impossibility".'[55]

The plot seems a fantastic one, but it had many adherents in both the German states and Britain in the 1830s. An article on the social condition of Germany in *The London Dispatch* of 8 April 1838 records discontent in Baden over the accession of the new Duke:

> The present Grand Duke Leopold came to power in 1830 . . . Caspar Hauser, subsequently murdered at Anspach [*sic*], in Bavaria, was then alive and considered throughout Germany as the son of the Grand Duke Charles, who died in the year 1819 and Stephanie Napoleon his wife, and consequently the legitimate heir to the ducal crown of Baden . . . The notoriously abandoned conduct of the Grand Duke Louis, who governed the territory of Baden from 1820 to 1830, and who was with reason considered as capable of any atrocity, added to the credibility of the report that he had put the legitimate infant out of the way in order to seize upon his inheritance.[56]

Over fifty years later Elizabeth Evans is still telling this story plainly, but it receives a more curious expression in Feuerbach's work. In the old lawyer's account, the romance plot acts as a palimpsest, a story beneath the surface of the text. Therefore Feuerbach's main method of introducing the romance narrative into his story is through the indirect means of allusion. (He did write directly of his beliefs about Hauser's birth in a text called the 'Mémoire'. Written in 1832 as a letter to Queen Caroline of Bavaria, this document remained unpublished until 1852.)[57] There are three such hints in Feuerbach's narrative, and in each case Feuerbach alludes to Calderón's seventeenth-century romance, *La Vida es Sueño* (*Life is a Dream*). Other than the epigraph to the work, which quotes the opening lines of the play, there are two concealed references in the text itself.[58]

In Calderón's play, Prince Sigismund of Poland is imprisoned in a tower by his father and left in absolute isolation, as his father has heard a prophecy that his son will one day become a terrible and murderous tyrant. When he reaches young adulthood, Sigismund is temporarily released and allowed to become king for a day. However, during the course of the day it seems as if the prophecy is to be fulfilled as Sigismund kills a servant in a fit of blind rage. He is returned to his tower, where, on awaking, he is told that he dreamt yesterday's adventures. He experiences guilt for what he has done to the servant, while nonetheless believing that the murder was in fact simply a dream. He comes to the conclusion that even in dreams one must act with moral responsibility. The Polish people, hearing that Sigismund has been locked away, rebel and place him on the throne. Sigismund now has his father and his captors in his power, but refrains from exacting revenge, owing to the humanizing influence of his still firmly held belief that everything that happens to him is a dream.

The first reference to Calderón's play occurs in a context where Feuerbach intends to depict Hauser's disadvantages in being isolated from the world. It is in the second reference that Feuerbach alludes to his private beliefs concerning Hauser's origins. He describes how he hopes that those who damaged Hauser might be brought to justice:

But not all heights, depths, and distances, are accessible to the reach of civil justice. And, in respect to many places in which justice might have reason to seek the giant perpetrator of such a crime, it would be necessary, in order to penetrate into them, to be in possession of Joshua's ram's horns, or at least of Oberon's horn, in order, for some time at least, to suspend the action of the powerful enchanted Colossuses that guard the golden gates of certain castles.

But what is veiled in blackest shades of night,
Must, when the morning dawns, be brought to light.[59]

The last lines quote Calderón. Such circumspection was by no means merely a literary game in Metternich's repressive Europe: so it is that Feuerbach's belief about Hauser's origins are all but concealed in a quotation that is itself about concealment. Even such an elaborate attempt at saying and unsaying was felt by some to have been insufficient to have saved Feuerbach from the effect of his suspicions. Rumours abounded that Feuerbach's death was the result of his being poisoned by agents of the usurping Duke. These rumours even reached London – that same article in *The London Dispatch* already quoted above darkly hints as to the old lawyer's fate:

This opinion [that Hauser was the rightful heir to the Duchy] was founded upon a combination of a variety of circumstances, and strengthened by the guarded but intelligible hints of Feuerbach the distinguished criminalist and president of the tribunal of Anspach [*sic*], who died shortly afterwards at Frankfort of a violent colic, in consequence of having accepted an invitation to a diplomatic dinner.[60]

'Men must not walk too late.' So it was not until Evans's text that the full romance implications of Hauser's story could be written out clearly. Unfortunately, although Evans describes a narrative that in

itself corresponds to the conditions of romance, it was undoubted-
ly Feuerbach who was most aware of the meanings inherent in the
romance narrative – one that, for legal and political reasons, he was
unable to write.

There are several ways in which the Hauser story repeats the the-
matic patterns we have already witnessed in the earlier romances of
the abandoned child. First, there is the question of the identification
of the abandoned child with Christ – Hauser's death-bed scene as
quoted above from Evans's book implicitly urges just such an identification. This image of Hauser as Christ is both sentimental and
intrinsically connected to a crucial unspoken proposition, namely,
that Hauser is an individual without sin. The presentation of Hauser
as a suffering Christ, an individual of intrinsic goodness and perse-
cuted virtue, is of particular interest when we consider that
Feuerbach, Evans, and Hauser himself all express an antagonism to
Christianity. In the same year as her work on Hauser was printed,
Evans published a 'free-thinking' work on the errors of Christianity.
It may be that Evans's hostility to Christianity created a need for a
Hauser figure, a 'natural man' who displays an integral human
goodness. Hauser's 'unspoilt' life also implicitly proves such goodness to be essentially human: Feuerbach also thought of Hauser as
proof of humanity's natural goodness. Of course, these ideas return
us to Rousseau's image of the 'child of nature'. Such a figure of
apparently unmitigated goodness elicits pathos through being victimized, and in this way can rapidly assume the function of a traditional 'Man of Sorrows'.

From another point of view it may be that some complex form of
anti-monarchical dissent informs this use of romance in telling
Hauser's story. It is difficult from this distance to effectively place
Hauser in the politics of the period. Baden was, surprisingly
enough, one of the more liberal states; however, radicalism tradi-
tionally flourishes in more liberal regimes. Ansbach, the home of
Feuerbach, was judged by an English visitor in the mid-1830s to be

the most radical town in Germany, though interestingly he ascribes this radicalism to a wish to have the royal family living in the town – a wish symbolized in the presence of the empty Palace there.[61] There *was* peasant and middle-class disaffection in the German states of the 1820s and 1830s; the populace 'were only too ready to see Divine Right discredited and sovereignty reduced to dynastic gangsterism'.[62] Yet, in the southern states paternalistic relationships to the monarchies flourished: kings were seen as familiar and accessible, and were often well liked and respected.

Nonetheless, the bourgeois political radicalism of the period would appear to receive tacit expression in the romance elements of the Hauser legend. The discontent concerning the monarchy was tempered, as we have seen, by a sense of deep personal affection and identification towards particular monarchs (though not, it would appear, to Duke Leopold of Baden). It is possible, therefore, that the radical agitation implicitly present in the Kasparite texts is provoked neither by republican nor modern democratic sympathies, but by an implict belief in the institution of monarchy itself. There is a feeling that kings should be good and should rule decently, and a concomitant sense that the monarchy is in any case losing power and prestige in the face of a process of state centralization and modernization. The criticisms of the monarchy that begin to appear in the 1830s and 1840s tend to concentrate on the 'personal silliness or inadequacy of individual rulers'.[63] Yet this need not obviously imply an attack on monarchy itself; rather it may embody a wish that the institution were stronger. The king, for all his 'silliness', at least remains an individual with whom the subject could feel an affinity – something unavailable to the impersonal and abstract operations of bureaucratic rule. Attempts to read the Hauser legend as republican, therefore, become more ambivalent. Any radical potential merges with a reactionary conservatism; and this is precisely the kind of thing that one would expect to find contained within the romance form. However, one fact complicates this discussion of the Hauser fable: while his story begins as romance, it ends as tragedy.

So Kaspar Hauser both acquires prestige through his connections with the royal family, and yet exists in antagonism to the monarchy. He becomes a symbol both of the divine right of kings and of 'the wretched of the earth'. This is made apparent in Werner Herzog's film on Hauser, where Bruno S., the actor who played Hauser, had spent long periods in asylums and prisons and had lived as a down-and-out. If Hauser was just a peasant on the make (and pauperism was a wide-scale social problem in the German states of the period) this would still hold true. In this way, he assumes the position of one who can be used for attacks upon the monarchy, despite the fact that, according to the Baden Thesis, he continues to be the rightful ruler. Hauser's legitimacy expresses the right of the oppressed and victimized to rule.

Was Hauser a king in exile or a liar? It may be the idea of Hauser's imposture that most looks forward to cultural 'modernity' – particularly in the way imposture begins to ally itself with the image of celebrity. Besides these intimations of cultural change, it is important to remember that the 'Kasparites' rely upon forms of narrative that are fundamentally, indeed defiantly, old-fashioned – though, of course, this desire for the past is itself a sign of the modern, particularly in those aspects of it that hint at a tribal nationalism. The difficulty that we cannot actually know if Hauser was an impostor or not is of course not such a problem as might be supposed. What the theme of imposture brings out is the necessity for the 'Kasparites' to provide a narrative that can authenticate his story.

Since Hauser's death there have been two such attempts. The first occurred at his post-mortem – an event reinterpreted by Elizabeth Evans in the 1890s in the light of the newest evolutionary theories. This is what the physicians found:

The brain was only slightly developed, but not diseased. It resembled the brain of a marten and of the human foetus, and its condition showed that its activity had been arrested at an early period of life . . . When restored to society he was a man in years and in outward development; but his brain had remained in its primitive stage of growth, and could not enlarge after so long a period of inactivity. Kaspar Hauser's peculiar character (his faults and imperfections, as well as his uncommon virtues) was thus accounted for. He was silly, vain, and untruthful, because he had only a child's judgement to guide his conduct; he was gentle, affectionate, and pure, because his stronger passions had never been awakened. More was expected of him than his fellows had a right to demand; he neither understood himself nor was comprehended by others; he was a being apart, and could never find his place in the world from which he had been so long excluded.[64]

Evans takes the evolutionary jargon of the period and uses it to try to explain Hauser away. He is a primitive in the modern world, a 'degenerate' whose stunted development has left him half-savage and half-beast, a child in both his foolishness and his innocence. Late-nineteenth-century evolutionary theory took the supposed facts of embryology, in which the individual foetus appears to recapitulate the primitive stages of human development, and applied this same model to the growth of the individual child and adolescent, which was then supposed to be repeating the history of the human race in its own life. Now Evans was using this analogy to explain Hauser: because he had no chance to develop normally, passing through the stages of savagery to civilization, his brain was both bestial and embryonic. What alienates Hauser from others, therefore, becomes not a matter of the condition of the world but one of biology: it is the effects on Hauser's physiology that constrain him as a 'being apart'. The biological arrest that he undergoes further identifies him as a perpetual child and, moreover, one who is doomed never to grow up.

Oddly enough, in our time we have used our own models of evolutionary development to examine the veracity of Hauser's story. So it was that this same process of establishing identity by recourse to the body was apparently re-enacted in Germany in the 1990s, when scientists are said to have dug up Hauser's body and examined his DNA to see if he shared any genetic links with the royal family of Baden. After over a century and a half, the suspicion was supposedly proved untrue: Hauser was not, after all, a royal foundling.

Yet Hauser's genetic origins leave the main issues unsolved. The essential mystery remains whether Hauser really did spend the first years of his life locked away, solitary, in a hole. Now that Hauser's family romance of royal kinship has dissipated into nothingness, revealed as the fantasy it always was, it may be that we can come closer to the truth about Hauser. He may not have been a royal child, but it seems highly likely that he was, as he claimed, stabbed and consequently murdered. Might nervous authorities have decided to kill Hauser simply as a way of removing a beacon of political discontent? Might Hauser have been stabbed not for what he actually was, but for what everyone thought he was – a prince in exile, the exceptional embodiment of an old myth?

The astonishing cultural persistence of his story shows just how greatly the need for a Hauser figure remains. Was he killed, the victim of the rumours circulated about him by credulous supporters? *Was* he an impostor? Perhaps the existence of other Hausers in our own century – children locked away and neglected by their parents, confined for years in the dungeons of suburban bedrooms, or in outhouses on lonely Irish farms – shows that we should not dismiss too quickly the story of Hauser's captivity. As for the myths that have grown around him – an infinitely compassionate, infinitely suffering being – these, like the story of the lost royal child, have a function to perform. It is Daumer after all who holds the key to understanding Hauser, as an enthusiast for the newest pseudo-sciences, a man desperately in search of a faith to sustain him. Hauser is someone to believe in, an uncertain point of certainty in a confused and foundering world.

To believe in innocence; to see in another a magical, animistic apprehension of the world; to re-invest the world with lost wonder; to feel that suffering and neglect lead to the most perfect and joyful apprehension of the world – those are powerful incentives for belief. His nonsense suited their nonsense; his being, whether it was pretence or natural feeling, was just the kind they wished to find. All these wild children are really mirrors; through them we feel the joy of the shipwrecked in finding their passage home.

If we are left only with doubt when we consider Hauser's story, then we are in good company. Feuerbach notes that the early discussions of Hauser, including the first official publication related to him, are marked by the desire of those confronted with the strange boy to make a story of him, filling out his blanks with their own conjectures and guesses.

There is no final truth to Hauser; there are only ways of telling his story. The invisibility of Hauser's past, the absence of a witnessed history, means that conventional narrative will not work in his peculiar case. He arrives in Nuremberg on that empty Whit Monday from nowhere; it is as if he genuinely had only just come into the world at that moment. For if Hauser were an impostor, why did no one recognize him? His picture was circulated in numerous publications, including Feuerbach's book, across the princedoms and duchies of Germany – but not one childhood companion, not one schoolmate or fellow peasant came forward to authoritatively identify the mysterious boy.

Hauser's self vanished in the obscurity of his childhood. His history is a condition that he has slept through, with no consciousness even of being asleep. The crime committed against him robbed him of the human development necessary to create the sense of self:

Having commenced the life of infancy at the age of physical maturity, he will, throughout all his life, remain, as regards his mind, less forward than his age, and as regards his age, more forward than his mind. Mental and physical life, which in the regular course of their natural development go hand in hand, therefore, in respect to Caspar, have been as it were separated, and placed in an unnatural opposition with each other. Because he *slept* through his childhood, that childhood could not be *lived* through by him at its proper time; it therefore still remains to be lived through by him; and, it consequently follows him into his later years, not as a smiling genius, but as an affrighting spectre, which is constantly intruding upon him at an unseasonable hour.[65]

Here Feuerbach portrays Hauser's childhood as though it were embodied in that dark and murderous man who pursued him to his grave. Yet Hauser's identity might be found again in a narrative that could bring the adult back into contact with the lost childhood. It seems Feuerbach instinctively grasped that romance was the form by which to achieve this aim.

For romance is the genre in which the lost are found. An abandoned child on a far seashore; a few tokens and letters; a long childhood among a family of strangers; a journey; a chance meeting; the recognition of the lost one, proved by those forgotten relics – these are the elements of the old romances. It is to this model that the wishful belief in the Baden Thesis tends. What if Hauser really were a royal child? What if the old stories were true? Then everything would end as in an old tale – the lost one found, the throne restored, rightness returned, the years' secrets told.

For Hauser, however, the transcendence that Feuerbach had hinted at and waited for never came. At the end Hauser's story ceases to be romance and becomes tragedy. Always the position of abandoned children is inherently tragic in potential. They are persons without a place in the world, with no knowledge of themselves or of their relation to the world in which they live. Hauser falls into a knowledge of his placelessness, his otherness, but never achieves the epiphany of recognition that might heal that knowledge. His story is a romance plot in which the saving moment of 'recognition' is perpetually deferred. The reconciliation of past and present that would draw him into the social domain as a person with a history simply never occurs.

So Hauser remains an eternal child, for ever exiled from the state of childhood, a self unable to cohere or consolidate itself in terms of its own history, and so cut adrift within the process of time – a process that never appears to amount to anything.

This is soul murder: the crime that eradicates the self. Deprived of the identity realized in ordinary development, Hauser's self dissolves into bewilderment. The traces of a personality that is thoughtful, wondering and sensitive are only briefly visible within the unsteadiness of his body, and the self that it manifests. So Hauser remains as mysterious as he was when he first wandered into Nuremberg. That Nuremberg is gone, destroyed by Allied bombing; Karlsruhe, Hauser's supposed birthplace, was similarly destroyed. The condition of Hauser's existence, both for himself and for others, remains for ever one of confusion and unknowability:

> Kaspar Hauser's grave in the public cemetery of Ansbach is marked by a low headstone of granite bearing the inscription: Hic jacet Casparus Hauser Ænigma Sui Temporis Ignota Navitas Occulta Mors. MDCCCXXXIII. In the royal park the site of his murder is indicated by a small granite column with the words: Hic Occultus Occulto Occisus est. XIV Dec. MDCCCXXXIII.[66]

'Here lies Kaspar Hauser, enigma of his age – unknown birth – mysterious death'; 'Here the unknown one killed the unknown one.' They are fitting epitaphs.

CHAPTER SIX

The Wolf-Children

I: Kamala and Amala

Koko is also creative . . . She signed ME CRY THERE when she saw a picture of a gorilla in a bath, apparently a cry of sympathy, since she herself
hates being bathed. And in a flurry of fury, she once signed PENNY TOILET
DIRTY DEVIL when she was angry with Penny, her trainer. Her most
impressive conversation is one in which she supposedly apologised for a
biting incident which had taken place three days previously. When shown a
bite mark on Penny's arm she allegedly signed SORRY BITE SCRATCH.
WRONG BITE. 'Why bite?' queried Penny. BECAUSE MAD, Koko replied.
'Why mad?' asked Penny. DON'T KNOW, responded Koko.

Jean Aitchison, from *The Articulate Mammal*

Kaspar Hauser's story blurred the lines between life and art, as the
young man lived out a romance that would not have looked out of
place in the writings of Hoffmann or Kleist. The next seventy years
were to witness the most famous fictional versions of the wild child
myth. In the last years of the nineteenth century, Rudyard Kipling
dreamt up Mowgli, the wolf-child of the Imperialist Indian forests;
and then, just twenty years later, Edgar Rice Burroughs 'jazzed' that
story and created Tarzan, the white lord of the African jungle. Then,
most strangely of all, just as it seemed as if the myth was passing
into the realms of mere fiction, these stories once more came to life
in the same jungles of the British Empire, as two wolf-children, wild
young girls, were trapped in the Indian forests.

The Reverend J. A. L. Singh had long been a missionary to the
aboriginal tribes around Midnapore, a town about eighty miles
south-west of Calcutta.[1] With his wife he ran an orphanage there,
made up of waifs and strays that they had found in the nearby villages. Singh was a man with a vocation, a missionary fired with the
call to bring Christ to the jungle, which could have been an Eden

but instead was the home of idolatry and ignorance. Various tribes lived out there: Santals, Koras, Lodhas, Mahatos, Goalas, Urias and Kols.[2] These tribesmen were all heathens, but ones who the missionary could see lived according to an honourable and decent moral law. They were not beyond the reach of Christ.

So Singh went out to find them. With up to thirty men, many of them there to hunt for animals to eat or sell, he would make expeditions into the wide jungle – lost in its silence and its leaf-shrouded half-light at noon, its thick gloom at night; armed with rifles; resting after dark in a circle of fire, outside which roamed the wild animals of Kipling's *Jungle Books*: bears, wolves, panthers, tigers, snakes. There were other, stranger creatures out there too. On one journey in the late September of 1920, the missionary and his entourage of hunters stopped for the night in a villager's cowshed. While they rested in the little hut, the villager came to them and declared in fear that there was a ghost out in the jungle. He begged Revd Singh to perform an exorcism, for it was terrifying the villager and his wife. Curious, Revd Singh agreed to go with the villager the next evening and see the ghost for himself.

All that dusk they waited, but saw nothing. Interest waning, only the fearful protestations of the villager brought the priest back to the place in the jungle a week or two later. Singh journeyed in with five other men, including Janu Tudu, a jungle guide. They went by day to where the ghost was usually seen and there found a huge anthill, 'as high as a two-storied building'.[3] There were large tunnels burrowed into the ant-hill, all leading inwards to a hollow at the base of the mound. A local path that passed by had once been heavily frequented by the local villagers but was now abandoned. They feared too much the ghosts that came there at twilight.

All day Revd Singh and his party lingered there. Then, just as the sun was setting, a wolf stole out from one of the tunnels in the mound. Another followed, and then another, and another, and some wolf-cubs trotting along behind. After the cubs, the ghosts came out. There were two of them, both horribly ugly, the heads like large, shapeless globes within which, among the matted hair, a small fragment of face could be seen: a human face with brilliant bestial eyes.[4]

They ran on all fours, bowed head-down in the dust. The others were ready to shoot them, but Revd Singh stayed their hands. He could see that these ghosts were, in fact, children. The problem was how was he going to get them out of the wolves' den? He decided that he and his men should come back in the daytime, while the wolves were sleeping out the sunlight and the jungle heat, dig into the ant-hill and pull the children out. The local villagers refused to help, far from convinced that these jungle phantoms were merely children. So Singh simply went to the next village and persuaded the people there, who had heard nothing of the ghosts, to come and dig with him. The excavation began on an October Sunday morning. As they burrowed into the hill, suddenly first one and then another wolf darted out from the tunnels and ran for shelter in the jungle. A third wolf, however, would not budge from the mound and charged at the diggers, furiously snapping, snarling and not yielding any ground to the invaders. Singh guessed that this must be the mother wolf, acting out of maternal instinct. She filled him with wonder:

> I was simply amazed to think that an animal had such a noble feeling, surpassing even that of mankind – the highest form of creation – to bestow all the love and affection of a fond and ideal mother . . . Whoever these peculiar beings [were], and whatever they might be, certainly they were not her cubs, but had originally been brought as food for the cubs. To permit them to live and to be nurtured by them (wolves) in this fashion is divine.[5]

But while Singh wondered, the villagers acted: they took their bows and arrows and shot the wolf dead.

They dug on, and at last the mound collapsed, leaving a central cave intact. There they found the two cubs and the two ghosts, all huddled together in their fear. Eventually they managed to prise the two snarling children apart. The cubs were given to the villagers, who took them to the local market, where they sold them for a good price.

The children were half savage, more like beasts than humans, wildly showing their teeth to their captors. For now, nothing could be done with them except keep them fed and clean. So Singh left the children with the local villagers, while he continued his missionary tour: he would consider what was to be done with them on his return. However, Singh had not reckoned on the fearfulness and superstition of the villagers. Even though the two children were kept secure within a barricade, the presence of these strange, inhuman ghosts scared the villagers away. When Singh came back five days later, he found the village deserted and the two creatures tied up, soiled, half starved and pitted with terrible sores. Restoring them to health with a handkerchief soaked in tea, Revd Singh thanked God that He had not let them die through his negligence in leaving them, and he headed back to Midnapore orphanage with his strange find. There was simply nothing else to do.

They were girls. Many unwanted children, particularly girls, were reputed to be exposed by the tribes in the forests around Midnapore. The elder was about eight years old and the younger only about a year and a half. They named the elder Kamala and the younger Amala.[6] They washed the sores, and fed them on milk. The girls permitted the care but remained detached, indifferent, taking nourishment but forging no connection, true to their wild selves.

Singh was watching them. By now, the traits that he discovered in the girls will be familiar to readers of this book. They were aloof and shy of others, particularly hating contact with the other children. They did befriend one other baby at the orphanage, while he was still crawling like themselves. Yet one day, without warning, they suddenly turned and attacked, biting and scratching him hard. From then on, the two girls refused to have anything to do with the little child. Singh speculated as to what had motivated the attack: 'It is presumed that when they found some difference and understood that he was quite different from them, then they commenced to dislike him. After this when they fully came to know that he was not one of them, then they fought with him, which frightened him so much that he left their company altogether and never approached them afterwards.'[7] The girls lived within themselves, choosing only each other for companion, shunning human society, longing to return to the jungle from which they had been dragged. Strange physical changes had occurred to them during their life in the woods: their jawbones had altered shape, the canine teeth lengthened, and their eyes in the dark had the peculiar blue glare of cats or dogs.[8] Their night vision was preternaturally acute, as was their sense of smell; also they could hear the minutest sounds at astonishing distances. They ate, drank and walked like dogs, lapping at their bowls of water and milk, running on all fours. Even when sleeping they were 'like little pigs or dog pups', the two of them lying together and overlapping each other for warmth and comfort.[9] They liked the dark, and loved to wander the orphanage compound after nightfall. At sunrise they whined to go inside and shelter from the sun. They had become nocturnal animals, fearless of the dark.

They had no sense of humour, no sadness or curiosity or connection to others. They never laughed, and Kamala shed tears only once – on 21 September 1921, when Amala, her little companion, died. Both girls had been sick for several weeks, after dysentery had set in. Six days into the illness, they began to excrete thick red worms, each about six inches long, and many of them alive. 'Amala brought eighteen such worms, whereas Kamala brought out 116.'[10] They grew weaker, were often unconscious, sometimes for days on end. Kamala began to rally, but her 'sister' went under as her temperature dropped, rose again, and then sank once more. She died in the early morning. For six days Kamala sat by herself in the corner of the room, always silent, never moving.

Kamala's grief lasted a long time. Beneath the blank exterior, she was genuinely bereaved. A few weeks after the other girl's death, Kamala went to smell all Amala's things – her clothes, her plate, her bed – roaming around the garden 'as if searching for something but not finding it'.[11] She was quiet, even more distant than before, scarily adrift from human contact. The missionaries began to wonder if she too might die, simply of her loneliness; but Singh's wife contrived to draw the little girl back into contact with the living, firstly by the use of repeated massages. She would rub the girl's body, affectionately talking to her at the same time, subduing her wildness. The girl returned from her impenetrable distraction; slowly she became livelier; she began to seek out Mrs Singh. If Mrs Singh was absent, Kamala would grow sad and listless; but on her return, she would become impossibly excited, allowing herself to be kissed and petted by the motherly woman. Mostly she paid little attention to Revd Singh.

Singh and his wife pressed on with Kamala's reclamation. They taught her, as best they could, to move, eat, play like any other child. In all her actions, Kamala, although a full-grown child, behaved like a one-and-a-half-year-old baby. She learnt slowly, but nonetheless progress was made. She began to feel the ordinary human fear of the dark, and on night-time walks would now look furtively about her, keeping close to her foster-parents. If the Singhs were present, she would now go to urinate in the bathroom; if left alone, she would pass water wherever she was, as she had done since first being discovered in the woods. Above all, although still silent, she began to understand words, sometimes showing by a gesture that she had taken in what was said. Then she too began to utter a word or two: 'Hoo' for yes, and 'Bha' for 'Bhat', which in Bengali means 'rice', and 'Bhal' meaning 'all right'.[12] There were other words too: Kamala was picking up language.

For eight years Kamala grew up in the orphanage, cared for, slowly learning the rudiments of human behaviour; but like most Indian wolf-children, she was not destined to live long. In 1928, her health mysteriously broke down. An invitation to the USA had to be turned down, as Kamala was too weak to travel. And then, on 26 September 1929, she became very ill. The doctors could do nothing to save her. She died in the small hours of a November morning of that same year.

From the beginning Singh had decided to keep the children from the attention of the Press. Instead he decided to record for himself and posterity a diary account of his treatment and education of the two girls. They would live in the seclusion of the orphanage until such time as they were well enough and socialized enough to fend for themselves. He made his wife swear not to reveal the girls' strange history. As far as the others in the orphanage were concerned, the girls were just two neglected children. Publicity would only ruin them; they needed time and privacy. Moreover if they were ever to marry, it would hardly do to spread the story of their incredible childhood far and wide. Moreover, Singh feared the incursions of the outside world into his orphanage, confusing the purity of the place, taking up his time.

The outside world, however, was not so easily dismissed. Although he and his wife kept the story a secret in the orphanage, when Amala was dying, Singh had to tell the local doctor the history of the girls in order to facilitate their treatment. The doctor gossiped; word got out and visitors started to arrive. Some of the strangers were journalists in disguise: within a few months the whole of India knew of the wolf-girls.

When the news first carried to the West, the response was inevitably one of doubt. Yet Kamala and Amala were far from being the first reported wolf-children to be discovered in India. Many rumours and accounts of savage girls and wild boys appear in the writings of nineteenth-century British Imperialists.

These stories were well enough known to have influenced Rudyard Kipling when he had first come to tell the story of Mowgli, Kamala and Amala's fictional predecessor, over thirty years before. On 24 November 1892, Rudyard Kipling wrote a letter to Mary Mapes

Dodge, the editor of the *St. Nicholas Magazine* for children. He had first submitted a poem to Dodge in 1879, when a fourteen-year-old schoolboy. Now he was letting her know, in a rather proprietorial way, of the origins of Mowgli, perhaps the most famous of all the fictional wild children: 'Also, there will be (D.V.) a wolf-tale, 'Mowgli's Brothers'. *He* was a wolf-boy (we have them in India) but being caught early was civilized.'[13] Kipling was all too aware of Indian tales of children being reared by wolves, and that letter to Mary Mapes Dodge indeed shows that he considered this kind of story to be specifically Indian.[14] Kipling would have already encountered wolf-children in his father's book, *Beast and Man in India* (1891). There John Lockwood Kipling writes: 'India is probably the cradle of wolf-child stories, which are here universally believed and supported by a cloud of testimony, including in the famous Lucknow case of a wolf boy the evidence of European witnesses.'[15] There are many other mentions of Indian wolf-children – such as this from Robert Sterndale's *Natural History of the Mammalia of India and Ceylon* (1884):

Stories have been related of wolves sparing and suckling young infants so carried off, which, if properly authenticated, will bring the history of Romulus and Remus within the bounds of probability. I have not by me just now the details of the case of the 'Boy-Wolf' of Lucknow, which was, I believe, a case vouched for by credible witnesses. It was that of a boy found in a wolf's lair, who had no power of speech, crawled about on his hands and knees, ate raw flesh, and who showed great wildness in captivity. I think he died soon after being caught. The story of the nursing is not improbable, for well-known instances have been recorded of the ferae, when deprived of their young, adopting young animals, even of those on whom they usually prey.[16]

The most important single nineteenth-century account of Indian wild children is W. H. Sleeman's pamphlet, 'An Account of Wolves Nurturing Children in their Dens'.[17] Sleeman was an English soldier, famous for conducting the inquiry into the activities of the Thugs, a murderous nineteenth-century Indian religious cult who believed that strangling their victims would serve as an act of worship to the god Kali. In his pamphlet on wolf-children, Sleeman records an incident of February 1847, in which a boy was discovered at Sultanpoor living in a wolves' den. The child behaved like a wolf; he was unable to speak, and could only growl or snarl:

> He understood little of what was said to him, and seemed to take no notice of what was going on around him. He formed no attachment for any one, nor did he seem to care for any one. He never played with any children . . . When not hungry, he used to sit petting or stroking a pariah, or vagrant dog, which he used to permit to feed out of the same dish with him. A short time before his death, Captain Nicholetts shot this dog, as he used to eat the greater part of the food given to the boy, who seemed in consequence to be getting thin. The boy did not seem to care, in the least, for the death of the dog . . . He had lived with Captain Nicholetts' servants for about two years, and was never heard to speak till within a few minutes of his death, when he put his hand to his head, and said, 'it ached,' and asked for water. He drank it and died.[18]

This air of torpor and depression doesn't belong to all the cases that Sleeman describes. The following incident comes closest to forecasting the wistfully magical tone of *The Jungle Books*. Janoo was a surgeon who had helped a newly discovered wolf-boy:

> One night, while the boy was lying under the tree near Janoo, Janoo saw two Wolves come up stealthily and smell at the boy. They then touched him, and he got up; and instead of being frightened, the boy put his hands upon their heads, and they began to play with him. They capered around him, and he threw straw and leaves at them. Janoo tried to drive them off, but could

not, and became much alarmed . . . The night after three wolves came, and the boy and they played together. A few nights after four Wolves came, but at no time did more than four come; they came four or five times, and Janoo had no longer any fear of them; and he thinks that the first two that came must have been the two cubs with which the boy was first found, and that they were prevented from seizing him by recognizing the smell; they licked his face with their tongues as he put his hands on their heads.[19]

Here Sleeman, the careful English soldier, shows abandonment to be a blessing, only another way of being found; the child inhabits the animal world, and there is at home; a gap is bridged; something lost is restored.[20]

Edward Burnet Tylor, the most important of all the Victorian anthropologists, has something to say about Sleeman and his wolf-boys in a short essay on 'Wild Men and Beast Children', printed in the first volume of *The Anthropological Review* (1863)[21] In reviewing such accounts, Tylor is fundamentally sceptical: 'The whole evidence in the matter comes to this. First, that in different parts of the world children have been found in a state of brutalization, due to want of education or to congenital idiocy, or to both; and secondly, that people often believe that those children have been living among wild beasts, a supposition which accounts for their beast-like nature.'[22] But there are other witnesses ready to back up Sleeman's tales. There is Valentin Ball's *Jungle Life in India* (1880), a bizarrely stoical volume of Victorian hunting reminiscences in which, for instance, the author hints with whimsical unconcern at jungle cannibal experiences during a wayward youth. Ball describes the wolf-boy of Sekandra, whom he himself saw, considering the child to be a 'perfect beast'. He also runs through Sleeman's case histories, and pointedly remarks that these kinds of incident only happen to boys. Yet another case mentioned in the March 1893 edition of *North Indian Notes and Queries* proves him wrong:

A correspondent, writing to the *Statesman*, says: – We have heard of Peter the wild boy discovered in 1725 in the forest of Hertswold, and the wild girl, Mddle. Lablanc [*sic*], found near Chalons, in 1731. But here is a living wild girl come down to Calcutta who was nursed by a bear. She is really an unsophisticated specimen of the *genus homo*. She was found sitting by a huge bear near a den in a forest in Jalpaigori, by the coolies of the tea gardens. The latter, seeing this strange phenomenon, ran to their *Saheb*, who, on hearing the account, went up with a gun, frightened the bear away, and took over the girl, who was then about two or three years of age, to the local Commissioner, and through him placed her in the Jalpaigori hospital. At first the poor creature used to walk on all fours, and bite and scratch, but gradually she became tame, and was taught to walk on her feet and wear clothes, but could not articulate a single word. The Civil Surgeon, after trying unsuccessfully for three years to teach her to speak, discharged her. She then lived on the mercy of the children and women of the place, till at last Babu Pran Krishna Datta, a Brahmo Missionary, took pity on her, and with the permission of the Civil Surgeon, brought her to Calcutta, and placed her under the hospitable care of the *Dassaram* – a friendly institution for suffering and helpless humanity at large, – at Mohendra Nath Goswami's Lane, Simla, Calcutta.[23]

From the evidence of all these accounts, it is clear that when news of Kamala and Amala hit the sceptical West, it could seem part of a rich tradition of Indian wild children.

Yet despite, or even because of, these earlier stories, few believed in Singh's account of Kamala and Amala. The story was too fantastic, and at first many simply scoffed at the notion of human children being nurtured by wolves. Besides, in Britain at least, many were predisposed not to accept the word of mere native witnesses – and here we may recall John Lockwood Kipling's passing comment that even Europeans had testified to the existence of at least one Indian wolf-child. The anthropologist and philologist Max Müller had similarly complained of the doubtfulness of native witnesses,[24] and in the 1890s and afterwards the prejudice against native evidence was still endemic.[25] Suspicion in many Western circles regarding the Indian independence movement of the 1920s ensured that the old distrust against native veracity remained strong. As readers of E. M. Forster's novel of 1924, *A Passage to India*, will know, it was a central part of the justification for British rule that the Indians were too primitive and superstitious to run their own affairs. Strange stories of wolf-children served to endorse this deliberately unflattering view of the native Indians. Moreover, the story was so undeniably fantastic. Scientists exposed aspects of Singh's account to the most rigorous examination. Could children's eyes really change so as to glare in the dark like a dog's? Did their jawbones and teeth actually metamorphose under these supposed wild conditions? The whole thing seemed improbably far-fetched.

Yet Singh found supporters. Sir John Hewett, the author of one of those comfortably Blimpish volumes of hunting reminiscences, put his substantial weight behind the story; and there were other, more influential figures prepared to vouch for the tale's truth, among them Western psychologists and sociologists such as Arnold Gesell, an expert in child development, and Robert Zingg, an academic and anthropologist. For these men the possibility of Singh's story being true was tantalizing in the extreme. If the story *was* true, then this was the first well-documented case of a wild child since Itard's account of his education of Victor. The potential for advancing knowledge was inestimable.

The various Western scientists who were captivated by the case each brought to it their own manner of interpretation. For Professor Ruggles Gates, Chairman of the Human Heredity Bureau on Gower Street, London, an institutional legacy of Francis Galton's evolutionary theories and Karl Pearson's eugenicism, the case proved that there was an 'embryology of the mind' in childhood.[26] In other words, the children provided evidence for the still fashionable belief in recapitulation.

For Professor Francis N. Maxfield of Ohio State University, Singh's story showed that children were born wild and 'domesticated' (or civilized, if you prefer) during infancy. This theory revisits the arguments of Johann Friedrich Blumenbach, the early-nineteenth-century anthropologist who described the human as the only animal that domesticates itself. Therefore for Blumenbach, wild children are a meaningless phenomenon: being essentially a domesticated animal, a wild, solitary individual tells us nothing more about human nature than a wild, solitary bee would tell us of the habits of bees.

For Professor Kingsley Davis of Pennsylvania State College, the wolf-children were essential human beings, clearly seen since removed from the misleading local influences of culture. What they showed was that 'what we call *homo sapiens* is a species whose characteristics and behavior are standardized by the possession of culture. Without culture the behavior of this mammal would be unpredictable, depending upon the peculiarities of the particular environment in each case.'[27] More vitally, such children dismantled the Aristotelian notion that 'Man is by nature a social animal.'

For Bishop H. Pakenham-Walsh, Singh's immediate source of religious authority, there was another truth there to be found. He himself had met Kamala at a Student Christian Camp in 1926, and been impressed by the transient sweetness of her smile, and by the stony blankness that succeeded it only an instant later. She was strange to him, unsocialized, curiously empty, and yet even in her he could find grounds for consolation: for though the girls had inherited no human graces, none of the beauty of human connection, they also had learnt nothing of human guilt or shame:

> If one accepts as natural the use of teeth and nails when they felt
> themselves annoyed, there was no malice, nor was there any fear,
> as for instance of thunder or lightning, of big animals, of the dark,
> etc.: nor, so far as I could ascertain, was there any trace of pride or
> of jealousy. Human vices seem to have been as little inherited as
> human virtues, and this fact seems to me to have a very pertinent
> bearing on the consideration of what we mean by 'Original Sin'.[28]

Singh shared his bishop's interpretation. For here, more clearly
than anywhere else in this book, we find the invisible battle-lines
between science and piety drawn. While Singh recorded all the
information that the scientists would want, his motives were not
quite the same as theirs. He saw in the fate of these girls, much as
had the writers of the medieval romances, God's curious proving of
His miraculous providence. More than that, the slow awakening of
Kamala's human nature, her reclamation from the borderline of the
bestial was a true sign that no one was beyond the reach of Christ's
mercy. The forest ghosts had come to life; the beasts had shown
themselves to have an innocent human soul. The jungle had proved
an Eden after all.

II: White Savages and Irresponsible Places

'Dis man haf lived, and he is an anachronism, for he is before the Iron Age,
and der Stone Age. Look here, he is at der beginnings of der history of man
– Adam in der Garden, und now we only want an Eva! No! He is older than
dat child-tale, shust as der rukh is older than der gods. Gisborne, I am a
Bagan now, once for all.'
    Rudyard Kipling, from 'In the Rukh'

For Kipling, as that already-mentioned letter to Mary Mapes Dodge
shows, wolf-children meant India. '*We* have them' there: was it this
peculiarly Indian quality that drew Kipling to these stories, that fed
the hidden resources from which Mowgli and his brothers sprang?
What did Mowgli, the wolf-boy, really mean to Kipling?

Born in India, Kipling left Bombay at the age of four, as was the custom, since Imperial parents feared the effects of the pernicious-ly sultry Indian climate on their children. There was the obvious risk of disease, but behind that there were subtler terrors, especially that India would render a British child degenerate.[29] So for Kipling, as a child, England became the place of exile, while India meant the lost home. Mowgli could represent the wish to belong properly in that home; yet Kipling's position as a white Imperialist in India made any notion of such belonging ambiguous and strained.

From Mowgli's first appearance in Kipling's short story for adults, 'In the Rukh', the idea of possession and ownership clings around him. ('Rukh' is a vernacular word meaning forest or wood.) In this story we see Mowgli as a young adult, voluntarily leaving behind his life as a wild child for a position in Imperial service. (Surprisingly, this is not as far-fetched as might seem: a wolf-boy discovered some thirty years before had ended up serving with the police.)[30] One question nags throughout Kipling's first Mowgli tale: who owns the forest – Mowgli, young and beautiful as a pagan god, roaming there, free and happy; or Gisborne, the orderly, punctilious British bureaucrat?

The story's answer is clear: Mowgli defers to Gisborne. Although the wolf-boy is the god of the forest, wandering through the place at will, in complete possession, he acknowledges the ordinary, unex-ceptional Englishman as his master. There seems no doubt that Kipling intends us to judge this act of Imperial deference as a kind of liberation: '"It is the sahib's rukh," said Mowgli, quickly looking up.'[31] Mowgli has previously served no one but himself. Now, by entering service, Mowgli assumes a place in society; he is no longer solitary; he is no longer the forest god.

So Mowgli assumes the necessary burden of duty, an action that is intrinsic to Kipling's work. For Kipling, duty is the psychological limit that staves off the nightmare of the world; the stoicism of ser-vice defends you from suffering. The characters of Kipling's stories for adults rely on reticence and stoic endurance as a means of subduing their too-strong imaginations, their too-violent sufferings. They endure in a world where to think deeply is to invite madness and despair, and undertake their duty against an unshifting background of horror.

For those who first encountered *The Jungle Books* in childhood, or, more likely, the Disney cartoon version, their grim underlying atmosphere of oppression and violence is shocking when turned to in adult life. Here nature is in a state of war: humans oppress the animals; the animals oppress each other. Hoping to live in freedom, Mowgli would like to opt out of this eternal oppressive order; in Kafka's words, he would rather lie down with the animals than stand up with the men.

Such escape, however, is a dream. Just as the animals must fulfil their nature, so must Mowgli. In *The Jungle Books*, Mowgli moves away from the jungle, from savagery and childish irresponsibility, towards a tentative maturity, an acceptance of his place in the human world. So even while Mowgli plays in the jungle, we remain aware of how his time is only leased, a postponement of an unavoidable end: '"Man goes to Man at the last."'[32]

The awakening of sexuality prompts Mowgli's assumption of his true nature. This is one responsibility that he cannot shirk; he must end his solitude, and join with a mate. When he first quits the woods, Mowgli disavows his old wild nature and resumes his lost human name, Nathoo, son of Messua. In taking the name that his parents gave him, Mowgli lays claim to his position in human society. Yet strangely, when Mowgli returns to social life, he does not go to a wife but back to his mother, although the last illustration in the book, by Kipling's father, John Lockwood Kipling, makes it plain that Mowgli does marry. The drawing depicts a middle-aged Indian in a turban, sitting in a room with a woman of his own age, with a child at her knee. The man stares out thoughtfully through the open door into the jungle beyond. He has a full moustache and more than

a passing resemblance to Kipling. Is Kipling's father teasingly suggesting that *The Jungle Books* were a wish-fulfilment on his son's
part? After all, Kipling wrote the Mowgli stories shortly after his
hasty marriage to Carrie Balestier, following the death of her brother, Kipling's beloved best friend, Wolcott Balestier. Are we meant to
guess that his son is hankering in these stories for a time when he
felt his own personality to be free, before he entered the fixity and
responsibility of marriage?

Yet this misses Mowgli's deepest meaning for Kipling. For while
asserting the necessity of maturity and duty, *The Jungle Books* vivid-
ly celebrate freedom and play. Mowgli's life in the jungle is almost
pre-lapsarian: there is no need to struggle for survival; he wants
nothing from the animals; they want nothing from him. We never
see him embarked on a kill, or hunting for food: Mowgli is always
either at play, or by mischief and trickery ingeniously getting the
better of some enemy.

In the jungle, Mowgli possesses a double identity: he is both man
and animal, as all wolf-children must seem. He can, for a while, be
anything: '"Mowgli the Frog have I been," said he to himself,
"Mowgli the Wolf have I said that I am. Now Mowgli the Ape I must
be before I am Mowgli the Buck. At the end I shall be Mowgli the
Man."'[33] Yet in the end, Akela, the wolf-father tells his foster-child:
'"Mowgli will drive Mowgli. Go back to thy people. Go to Man."'[34]
Mowgli's multiplicity ends; he becomes simply a man. However,
there remains a sense of a plenitude of choices, of possibilities and
potentialities. Even Mowgli's solitude itself is, while he is a child, an
opportunity and a freedom. He is responsible to no one.

So Mowgli in the jungle glories in his dispossession; all of his
songs unabashedly triumph over his enemies and celebrate his own
identity. This is why 'In The Rukh', the first written and the fitting
end of the Mowgli stories, remained in Kipling's eyes 'a story for
grown-ups'. In that story, and for an adult reader in *The Jungle
Books* themselves, the emphasis falls on responsibility, on the

necessity to live our lives as human beings. For child readers, this responsibility is still waiting to be born; for an adult, Mowgli embodies a wish that ought to remain unfulfilled. Yet the reader, like Kipling himself, remains nostalgically, sentimentally, powerfully divided. Like all of us, Kipling knows that we cannot simply be animals, trying out different natures in complete freedom; but, living in what G. K. Chesterton once named an 'irresponsible place', Mowgli can be anything for a while, in the jungle, as a child and a savage. *The Jungle Books* celebrate that indeterminacy, for all that they point to its eventual close. Lost for a while in the wild possibilities of play, Kipling, the apostle of rule and duty, offers for himself and for us a momentary escape, a savage childhood where individuals may dream of establishing a free place, where they can, for a while, be someone else.

This division between duty and play permeates the next surprising turn in the history of the wild child. For there were other ways that Mowgli could be used as a symbol of how to grow up. As an animal-child, a wolf-boy, Mowgli embodied an evolutionary origin and the lost life of childhood. It was in this symbolic way that he became, along with Kipling's other abandoned child, Kim, the basis of the most extraordinary development of the wild child motif: that is, its absorption into the iconography of Baden-Powell's cub scout movement.

How is it that Mowgli could seem so fitting a symbol for the ideal cub scout? In order to answer this question, we must first make a strange detour. Since the eighteenth century, observers had imagined wild children as belonging to the state of nature, the fictional period before society and politics began. They thought of wild children as being like those who lived in a pre-political realm that was either distant in time (Europe over three millennia ago) or removed in space *and* time (like the savages in the New Worlds of America or the South Seas). So wild children became identified with a lost state, one that stood as a symbol for an essential human nature. They embodied silence over words, solitude over society, and passion over reason. Following Rousseau, children of nature therefore symbolized a lost personal authenticity, an imagined self prior to that which had grown up within the social and the historical. They retained the power and the clarity of origins from which the civilized observer had been estranged.

Such ideas appear in a different form in the work of Sigmund Freud. Freud thought that the inner, essential self was both like a child and like a 'savage' – more than that, the ordinary child is himself a kind of savage, his or her mental traits resembling the primitive origins of humankind. In this way, Freud disperses the experience of childhood 'savagery' described in this book, so that it becomes everyone's experience. Similarly he internalizes the condition of being a wild child: it becomes everyone's psychological history.

It is precisely this same process that can be seen in the work of Robert Baden-Powell. For him also the childhood of each individual repeated the universal childish savagery of primitive humanity. His use of Kim, Mowgli and *The Jungle Books* in creating the scouts and cubs might mystify us, until we recognize that, like Freud, Baden-Powell believed that the young boy who pretends to be a member of Akela's wolf-pack enacts an essential truth about himself. The cubs aren't just acting being wolf-children; in a psychological sense they *are* wild children. The cubs manifest in an adult-directed ritual their supposed 'savagery', their momentary position on the evolutionary scale. The essential discipline of Kipling's playful world, its subjection even as play to law, authority and hierarchy, made Baden-Powell's choice of *The Jungle Books* even more fitting. Play would create a good potential Imperial soldier; yet nonetheless in play, at least, anyone could become a wild child.

Mowgli then is the quintessential fictional wild child. However, if asked what their first experience is of the wild child story, although many people will choose Mowgli, or Romulus and Remus, the figure that most often leaps to mind is Tarzan. This is the wild man who dominated Saturday morning television, a white man who was lord of the African jungle, Hollywood's all-American savage Englishman. Tarzan haunted the playgrounds of my own childhood: those skinny kids in recreation grounds mimicking leaping from tree to tree, swinging on imaginary jungle vines, beating their scrawny chests and letting out primitive, high-pitched yodels in imitation of Johnny Weissmuller's full-throated cry. As a child I fell for the romance of that athletic figure, racing through the black-and-white jungle, fighting off savages and defeating the duplicitous greed of the over-civilized, pith-helmeted interlopers. I loved the weirdly shaggy vegetation that draped from the heights of trees; I yearned for the chasms, the waterfalls, and the menacingly beautiful lakes. I didn't even mind the stock footage repeated in film after film, in which Tarzan wrestled underwater with an enormous crocodile, or fought with a charging lion. Even the nuclear family, the wild mirror-image of my own, could entice me at times, though 'Boy' bored me a little and my feelings for those domestic jungle arrangements were indifferent. I loved comfort, but felt ambivalent about the nannying presence of women. For what I really loved was the relationship of that family cosiness to something more dangerous for which I placidly longed. Tarzan meant adventure; and in that safe sitting room of childhood, I, like thousands of others, could dream of treasure, immense physical strength, and a savage nobility out in a wilderness where the only rules sprang from my own goodness.

Kipling was in no doubt where Edgar Rice Burroughs, the American pulp writer of pot-boilers and Martian romances, had found his inspiration. In his autobiography, *Something of Myself*, he acidly made the point clear:

And, if it be in your power, bear serenely with imitators. My *Jungle Books* begat Zoos of them. But the genius of all the genii was one who wrote a series called *Tarzan of the Apes*. I read it, but regret I never saw it on the films, where it rages most successfully. He had 'jazzed' the motif of the *Jungle Books* and, I imagine, had thoroughly enjoyed himself. He was reported to have said that he wanted to find out how bad a book he could write and 'get away with', which is a legitimate ambition.[35]

Understandably Burroughs did not relish this spirited 'praise'. A career dogged by charges of plagiarism made him in any case noticeably reluctant to pinpoint specific sources for *Tarzan of the Apes* (1914). Comparison with *The Jungle Books* pained Burroughs; confessions of indebtedness on Burroughs' part were always stated equivocally, as in this letter to Professor Altrocchi, of 31 March, 1937, where the author of *Tarzan* seeks to explain the origin of his story:

> I believe that it may have originated in my interest in Mythology and the story of Romulus and Remus. I also recall having read many years ago the story of a sailor who was shipwrecked on the Coast of Africa and who was adopted by and consorted with great apes to such an extent that when he was rescued a she-ape followed him into the surf and threw a baby after him.
>
> Then, of course, I read Kipling; so that it probably was a combination of all these that suggested the Tarzan idea to me. The fundamental idea is, of course, much older than Mowgli, or the story of the sailor; and probably antedates even Romulus and Remus; so that after all there is nothing new or remarkable about it.[36]

Here Burroughs both concedes his debt to Kipling and diminishes it. Even the timing of this confession is intriguing: Kipling's recent death had probably ended any acute sense of rivalry on Burroughs' part.

If the ultimate meaning of Mowgli is the uncomfortable mixing of the desire to belong and the desire to escape, then the ultimate meaning of the Tarzan story is also clear: nothing matters so much as being white. Burroughs draws out from the wild child myth the racial meanings that had been collecting around it at least since those considerations of the origins of poor Memmie Le Blanc. Burroughs' story explores the borderlines between races, as between the human and the simian, not in order to subvert or transgress them, but rather as a means of acting out what he considers their defined and permanent lines of demarcation.

Everyone knows the Tarzan story, yet few have read Burroughs' original novel. So here for the benefit of the reader is Burroughs' own précis of the tale:

> The story I am on now is of the scion of a noble English house – of the present time – who was born in tropical Africa where his parents died when he was about a year old. The infant was found and adopted by a huge she-ape, and was brought up among a band of fierce anthropoids.
>
> The mental development of this ape-man in spite of every handicap, of how he learned to read English without knowledge of the spoken language, of the way in which his inherent reasoning faculties lifted him high above his savage jungle friends and enemies, of his meeting with a white girl, how he came at last to civilization and to his own makes most fascinating writing and I think will prove interesting reading, as I seem especially adapted to the building of the 'damphool' species of narrative.[37]

Burroughs' self-deprecation is not unjustified. A more enthusiastic account of the story appeared in the September issue of *All-Story* advertising *Tarzan's* appearance in the following month's issue:

> If you will stop and realize how many thousands of stories an editor has to read, day in, day out, you will be impressed when we tell you that we read this yarn at one sitting and had the time of our young lives. It is the most exciting story we have seen in a blue moon, and about as original as they make 'em. Through a series

of catastrophes an English baby boy is kidnapped by a tribe of huge anthropoid apes. He grows up among them. The fact that he is a reasoning animal makes a difference in his development, and then the forces of civilization obtrude. Zowie! but things happen![38]

Burroughs' account of his own work, with its 'anthropoids' and contrast of heredity and environment, clearly reveals the influence of evolution and of racial theories. Burroughs was an amateur student of such matters: in January 1899, he bought Darwin's *The Descent of Man*; he sketched a crouching ape on the flyleaf and to the right of the drawing wrote 'Grandpa'. From its inception *Tarzan of the Apes* was obviously a post-Darwinian tale of 'the struggle for existence'; but Burroughs' natural white man is no animalistic brute: he possesses reason, the innately superior inheritance of his English aristocratic origins.

Burroughs knew that his tale was in essence a comforting fiction, and speculated as to what a wild child would really be like: 'The more I thought about it, the more convinced I became that the resultant adult would be a most disagreeable person to have around the house. He would probably have B.O., Pink Toothbrush, Halitosis, and Athlete's Foot, plus a most abominable disposition; so I decided not to be honest, but to draw a character people would admire.'[39] So it is that Tarzan is the typical natural man of American fiction – the frontiersman, the man's man, the skilled tracker, the chivalrous backwoodsman, the gentlemanly white savage. His senses are preternaturally acute, attuned to all the life of the forest. Yet, being white and an aristocrat, Tarzan lives at an even higher evolutionary level than the customary natural man; he is the furthest, most advanced point of civilization honed in the evolutionary origin of the African jungle. Throughout the novel, Burroughs ironically contrasts Tarzan's jungle life with that of his civilized brother, Clayton, having the aristocratic English-bred lord appear decadent beside the jungle-fit noble savage. At one point Tarzan lets out a roar in the jungle once he has killed Sabor, the lioness, while 'in London another Lord Greystoke was speaking to *his* kind in the House of Lords, but none trembled at the sound of his soft voice'.[40] In the end, Tarzan's savage childhood gives him an evolutionary advantage over the delicate, public-school lord when, in the matter of sexual selection, Jane Porter, the clean-limbed American beauty, chooses Tarzan over his genteel brother.

So, as with Mowgli, sex enables Tarzan to discover his true nature. The 'Me, Tarzan; you Jane' exchange that has passed into modern folklore is, after all, the key to the story. In the book version of their romance, Burroughs writes a semi-pornographic chapter, 'The Call of The Primitive', in which Jane is saved by Tarzan from being raped by the ape Terkoz. As she watches 'the primordial ape battle with the primeval man for possession of a woman – for her', 'the veil of the centuries of civilization and culture was swept from the blurred vision of the Baltimore girl . . . it was a primeval woman who sprang forward with out-stretched arms towards the primeval man who had fought for her and won her.'[41] Tarzan does 'just what his first ancestor would have done' and takes her in his manly arms and kisses her.[42] That this 'first ancestor' is not just some evolutionary progenitor is made clear later on: 'Never, she thought, had such a man strode the earth since God created the first in his own image.'[43] The Baltimore girl and the English lord are back (with Kamala and Mowgli) in Eden, a place of primeval purity free from the taint of civilization. Of course, Jane falls in love with this Adamic man; indeed, when she sees Tarzan in civilized mode she is vaguely disappointed. No wonder they decide to stay in the jungle for that much-beloved fictional 'for ever and ever'.

Burroughs' wild child means yet another American rejection of European civilization: Jane flees society in favour of the savage jungle; Tarzan rejects his inheritance as Lord Greystoke, denying his European heritage in favour of Africa, and embracing the new and the American girl. Together they will start again in the heart of the jungle, free from the constraints of civilization. Tarzan and Jane remain in the jungle in perpetuity, in a timeless world; they reject the world by returning to its beginning. So it is that only twenty or so years after the official close of the real American frontier, Burroughs, America's first pulp-laureate, opens up new frontiers, new landscapes for the American drama, for Tarzan in the jungles of Africa, and for his other hero, Carter, on the planet Mars, in his Barsoom chronicles.

Tarzan assumes his real identity as the jungle's lord by going back to the scene of his savage childhood. Like Huck Finn lighting out once more for the territory, it is a quintessentially American gesture. He refuses the name of Greystoke, and keeps instead his savage name, his 'real' name: 'Tar-zan' means in Burroughs' invented anthropoid language 'white-skin'. In this way Tarzan's name expresses not just his individual, but also his racial identity.

By doing so Tarzan opts out of a civilization that is seen throughout the *Tarzan* books as inherently 'savage'. This reflects contemporary fears of the decline of the West, the decadence of European civilization. Burroughs' response to this 'decadence' was one often favoured by writers and artists of the 1910s. Many thought that 'regeneration' and renewal would only occur when we leave the cities and return to nature and to adventure. We can note that Rupert Brooke's Tahiti poems, Jack London's stories, and Norman Douglas's *South Wind* (1917) are all roughly contemporary expressions of an artistic trend that goes back at least as far as Rousseau. Tarzan embodies another such return to the primitive, by moving back to an origin, to a state before history – a history that then seemed inevitably to be a record of decline. Burroughs' original *Tarzan* novel was published in an America looking on at a Europe ravaged by an increasingly bloody and senseless war. Against the contamination of the modern, Tarzan's jungle exists outside the historical   process,   despite   the   plunderings   of   European

Imperialists. It is an evolutionary origin and a place of perpetual renewal. Out of a real, historical Africa, Burroughs imagines an America in the jungle, and the wild child as a symbol of an American future.

So it is that the fate of Kamala and Amala stands in vaguely disappointing contrast to the wish-fulfilments of Imperial fictions. Their story has hardly resonated in the popularly mythic form of Mowgli or Tarzan; and yet the context for all three tales remains strikingly similar: they all belong to a shrinking world in which the dark spaces of Empire could still provide a space for narratives of wonder. Of course, for Singh and Kipling the jungle was not really like that. Well-worn village paths crossed near the wolf-girls' den; and the only place that seems truly exotic in Kipling's autobiography is Sussex. Yet the jungle had nonetheless once hidden the girls in a dark mystery, holding them like ghosts; and the secrecy that enfolded Kamala and Amala for a few years after their discovery allowed their childhoods to go on in a wonderful domesticity. The next case to grasp the attention of the world was to occur in quite different circumstances: in the heart of the richest country in the world, and in the brilliant publicity of international media attention.

CHAPTER SEVEN

Where Is Tomorrow, Mrs L.?

I: A Small Ghost

It was something quite special, that feeling: an oppressive, hideous constraint as if I were sitting with the small ghost of somebody I had just killed.
  Vladimir Nabokov, *Lolita*

At first, though, she responded hardly at all. Her usual comportment, Kent noted, was a 'sombre detachment'. If not deliberately engaged, she drifted around in her new physical world, walking with bent elbows in her strange 'bunny walk', spitting into her clothing or into a curtain hem, far more aware of the room than of the people in it . . . Some observers referred to her as 'ghostlike'.
  Russ Rymer, *Genie: A Scientific Tragedy*

She hadn't expected her to be pretty. The strangeness she had prepared herself for; and sure enough, the girl was strange. True, the girl's teeth were yellowed and even slightly fanged. Yes, you could see the anticipated oddity in the too-long dress and the stuttered movements. Even when she was still, you somehow knew that something was wrong; but how could she have guessed about the prettiness – the slightly retroussé nose, the softness of her expression and her flesh, the softness with which she gazed on things, and that soft, pale skin flushed with rose? Yet most entrancing were her eyes – grey and dreamy with distance, brimful, it seemed to Susan Curtiss, of the pain and suffering of the girl's story. She was even beautiful.[1]

Susan Curtiss was no nurse; she hated hospitals, and was apprehensive of that first meeting with the girl in the children's hospital. So she hung back at first, watching from a distance.

The girl was so small. When they had first found her, that day in November 1970, in the family aid centre, looking brutalized and spastically dazed, they had thought her to be about eight years old.

She was skinny and short, weighing no more than sixty pounds, and was only about four and a half feet tall. In fact, she was thirteen, a teenager under an enchantment, confined in the body of a child.

She came from a low, sand-coloured house on Golden West Avenue, Temple City, just on the borders of the Los Angeles suburb of Arcadia. Temple City is the Los Angeles equivalent of Surbiton. The house was just like every other on that street – a strip of lawn, the suburban trees – but she had been left in there, day after day, year after year, for nearly twelve years, spellbound in a little room, tied to a potty chair, sewn into a harness to attach her to the seat, only able to move her hands and feet, naked. All day, every day, she was left like that, until the potty chair wore a calloused ring into her buttocks. At night, if her parents remembered to do so (they didn't always remember), she was put in a sleeping bag of her father's own design. Here again she was pinioned so as not to be able to move her arms, and lifted into a crib caged with a wire mesh. Meanwhile, the rest of the family slept together in the living room, the son on a pallet, the mother on the floor, and the father in an easy chair, a gun resting on his lap.[2]

The girl's room was next to a bathroom and her dead grandmother's bedroom. No one was allowed to enter the dead woman's room; the dust settled there silently. The girl's room was at the back of the little house. No sound reached there from the street out front.[3] Tied there all day, she heard no voices, except her father's occasional distant cursing, no sound at all except the water in the pipes as the toilet flushed or the bath filled. Only sometimes she could hear a child neighbour at the piano, practising scales or trying out simple tunes.

If she called out, she was beaten, or threatened with being beaten. Her father kept a piece of wood in the room especially for the purpose. He never spoke to her, but only growled or snarled – or barked – like a dog. Sometimes he would bark at the door to frighten her. He taught her brother to bark at her like that too. Her father would stand in the dark and bark and growl, scratching at the door with the nails he'd grown especially long.

Her mother was going blind. She was frightened of her husband and obeyed his rules regarding their daughter. The loss of her sight meant that, as the years went on, she spent less and less time with the girl.

There was little for the girl to look at in the bare room. Sometimes she was given the TV magazine, once her father had flicked through it, ripping out any potentially erotic images: a man and woman in swimsuits on a sunlit beach; a girl in a suburban house dreamily sitting by the fire in a nightdress. Otherwise she could sometimes play with a pair of plastic macs, one yellow and one see-through, or things like an empty cottage cheese packet or empty thread spools left by her mother, who had once been a seamstress. She was fed quickly so as to keep contact minimal: baby food, cereal, sometimes a soft-boiled egg. The food was just shoved in her mouth; if she choked, her face was rubbed in it.

Her father, 'Clark', had grown up in a series of foster-homes in the north-west of the USA. Her mother, 'Irene', came from Oklahoma, growing up there in the dustbowl years. Clark had been twenty years older than Irene when they married.

Clark was intensely attached to his mother, despite the fact that she had effectively abandoned him to be brought up by others. She was what is sometimes called a 'character'. She had owned a brothel at one time, and was authentically wild, an untameable vestige of American frontier stock.

Clark and Irene weren't happy. He was cruel, authoritarian, and sometimes he hit her. Irene said that 'when she married, her life ended'.[4] Clark didn't want children. He hated kids, hated the noise, the smell, the nuisance; but then, after five years of marriage, Irene fell pregnant. She gave birth to a little girl. Clark banished their first daughter to the garage, where at the age of two and a half months she died of pneumonia and exposure. Some time later a boy was born to them, who also died at two days old. When another son was born, and also looked unlikely to thrive, exhibiting early behavioural problems, Clark's mother took the boy in. Living with his grandmother, the boy began to do well and, cured of most of his problems, he was sent back to his parents.[5]

Their last child was born in April 1957. It was another girl. She had a difficult and disrupted infancy, with developmental problems. Yet she looked likely to live. They named her Susan.

At fourteen months, while the little girl had a fever, a doctor (wrongly) declared that she might possibly be retarded. Jealous of the attention that the girl received from her mother, Clark used this diagnosis as an excuse for the abuse that followed. He decided that he would protect the girl from the evil of this world. If she was retarded, then she would need even greater care, even stronger vigilance.

Clark hated the world. It was a place of degradation, fear and injustice. Only recently his beloved mama had been killed by a drunk teenage driver. The car had dragged the old woman down the street. Once the boy had driven off, the body was too badly damaged to be identified. When the boy got off without any punishment, Clark was furiously upset. He moved himself and his family into his dead mother's home; and there ended his contact with the world. He kept a gun to deal with intruders. Sometimes he left the electric lights on all night so that he could see if anyone came near the home. Even his son had to make signals before he could be permitted to enter the house. The family was to be isolated, protected. And Susan, his little girl, was to be the most protected of all.

So the abuse began – abuse in the guise of a vindictive care, a punishing protectiveness. Sometimes Irene would ask if her daughter might be seen by an outside doctor. Clark made a pact. Believing that the girl was sure to die anyway, he promised his wife that if she survived until her twelfth birthday, then he would allow her to be examined. Years passed. The birthday came and went. Clark reneged on his promise. Nothing happened.

Irene was almost completely blind. She was helpless, not even allowed to call her own mother and father. Then, in 1970, Irene had finally had enough. After a terrible argument, she fled with her daughter, going to live in her own mother's house in Monterey Park. Their son John left home at the same time, going to live with friends.

In November of that year Irene, wearing heavy black sunglasses, and Susan went to a local welfare centre in search of the department giving aid for the blind. Irene's eyesight was so bad that they wandered by mistake into a family aid centre. A helper spotted the girl, and her strange behaviour. Mother and daughter were led aside; questions were asked and, on the basis of the almost unbelievable replies, the girl was taken into care and charges brought against both the father and mother of 'wilful abuse'.

The news hit the Los Angeles papers on 17 November 1970. In the atmosphere of the time the case must have seemed just one more instance of a war between youth and age. The papers that week were full of similar stories: the professors at Berkeley were lamenting the breakdown of the university community; Vincent Bugliosi and the state prosecution were just resting their case against Charles Manson in the Tate–La Bianca murder trials; the court martial was beginning of William Calley over the My Lai massacre; longhaired male students in Reseda High School were required to present parental consent forms if they were to keep their hair long; rumours were spreading of razor blades concealed in apples given to Hallowe'en trick-or-treaters; a young girl had vanished on the freeway; Dr Thomas Mintz was lecturing at UCLA on the adolescent's need for love. The spirit that hung over LA was like a miasmic sickness. Susan's fate could seem not so much outrageously cruel as symptomatic.

Reporters came to the house and spoke to Clark and his son John. Trying not to cry, he told them that no one outside the family would understand what had happened. A photograph of the two of them shows two blandly ordinary men. John is a typical American teenager, with a side parting and mid-sixties Beach Boys haircut, a dark shirt and jeans. Only his posture looks odd, his arms folded defensively, his eyes threatened and suspicious, the face somehow prematurely old. Clark looks like an old buffer just back from a fishing trip, his posture relaxed, his eyes mischievously inscrutable behind large glasses, a little sun hat perched jauntily over his brows. There is no sign of threat or strangeness – nothing really to see unless it is the striking age difference of a seventy-year-old man with a teenage son. Behind them, stairs climb up in the hazy November sunshine to the porch, and to the door behind which Susan was tied down for thirteen years.

Clark pre-empted justice. Curious neighbours began to drive by the house, slowing their cars or stopping outside to point at the place where the little girl had been imprisoned. They enraged and confused Clark. To comfort him a little and help deal with these intrusions, his son John and one of John's friends moved back into the house with Clark. On Friday 20 November, the day of the trial, John and some friends were taking the family car out of the driveway, ready to drive his father to the court. Clark had told them that he would be out in a moment. Instead, alone in the house, he spread a blanket and some cellophane across the living-room floor, wrote out two notes, one for John and one for the police, took his .38-calibre revolver and fired a single shot into the right side of his head. He had killed himself with the gun he had always kept with him as he slept each night on the easy chair, ready to protect his family from the horrors of the outside world. His suicide note added a last gesture of resigned defiance, saying once again, 'The world will never understand.'

Across town in the courtroom Irene was entering a plea of 'Not guilty' at her arraignment before the Alhambra Municipal Court. After the hearing they told her that her husband was dead. She said nothing. When she appeared in court a few days later, all charges against her were dropped. It was clear that she had been as much of a victim as her daughter.

*

The girl had been taken to the children's hospital of Los Angeles, and put in the care of a team led by Dr Howard Hansen, the humanely urbane Head of Psychiatry. Another psychologist, David Rigler, began to work out a research plan; James Kent, an expert in child abuse, became Susan's therapist; Jay Shurley, a visiting psychologist and expert on social isolation, flew to Los Angeles to test the young girl. There in the hospital they gave her a new name. Susan became Genie. She was like a girl who had lived in a bottle, as though trapped in its confines by a harsh spell. Susan Curtiss, the linguist who was to study Genie's language remarks: 'It is a name given to protect her privacy, chosen because it captures, to a small measure, the fact that she emerged into human society past childhood, having existed previously as something other than fully human.'[6]

The girl's condition beggared belief. This was someone suffering from a level of abuse beyond anything seen in the hospital before – or indeed ever since. She was malnourished, tiny, incontinent. Her short, dark hair was sparse; her eating habits disgusting; she salivated and spat constantly. She would only glance at you, then look away; she smelled objects by holding them close to her pallid face. Stooped and frail, her gait pigeon-toed, her body was bent at the waist, her shoulders hunched forward, her hands held up before her like a rabbit or a comic zombie returned from the dead. She could only make strange sounds in her throat; language was beyond her. On first seeing her, Jay Shurley recalled how she seemed like a shy, tiny, blind child, touching the world through her fingertips. Again Susan Curtiss thought of her as 'unsocialized, primitive, hardly human'.[7] Unwittingly Genie's carers were repeating the tropes employed by all the previous educators of 'wild children'. She had fallen into the pit of the other than human. She was like a ghost, a sprite, a changeling child. She was the beautiful victim – beautiful because she has suffered – the archetypal doomed adolescent, the troubled child storing for everyone who cared for her that part of themselves that was also lost, confined and damaged.

Yet Genie was not just a cute, soulful-eyed child. She could disturb and shock too. She spat continually, wiping the spit and mucus on to herself. She stank as the spit seeped into her clothes, glistening on her body, her hair. Her eating habits were revolting. As a result of being fed so quickly while tied to her chair, Genie had never properly learnt to chew. So instead she would just store the food in her mouth, waiting for the saliva to break it down, often spitting out the resulting unmasticated goo on to her plate or the table, mushing it up with her fingers. Sometimes she would spit the food out generously, but unwantedly, on to someone else's plate.

Like Peter the Wild Boy before her, she had yet to develop a sense of property. She took people's things wilfully, pulling on their clothes, invading their space. She would go up to them, getting very close, making eye contact and pointing at the thing of theirs that she wanted, demanding possession. On occasion, she would walk up to strangers and charmingly or embarrassingly link arms with them suddenly, ready to stroll on together.

Most difficult of all, she masturbated continually. Many of the things she coveted or stole were for masturbating with. Often she would try to involve older men in her masturbation. Was this evidence of other, even worse forms of abuse?

Yet most importantly, Genie had not learnt language. She was a child buried in silence – silently watching, silently scared, silently crying. Even her wild temper tantrums – when she would flail manically, scratching, striking, tearing at herself and smearing her face and hair with her own mucus – were silent.[8]

Now this silence, this absence of language, struck the doctors and scientists and psychologists and linguists examining Genie as an immense opportunity. They could learn something from her; but what could be learnt? Immediately questions arose that were never satisfactorily answered. Was Genie retarded? Monitoring her sleep patterns led to the discovery of an unusually high number of what are called 'sleep spindles', thought to be a sign of mental retardation; but were these readings produced by a reaction to Genie's long-term abuse, or were they a sign of innate damage? No one could be sure. More vitally, was the damage reversible? Might Genie be taught to speak?

The scientists kept on with their examination of Genie; but an unexpected influence was about to enter into their work. At half past four one afternoon, the doctors left the children's hospital early and made the short walk up the street to the local Los Angeles cinema. A special screening had been arranged of a film that had just arrived in America, receiving its local première at the San Francisco Film Festival in the week when Genie's case hit the headlines. It was *L'Enfant Sauvage*, François Truffaut's film about Itard's relationship with Victor.

Truffaut's film remains one of the best cinematic treatments of a wild child story. As I mentioned in the first chapter, watching a screening of the movie on British television in the late 1980s was a defining moment in inspiring my own interest in these tales. The film begins saturated in a romantic forest light, before turning to a purely classical style of symmetry: calm interiors, white-painted rooms. As cinematographer, Nestor Almendros lets the camera dwell on illuminating symbols of enlightenment: a room suffused with light from a lamp; an adult's hand protecting a fragile candle-flame. Truffaut himself plays Itard in his finest acting role: cool, but passionately serious; a man completely engaged with the object of his own observation; both directing the film and the boy, turning him on screen into an actor. The relationship between himself and the boy – and in real life the boy who played Victor, Jean-Pierre Cargol, was a gypsy and a street urchin – replays the adult mentor–delinquent child relationship of *Les Quatres Cents Coups* (1959), itself a reflection of street-kid Truffaut and his film-critic mentor, André Bazin.

The film's brilliance impresses anyone who watches it. When those involved with Genie organized the screening shortly after her discovery, it quite simply blew them away. After it had finished, they sat in stunned silence. The entire drama of their potential relationship with the girl was there already set out for them. It had all happened before, nearly two hundred years ago, and the trajectory of their future involvement seemed mapped out before them in the past. The film helped to alert the researchers to the moral constraints on their investigation of Genie.[9] More negatively, the misleadingly upbeat ending of Truffaut's film (in which Victor appears to be heading for a full place in the human community) may also have subtly influenced the scientists' expectations about the possible outcome of their work. As evidence of how seriously the team took Truffaut's film, we should note that it was screened again for visiting linguists and psychologists as part of a special academic conference on Genie's case organized in 1971. The conference set out to determine what would be the best focus of research regarding Genie's case.

The film had placed Genie in a context. She, it turned out, was a wild child just like Victor had been. For some of Genie's investigators, such material was, in any case, all too familiar. Jay Shurley, for instance, says that he had been interested in feral child stories since the 1940s. By the time he met Genie, in November 1970, he had an extensive knowledge of the existing literature on the subject.

More than this, Victor's story might have helped to create for the Genie team a narrative in which the role of heroic educator was still uncast. Perhaps it was now that the subtle and in many ways understandable conflicts began in which each sought to assume the part of Genie's saviour.

Genie could understand one or two words, and had her own set phrases such as *stopit* and *nomore*, but was basically without language.[10] So a decision was reached that they were specifically to study Genie's linguistic progress. Susan Curtiss, a young postgraduate student from UCLA, researching childhood language acquisition, began work with her. Her account of this work with Genie was to be Curtiss's doctoral dissertation. The linguists' aim was to solve one vital new question: was there a critical period for language? Behind this lay another even more contentious idea: was language an innate property of the human mind, or a learnt acquisition?

The idea of a 'critical period' had first appeared only a few years before in Eric Lenneberg's *Biological Foundations of Language* (1967). Lenneberg had argued that the origin of language lay in human biology, and was a natural product of being human. He saw clear evidence for this: the existence of anatomical specializations or, in other words, physiological equipment that could only be used for speech; the fact that language cannot really be 'taught' to non-humans in such a way that the language use of the animal subject will correspond to the complexity of human language; the difficulty of suppressing language, even in circumstances of gross abuse or neglect; the presence of 'language universals' present in all human languages; and, above all, the sudden and fixed development of speech, that begins in all children at roughly the same time and occurs invariably in the same order.[11] (Many of these assumptions have since been shown to be open to question.) Our linguistic abilities begin when we are around eighteen months to two years old and, according to Lenneberg, end around the age of thirteen. If individuals fail, for whatever reason, to learn language in that period, then they will never learn language. Genie was clearly an ideal test case for such a theory. If they could teach her language now, they would have disproved the critical period hypothesis.

Genie could also act as a testing ground for the theories of Noam Chomsky. Chomsky was an impressive advocate for his theory that grammar was an innate biological property of human beings. Chomsky had argued that we come into the world already equipped with the capacity for speech. Beyond the surface differences of apparently separate languages lurk the deep structures of human language: an ability to know when someone is literally talking non-sense; to create new, hitherto unheard sentences; to play with words within the rules of grammar. Genie could prove a vital test case for Chomsky's theories for, if she turned out not to be brain-damaged in any way and yet still could not acquire language, then this would show that the supposedly innate propensity for speech could be disrupted. We might not be able to teach someone language, but we could certainly suppress language in them.

How would Susan Curtiss and the psycholinguists know when Genie had authentically acquired language? There are certain marks of human language, some of which are givens, such as the arbitrariness of linguistic signs (there being no reason, for instance, why 'cat' should mean cat) and cultural transmission (the fact that a language is passed down within a culture from generation to generation, transformed in time while remaining itself). Other aspects of language seem more closely linked to the psychological development of the individual. These could include: displacement (the ability to talk of something no longer happening or of someone not then present); rule-following (the aptitude to discern and use the grammatical rules that create language); spontaneous and novel utterance (the gift of creating new sentences and coining new phrases for their expressive content). Human language, unlike animal communication systems, contains small talk, persiflage, chat – language that happens gratuitously and not for any instrumental purpose. Moreover, one end of language is self-expression – the person explaining and embodying their nature through words to others and to themselves. Then there are other social elements, such as the fact that conversation implies turn-taking and the inter-changeability of speaker and hearer.

Language therefore requires not only intellectual aptitude, but also a sense of the individual's place in the world and his or her relatedness to others. As Itard had found with Victor, language requires an awareness of another person. Speech emerges automatically in an infant, triggered perhaps by a biological trigger such as brain growth. Yet this automatic beginning in fact requires linguistic richness in the infant's environment if it is actually to acquire language.[12] If there are not enough words around or in use, then language cannot develop. Our 'nature' as linguistic creatures requires the 'nurture' of human contact; or, in other words, for language to develop, all that is required is a human brain, functioning speech organs and a sufficiently rich verbal environment. Genie's childhood had been deprived of that richness in every way, and her spontaneous attempts to articulate her feelings had led to beatings or threats that had effectively silenced her. If she was to learn language, she would first have to discover confidence in others and in herself.

So at the Los Angeles Children's Hospital, a team of scientists, therapists and linguists began working with Genie, determined both to plumb her secrets and to rescue her from the prison in which, imaginatively at least, she still remained. There was, as has been mentioned, James Kent, the kind, balding staff psychologist; Jean Butler, an ambitious special education teacher; David Rigler, the Chief of Psychology; Howard Hansen, the head of psychiatry; Jay Shurley, the expert on social isolation; and Susan Curtiss, the glamorous, dark-haired post-graduate student in linguistics. Under their care Genie rapidly improved at first – her cognitive abilities increasing markedly in the first year of her new life.

In his excellent book on Genie, Russ Rymer asserts that Genie became fodder for experimentation – almost the victim of another kind of abuse. She excited researchers, and they latched on to her as a wonderful testing ground for their theories. Rymer quotes Jay Shurley, one of the members of 'the Genie team', as saying that the questions asked of the 'wild children' talked about in this book depend on the kind of questions that already preoccupy the society into which they emerge. So just as Hauser entered a Germany ready for just such a person, primed with pseudo-scientific theories of the self and romantic notions of lost princes; just as Victor appeared in a country besotted with Rousseauist notions of the natural man – so Genie entered a scientific world excited by Chomsky's ideas that language was an innate property of *Homo grammaticus*, the grammatical man.

Yet this is only part of the truth. It is apparent that the 'Genie team' was also a group of individuals with very different views of what Genie's story represented. Jay Shurley saw her as suffering from some form of brain damage, while David Rigler saw her problems as very largely created by her deprivation and abuse. Moreover, all of the team genuinely cared for her – she somehow seemed to provoke such a feeling. Behind the accusations of alleged exploitation or incompetence lie genuinely heroic attempts to care for this girl, and a committed belief in her vital importance for scientific research. If the pursuit of knowledge somehow blurred the clarity of the intention to nurture her, we should never forget the difficulties of the case or the intensity of their commitment. In a television documentary on Genie by Linda Garmon, James Kent, the staff psychologist at the children's hospital, remarked: 'She had a personal quality that seemed to elicit rescue fantasies, and this in a group of people who were interested in taking care of kids and who specialized in early childhood, and were going to be powered by rescue fantasies anyway. She reached out and grabbed lots of us.'[13] Jay Shurley has also spoken of Genie's power to affect people: 'She grabs you and you can't get loose.' Perhaps it was her prettiness or the muted presence of all her suffering in her eyes, her fragile demeanour. She seemed to be making a silent appeal to them. She would come up close at times and just look deep into people's eyes, wondering, curious, importunate for something. Even strangers would fall for her, responding to her silent needs. Genie loved plastic. Sensing her yearning, people would hand over to her without a word the small things she longed for. Once a boy and his father passed Genie as they left a shop where they had bought a shiny new plastic fire engine. They walked a little way down the road, stopped, then the boy turned back, went up to Genie and without a word gave her the engine. Yet she had made no sign that she wanted the toy, never uttered a sound.

For the first months after her discovery, Genie continued to live in hospital. It was thought that perhaps what she needed was a family home in which her care could be focused and constant. Yet there remained doubts over who would be the best person to take her on. The break came when Genie apparently caught measles while she was staying with Jean Butler, her special education teacher. The Genie team could not bear the necessity of having to put her in an isolation ward so as to prevent an epidemic among the children in the hospital, so in the summer of 1971 it was decided that, to avoid that happening, Genie should remain with Butler.

Butler disapproved of the Genie team – the therapists and linguists such as Susan Curtiss, who worked with the young girl. For Butler, the research on Genie looked purely intrusive, as though it were being conducted at the expense of proper care; but the dislike was mutual: some of the scientists wondered about Butler's greedy desire to be the one to save Genie, the one to gain the fame of bringing her back to a full life. Of course, Jean Butler really did love Genie for herself, but from now on the girl became the passive prize of a struggle to gain possession of her.

For a while, Butler forbade Susan Curtiss and James Kent to enter her house. She put in an application to be Genie's foster-mother. But Butler was not going to win control of Genie: on 13 August 1971, social workers decided on the case. Butler's application was denied, and Genie returned to the children's hospital. She was not to stay there for long. A few weeks later, she was fostered to David Rigler, her therapist and chief scientific experimenter. Genie duly moved in with Rigler, his wife Marilyn, their children and dog.

Freed from Butler's interference, Susan Curtiss worked with Genie on a daily basis. The girl's vocabulary was already improving fast:

From the barest rudiments of a vocabulary, she began – at first slowly, then toward May, much more rapidly – to learn the names for everything around her. When she wanted to learn the word for something, she would take the hand of someone nearby and place it on the object of her attention as best she could. Hungry to learn the words for all the new items filling her senses, she would at times point to the whole outdoors and become frustrated and angry when someone failed to immediately identify the particular object she was focused on. The number of words she recognized grew sizably, probably totaling hundreds of words by June, 1971.[14]

Genie had begun a quest to label the world. She was learning language in ways quite unlike that followed by infants. She had a huge vocabulary, employing words that ordinary children would not use for years. Yet actual speech was hard for her. She would tense her body before beginning to talk, breathing in deeply. The tone was, as Memmie Le Blanc's had been, high-pitched, a breathy squeak, a voice like that used by someone deaf. Interestingly, and as living proof against Condillac's theory that for a 'wild child' their wordless time would be necessarily unremembered, since memory requires language, Genie began to talk fragmentedly of events from her past, events from before she had had language. She remembered her father. And she remembered the abuse: 'Father hit arm. Big wood. Genie cry . . . Not spit. Father. Hit face – spit . . . Father hit big stick. Father is angry. Father hit Genie big stick. Father take piece wood hit. Cry. Father make me cry. Father is dead.'[15]

With the help of the Riglers, Genie began to explore the emotions of those terrible years. Through role play they went back to the past. After one such session, caught on videotape, Genie comes into the kitchen where Marilyn Rigler is waiting. She tries to speak. 'Where's father?' Her voice is thick, high, hard to make out. 'You want to see your father?' Marilyn Rigler asks, her voice patient and contained. There's a look of concern and worry troubling Genie's face. 'Father is not living,' Marilyn Rigler patiently explains. Genie still looks anxious, bereft. 'Not living,' she says; and she shakes her head, disbelievingly, mockingly, and backs out of the room.

The linguistic experiments continued over the next few years. But the results were disappointing in the end, for despite her wide vocabulary Genie failed to use grammatical structures. She had words, but could not make correct English sentences. Her failure appeared to prove Lenneberg's thesis of the critical period for language acquisition. Yet in one sense, Genie really did learn to communicate through words, if communication means simply making oneself understood, though her linguistic attainments were perhaps not sufficient to enable a fully fledged conversation. In any case there is evidence that Genie had suffered some form of damage in the left hemisphere of the brain, leaving her a right-brain functioner. So she scored highly in tests that depended upon activities regulated by the right brain, such as face recognition, but poorly on left-hemisphere functions; and vitally, the aptitude for grammar is located in the left hemisphere of the brain. This meant that her quest to master language was hampered by more than the cruelty she had suffered as a child. Nonetheless, she mastered the essential facets of language: she could produce novel sentences, play with words, listen, take turns in conversation, speak spontaneously, and refer to people or events displaced in time.

Genie was learning to express her emotions, in words and gestures. She learnt to scream, to have a crush, to show joy, to share. At first, she would apparently not care if someone left her at the end of a visit, even though her greeting on their arrival had been ecstatic. It was as if she could only ease the burden of separation by refusing to feel its pain; abandoned once so completely, she could only cope with the little abandonments of parting by an anaesthetic response. Yet the shell of strangeness that still surrounded her was breaking up; she was allowing herself to be loved.

In some ways the only thing she had was her strangeness, itself the consequence of her special suffering. It was the extremity of her past distresses that had taken her from the periphery of abandonment to the centre of everyone's attention. Yet was it the right kind of attention? The emphasis was on pedagogy, not emotion. However, as Jay Shurley, one of the psychiatrists involved in the case, came to realize, it is love that lets you learn and grow. The thing was to enable Genie to gain connectedness to another. Love would help her to speak. Soon after her rescue from her family house, David A. Freedman, a visiting Professor of Psychiatry, watched her interact with two other children. The other children just did not exist for her; she was not really 'with' them at all.[16] She was still locked away in her exclusion and isolation, waiting for a mother, for an attachment to begin.

Did the scientists, the therapists and the linguists completely grasp that fact? Genie's most needy contacts were with the cooks in the hospital. It was to them that she ran one day when there was a Californian earth tremor, seeking human comfort for the first time ever. '"So Genie responds well to your intrasupportive initiatives?" a scientist asked one of the cooks. "I just give her love," the cook replied.'[17]

Yet the scientists loved Genie too. Those rescue fantasies were subtly at work; and more than that, the therapists and the linguists recognized something unique in Genie. James Kent and Susan Curtiss, in particular, established a genuine relationship with the disturbed girl. In her book on Genie, Susan Curtiss wrote: 'Much of what I have written in Part I does not follow the normal canons of scientific writing. To some extent it is an account of the interaction between this remarkable girl and myself.'[18]

However, this heartfelt awareness of Genie's character merged with a tendency to view her as a type. While Genie attempted to find herself in and through others, the scientists sought to find Genie through her belonging to the group of individuals that I and others have named 'wild children'. When the scientists working with Genie

watched Truffaut's film on the Itard case, it gave them a model history of which Genie simply formed the latest example. When
Curtiss's book on her work with the girl came out, its title was *Genie:
A Psycholinguistic Study of a Modern-Day 'Wild Child'*. Those quotation marks make little difference to the fact that Genie did appear
a 'wild child' – though what is particularly 'wild' about an incarceration in a Los Angeles bedroom is strangely unclear.

I, too, am linking Genie with wild children. After all, her story
closely resembles that of Kaspar Hauser, and her lack of language
places her with Peter, Victor and the Indian wolf-children. Yet does
she really fit? Are wildness and savagery the best modes for understanding Genie? They had found a template for Genie, the abused
and isolated child; but were the efforts of the whole team working
with this girl going to make any advance on the spontaneous pio-
neering efforts of Itard? With all the resources of American science
and psychotherapy on hand, could they save her?

Genie lived with the Rigler family for four years. They learnt to
cope with her antisocial behaviour (on her first day in their home
Genie defecated in their daughter's waste-paper basket) and with
her terrible self-directed temper tantrums. The Riglers tried to help
Genie as much as anyone could. They showed her love, care and
immense sympathy. Yet at the end of those four years, they were
exhausted. In the autumn of 1974 the National Institute of Mental
Health failed to renew their financial aid for the research on Genie.
Without it, the Riglers' home care could not continue. In 1975, their
foster-care ended.

On her eighteenth birthday, guardianship of Genie reverted to
her mother. She went back to live with Irene in 1975; but Irene could
no longer cope with the girl. So Genie was unsuccessfully fostered.
She was taken from one home after another over the next few years,
before finally ending up being handed out to unsympathetic, even
abusive, families. A terrible period began in her life, in which she
was moved from pillar to post, while contending factions fought for

control of her. The ins and outs of these struggles make confused and dispiriting reading. I have made the decision not to rehearse them all here. Suffice it to say that ownership, affection, exasperation, and dislike for opponents motivated the tangle. Accusations were made, lawsuits filed and counter-filed. Irene initiated legal action, accusing the scientists who had cared for Genie of 'extreme, unreasonable, and outrageous intensive testing, experimentation and observation'.[19] In 1984, a judge decided in Irene's favour but in such a way as to give access to Genie to her old helpers. Effectively, the tussle stopped Genie's education. Good people behaved shabbily; mistakes were made.

There is no doubt that this tug of war – as though Genie were a Maisie-like figure passed between warring divorced parents – affected her adversely. Her language, after great advances at the beginning, reached a plateau and would not progress – though with each year out of confinement her mental age had gone up by one year. Here was clear proof that she was not retarded.[20] Yet much of Susan Curtiss's amazing work with Genie was undone by the turmoil surrounding her. Beaten terribly for vomiting at one foster-home, she regressed, grew constipated and, worst of all, fell silent. The girl who had spent thirteen mute years, too frightened to speak, returned once more to that emptiness. Right now she is still alive, and living, as she no doubt always will, in private adult care homes.

Her few utterances, recorded by Susan Curtiss for her doctoral thesis, give us more than purely linguistic information. Her pain is there too: 'I want live back Marilyn house,' she said in November 1975, referring to her time with Marilyn Rigler and her family; and poignantly, in August 1977, she spontaneously said, 'Think about Mama love Genie.'

The issue that had been fudged from the beginning was the need for research on Genie versus her own need for treatment and care. Yet in the circumstances it is absolutely clear that the scientists who worked with Genie, researching her, exploring her nature, did so in ways that were essentially sympathetic. The tests they carried out were conducted in a spirit of play and even tenderness. Their failure to save her from further suffering unfortunately need not surprise us. It was, after all, the final fate of many of the wild children discussed in this book.

Poor Genie – saved from a nightmare life, and brought into the light of love, family life and intense caring attention, only, like Memmie, like Victor, like Hauser before her, to be consigned once again to a form of oblivion. In over three hundred years of dealing with such children nothing had really changed.

So what should we make of Genie's story? In his book on the case, Russ Rymer describes Genie's difficulty with personal pronouns: 'Most were missing from her lexicon entirely. "I" was her favourite, and "you" and "me" were interchangeable. Here the grammar reflected Genie's egocentrism – the lack of a border between her person and her world. She never figured out who she was and who was somebody else. "Mama love you," Genie would say, pointing to herself.'[21]

Like Hauser, Genie could not express anger with another, instead directing her intense rage against herself. She could never use her favourite phrases, 'stopit' and 'nomore', against someone else, or even call another person to her. Her entire selfhood was locked in the position of a victim. She was unable to bear, or even to comprehend, that her own self could actively affect others, and wrapped herself up within the sensation of her own powerlessness.

Though sometimes her words could evoke her sense of self, generally it seemed as though Genie's inability to communicate was found only in her weak use of language. Non-verbally she could reach anyone, convince them, draw them to her through the sense of her innocence, of her fragility. She could make a mute plea for love that could not be properly reciprocated, for a connection that could not finally be made.

One thing that Susan Curtiss found in Genie is that language ability is separate from cognition, and even from social interaction. Genie scored low on language tests, yet had a higher than average cognitive ability, a discrepancy that may have been caused by the damage to the left hemisphere of her brain. In the case of another damaged child, Marta, linguists discovered that you can have language and have no sense of others. Marta could reel off complicated sentences with a sophistication shown by few children of her age. Yet she showed no sign of comprehending what her words meant, or even how language operates within the world. Her sense of the structure of language was excellent, her sense of its meaning almost non-existent. Marta had language but no presence; Genie had presence but little language.

Genie was a person who could feel and experience deeply, but did not have the words there to express those feelings fluently. Instead she telegraphed her state of mind in short but expressive phrases. The undeniable presence that we feel when only hearing of Genie, Victor or Memmie is something that we need no longer feel troubled by: the self is there, whether or not it can be reached by words.

All through Genie's intense linguistic education, her teacher and investigator Susan Curtiss had one aim. She wanted Genie to outstrip her; she wished to educate Genie so as to lose her; her desire was 'that I will not be able to keep up with her, that she will have the last word'.[22] It was an aim that Itard had shared and, despite the ultimate sense of loss in both stories, we feel that both children did indeed get the last word. For though both Victor and Genie vanished – became invisible again – both left some unerasable trace of themselves as evidence against the small pointlessness of human unsuccess: a boy in the moonlight lost in his contemplative ecstasy; a curious girl awakened like a princess from a long sleep into a brightened world.

II: The Bye-Child

After those footsteps, silence;
Vigils, solitudes, fasts,
Unchristened tears,
A puzzled love of the light.
But now you speak at last

With a remote mime
Of something beyond patience,
Your gaping wordless proof
Of lunar distances
Travelled beyond love.
　　Seamus Heaney, from 'Bye-Child'

This book began with John and Ivan, two contemporary 'wild boys'. Since then we have traced the history of such stories from Romulus and Remus to Los Angeles in the 1970s. If at times this attention to the past has made our savage girls and wild boys seem remote and distant figures, then that is a sensation that we must quickly transcend. The twentieth century saw more than its share of such stories, continuing evidences of a persisting and curious fascination.

In the Himalayas we have tales of the yeti and in America folk legends of Big Foot, both strange humanoid figures – Darwinian fantasies of a missing link – as well as living remembrances of those Wild Men who once haunted the medieval woods. Of course, some wild men are not 'wild men' at all, yet have seemed to observers in our own time to be parallel examples of the stories found in this book. So there is Ishi, a middle-aged native American, the last of the Yahi, who appeared out of the wilderness in his native California in 1911. The press hyped the story, calling him a 'Stone-Age Man', 'The Wild Man', even the 'least civilized man on earth'. Ishi's fate was as strange as that of any of our wild children: he was taken to live in San Francisco's Museum of Anthropology, a living exhibit of the primitive. He died there in 1916, a last ironic exemplar of the savage, just as the technological savagery of the future was being unleashed on the Somme.

The children talked about in this book have themselves continued to lead a half-life of posthumous fame. Peter and Memmie are more or less forgotten, but Kamala and Amala were the subject of a great book by Charles Maclean. Victor has been the subject of two excellent books, Harlan Lane's *The Wild Boy Of Aveyron* and Roger Shattuck's *The Forbidden Experiment*; an extended essay by Lucien Malson; and formed part of Bruno Bettelheim's groundbreaking and somewhat misguided account of autism, *The Empty Fortress*; as well as becoming the subject of Truffaut's wonderful film.

However, it is Kaspar Hauser who, it would seem, most resonates for contemporary audiences. There have been several films on the case, including Werner Herzog's amazing portrait of Hauser as the suffering fool. Hauser has even had a weird afterlife among devotees of Rudolf Steiner, who apparently see the young man's death as the event that enabled the rise of Hitler. In this philosophy, spiritual struggles between good and evil, devils and angels, led to Hauser's death, thus preventing one of the great might-have-beens of history, in which Hauser would apparently have led a more peaceful and compassionate Germany reformed by the united power of Ferdinand von Lassalle and Bismarck.[23]

The scholarly industry on Hauser continues to thrive. There is the inspiring work of Johannes Mayer in Germany, while Jeffrey Masson's book on the Hauser story, *Wild Child*, is consistently excellent; and in Masson's book we see most clearly why Hauser should persist so strongly as an image for our times. Masson sees in Hauser an image of the abused child, as one senses in his book an idea that abuse in childhood is the root of all unhappiness. In this way, Hauser continues to flourish as an archetype of victimhood: the pure and innocent one abused by the foul and hideous; the absolutely pure Hauser, the son, versus the absolutely demonized Stanhope, the pseudo-father.

Many real cases – antelope-children, wolf-girls, monkey-boys – have cropped up over the last decades. However, perhaps it has been in cinema that some of the most poignant explorations of the myth have appeared. The Iranian film *The Apple* (1998), by Samirah Makhmalbaf, is a sensitive exploration of the theme, based on the true story of eleven-year-old twin sisters in Tehran confined from birth in their homes. Michael Apted's *Nell* (1994) adapted the wild child idea for Hollywood, casting Jodie Foster as a woman grown up in the American wilderness, who has developed her own language and is to be educated back into the world by Liam Neeson. Of course, there are the wonderful Disney cartoons, comedy versions of the story in *George of the Jungle* and *Walk Like A Man*, those innumerable Tarzan films, and the beautiful parable in David Lynch's *The Elephant Man* (1980).

Wild children have flourished in literature as well as in film. In 1978, Bruce Chatwin met a wolf-child, named Shamdev, in India; Thom Gunn wrote a poem about a sexualized wild boy in his 1957 volume *The Sense of Movement*; Jill Paton Walsh won the Booker Prize with *Knowledge of Angels*, a novel that deals with a medieval feral child; and Paul Auster's *New York Trilogy* meditates on Peter the Wild Boy and the Hauser case.[24] But for me, the most powerful conjuring of the wild child motif is found in Seamus Heaney's poem, 'Bye-Child', part of his 1972 collection *Wintering Out*.

The poem imagines a situation in which a boy enclosed in a hen-house looks up to the 'yolk of light' glimpsed in the back window of the home from which he is exiled. Real pity is here – both for the boy and for the woman, so put upon by social conventions as to cause his suffering out there in the dark. The poem does not exactly refer to that real case from the 1950s in Northern Ireland, in which a mother is reputed to have confined her child to a hen-house. As I said in the first chapter, this story was a point of entry for me in first forming the wish to write this book. In a beautifully chaotic Irish house, a few miles from Benone Strand, I first heard of the hen-house boy ('the talk of the country in the early 1950s', as Heaney remarks) from the family of a social worker who had worked on the case. The strangeness of the story struck home. Long before I came upon Heaney's poem, I found myself thinking of a boy locked out in the winter cold, surrounded by the smell of beasts and the mechanical, slightly deranged cluckings of hens. The image goes deep, and its resonance for Heaney goes beyond the complex and doubtful realities of the case. Here Heaney writes of what drew him to the story: 'What interested me about the boy, I suppose, was his persistent dream-presence in my mind. He is/was like a creature of myth, at one with those who might have been exposed on the mountainside or set adrift on a coracle.'[25]

Fittingly, we are back among the myths with which this book began.

And the myths go on. Just this summer, as I was finishing this book, two new stories emerged that parallel exactly the legends and histories we have been looking at. In the early summer, a boy appeared in Chile, who had apparently been brought up among wild dogs. And, in July 2001, closer to home in London, another even more startling case was discovered by the press.

No-one knew where the boy came from; no-one knew his name. He was first seen on March 8, a young teenage boy, dazed and lost, wandering on the south London streets near Tower Bridge. A passer-by saw him, grew concerned and contacted the police. When they picked him up, they found no signs of physical abuse. Yet something out of the ordinary was clearly wrong. Questioning him, they met a blank. He couldn't tell them his age, his name, or how he had come to be on the streets. Yet, in broken English, learnt, he said, from watching television, he told them how he had lived for the last eight years, confined to a north London house, beaten by the adults who kept him there, never allowed to go to school, and forbidden to leave the building on his own.

Could we imagine the boy's confusion on those springtime streets of Bermondsey, surrounded by traffic and the vast expanse of hurrying London? Could we inhabit this contemporary Kaspar Hauser's alienated sense of a world known only through television pictures or glimpsed from the windows of a London flat? Momentarily, his story touched a nerve for us. Perhaps he embodied our own buried sense of alienation, our own fears about a generation of children for whom the world is in any case a potentially scary place. But in his story the real object of our fears was not the streets, the exterior city, but the home in which he was incarcerated. The refuge we return to had here become a prison, a darkly protective and disconcertingly abusive place. The sanctuary turns out to be a dungeon.

For a day or two, the boy's story featured on the front pages of all the national newspapers and in the television news reports. And then suddenly, it was revealed that the boy's story was a complete fabrication. Like Caraboo before him, and as was suspected about Kaspar Hauser, the boy had lied in order to make himself more interesting, to raise his ordinary sufferings to the status of myth. In the instant he was revealed to be a liar, he became uninteresting; commissioned articles for an account of his story were cancelled; the photographs were returned to the files. He was simply an impostor.

It is hard to say which is more striking in this story: the boy's invention of his own myth, as though he had read all the old tales of Hauser or of Genie, or the authorities' and the media's readiness to believe him. In either case, the significance is unmissable. Clearly whatever motivates our interest in such stories, remains with us.

Often while writing this book, at parties or over a drink, people would ask me what conclusions I had come to: what did I consider it all meant? – even, on one occasion, 'Well, what's the hook?' And each time, embarrassment bewildered me with shame at my own discovered ignorance. For the more I thought about these stories, these children, the more my grasp weakened on those hard and fast conclusions that can be passed to an interrogator like a token of consolation. Yet, after the ten years or so that I have lived with the stories, it seems impossible to part from them without bidding them farewell. So this is my awkward bow – not a summing up, nor a final word, but a lingering glance backwards and a parting.

First of all, there may be an unanswered question lurking in the minds of some readers. Are these stories true? Of course, all these children actually existed and all the events described in this book are documented; but what of those parts of their stories that are hidden? Was Peter the Wild Boy really suckled by a bear? Did wolves nurture Kamala and Amala? Could Victor actually have lived for years alone in the woods of France? Was Kaspar Hauser truthfully imprisoned in a little cell?

For what it's worth, in the case of Victor and Hauser, I am inclined to answer 'yes' to these questions. I also believe that the evidence regarding Kamala and Amala is at times convincing – particularly as presented in Charles Maclean's book on the twins. There may well be cases of inter-species nurturing, and certainly human infants can thrive on the milk of any mammal. Yet in most of the cases described in this book it is now impossible to know the veracity of the stories. The evidence is too flimsy and is mostly lost; and of course that does not matter in the least. For the deeper point of interest in these stories is what was believed about the children. By becoming objects of speculation, they opened up the fantasies of a nation and, in the stories told around them, we glimpse into our dreams.

So although none of these children were blanks, the first thing that will strike any reader is the way that each generation has fantasized them, using them like a screen on which to project their own preoccupations. Silence is the great guarantee of mystery, but it also permits a thousand fancies, the projection of a multitude of needs. Sometimes those fantasies are shared by an entire culture. On those occasions, as with Victor, Kaspar Hauser, or Genie, fame bestows its ephemeral blessing on the child; for a moment, they shine, imbued with a surpassing attention. At other times, such children are merely the recipients of a brief curiosity and, as with Peter or Memmie, they slip away from our gaze like an opportunity wasted. So they have had to endure the exploitation of a culture's curiosity, or face the second abandonment of their neglect.

If each generation discovers its own source of interest in such children, then it seems best to close the book by asking what such stories might mean for our generation. When we returned to Romulus and Remus, and those medieval romances of the lost child, we found mystery, wonder and reverence. Would our modern scepticism allow us such experiences? What are our fantasies, our dreams?

There is a despair even deeper than scepticism. Despite the continuing presence of Mowgli and Tarzan, and other such myths in our culture (even in so anodyne a form as films like *George of the Jungle*), we seem to have lost that feeling of miracle. Instead, our wild children are victims of improbably cruel abuse or, otherwise, evolutionary puzzles – no longer as with Tarzan, in so far as they belong to a hierarchy of races, but just as illuminating symbols of our own evolutionary dethronement, exemplars of the precarious, mysterious and perhaps insignificant difference of being human.

Yet some of the old wonder remains. The wild children of the past moved from the empty woods to the public arena of the court or the city. Today's wild children also come from an elsewhere, but under the continuing influence of Freud and even Rousseau, we now see that elsewhere as a lost place within ourselves. Of particular importance is our perceived sense of the wild child's harmony with nature. It can seem as though the wild child lives a purer, 'greener' relationship with a world that the more civilized have polluted, suffocated and scarred.

Yet the facing of that lost self found in the wild child is far from easy. In Itard's relationship with Victor we see most clearly the mingled contempt and envy felt for the savage one. By symbolizing our own lost possibilities, one might momentarily symbolize something better than oneself. And so we yearn to imaginatively possess the experience of the child. However, this reaching out of sympathy encounters also a resistance, in which desire becomes contempt, through the recognition of the wild child's rawness, brutishness and bestiality; and so once again we erect barriers against the recognition of kinship. In its most extreme form, this denial of identity with the wild child enters into the apparently abstract question of the definition of humanity. So the civilized discover in such children a symbol of their desire to escape the human condition through a return to the origins of childhood and the primitive. Yet they also fear and reject those origins, for their existence threatens to unravel the fragile unity of the self.

So wild children exist in the fault line between disgust and desire. They embody our desire for escape, freedom and wonder; yet they also provoke the disgust felt for the merely corporeal, the wholly physical – the disgust for that which has no self, no love, and no remorse. Desire seeks escape by possessing another; disgust re-imagines that possession as a return to the most torpid, gross and inescapably material aspects of the self.

Yet it is in their embodiment of a primal solitude that these children can most affect us. The savage girls and wild boys are God's lonely children. Loneliness seems the crucial experience of our culture. Our secular faith in 'relationships', marriages, casual sex, drugs, lonely hearts columns bears witness to the deepest terror of simply being alone. People mock the thing they most fear, as the re-invention of the word 'sad' as a contemptuous term of abuse shows. And just to show that a fear is also a desire, we find the mass fascination with the suffering star (Marilyn Monroe, James Dean, Princess Diana), fêted and surrounded by the most elaborate trappings of fame, attention and success, but still internally desolate, irredeemably forsaken.

Wild children live out this fear and fantasy on an even more exaggerated scale. They embody the pain of the rejected, and yet seem free of their loneliness. Their selves are the products of an isolation that they no longer seem to feel. Hence Victor appears to us now as the triumphant hero who has defeated his own abandonment, transforming it into a sought-for solitude. Loneliness pervades his story; though it is Itard's isolation that may most strike us now. In Itard's story one loneliness encounters another. This is the pattern of all our tales. For they are all stories of unrequited love. Love seeks to gain the recognition of the beloved, both to bring to life the mutual humanness of feeling in the loved one, and even more to share a contact with someone always turned the other way, locked in what the psychoanalyst Bruno Bettelheim has termed 'the empty fortress'.

Is the fortress empty? Most of our observers were asking the same question: what makes someone human? Their answers are too various to permit a summing up here, but in writing this book one thing has become apparent to me: some residual element of human nature is not contained in language. It seems as though there is indeed an essence that makes us human – though every practical attempt to define that essence ends in failure. We know when someone is human – although what distinguishes an ape from a human, or a wild child, is unclear.

At times during the writing of this book, an anxious thought would recur to me: what if the question that has always been asked of these children no longer applies? What if the human is obsolete? Increasingly, the 'human condition' that once defined our lives appears to be on the point of ceasing to exist. We can clone ourselves, transform our bodies cybernetically, free ourselves from the inevitable consequences of our birth. The 'facts' of birth, identity, sex, ageing, and even mortality seem malleable or even avoidable. The only element of that age-old human condition that doesn't pass is the sense of our own passing.

The question as to what makes us human would seem to have been solved, the answer lying not in language, or shape, or culture, but in tiny strands of DNA, the minuscule difference of genetic material separating us from our primate cousins. The solution is so simple, and yet it fails to satisfy.

The observers and educators of our wild children shared a belief that human nature was not a given, but something that had to be attained. Some of them discovered that, through whatever hidden process, their wild children had already attained the human, and that its fine elements of wisdom, ecstasy, curiosity, compassion, kindness and love were something that they too had to learn. In his book on Genie, Russ Rymer remarks that the scientists examining the damaged girl had come to her with the question: 'what makes this person human?', only to find that she in her turn was implicitly asking the same question of them.

For it strikes me, as I finish writing, that all the stories included here are parables of care. The 'wild children' were not just objects of personal and cultural fantasy; they were also themselves. In each story we witness people's desire to take on responsibility for another human being; to offer continuing love, support, and refuge; to become to the most unrewarding of individuals a surrogate parent, a mentor, a friend. So often the desire fails. Again and again, ambition, intellectual curiosity, or artistic longing steps in and muddies the apparent clarity of that relationship. Often it is 'the simple people' – those who have no desire to speculate on the meanings of others, to make a name, to write a book – who can best show that care: the farming family who took care of Peter the Wild Boy and not Arbuthnot; Madam Guérin and not Itard. Yet however compromised their motives, however ineffectual their love, when I think of Burnett and La Condamine, Itard, Revd Singh, or the Genie team, it is not their ultimate failure that I now think of, but the quiet nobility of the attempt.

The stories in this book might distress us. After all, they contain in their most naked form the worst aspects of human nature: cruelty, barbarism, sadistic violence; a small child with his throat cut left to wander in the woods of France; a young girl strapped to a chair and threatened with violence for year after year. Yet the overall effect is, I hope, not depressing. Some of the wild children escaped to a nature that appears unexpectedly merciful and kind. Some of them embody a passionate attentiveness; and some of them, though beginning in the most abject suffering, end by discovering in their lives something else – not necessarily transcendent, but nonetheless foolishly gentle, incompetently compassionate, wrongheadedly thoughtful: in other words, something human.

Notes

Chapter One, 'The Child of Nature'

1 In his notebooks, Samuel Taylor Coleridge regretted the linking of the relationship of Jehovah to the Virgin Mary with that between Mars and the mother of Romulus and Remus. (Note 2670 in Coleridge, 1962, vol. 2.)

2 In *Les Origines de Rome* (Brussels: Facultés Universitaires Saint Louis, 1985), Jacques Poucet alludes with an air of embarrassment to the archetypal meanings of the foundation narrative: 'Ces motifs semblent surgir d'une espèce de fonds communs de l'humanité. Serions-nous en présence de "l'inconscient collectif" jungien? C'est possible.' (182).

3 Beard, 1996: 3.

4 Acca Larentia, the wife of Faustulus, was probably a late addition to the story, and may be traced to Ennius (Bremmer/Horsfall, 1987: 32).

5 Ovid, 1929: 79 and 81.

6 Dickson, 1929: 35–7.

7 Mills, 1973.

8 *Valentine and Orson*, 1937: 38.

9 Again there were classical precedents for such creatures. Lycaon, founder of the city of Lykosoura, lived for nine years as a wolf lost in the wilderness outside the city walls. The Bible too had its wild man: Nebuchadnezzar in his madness living out in the wilds like a beast of the fields. From the later medieval period a vogue for such wild men flourished, and they began to appear in pageants, masques and court entertainments. A wild man jumped from a rock to dance before Gaston de Foix in a 'mystère d'enfants sauvages'; they romped in the Twelfth Night celebrations at Greenwich of 1515; wild men prettily entertained Anne Boleyn at her coronation pageant. Indeed, the fashion for such creatures persisted for several hundred years: there were still wild men in the Lord Mayor of London's procession in the mid-eighteenth century.

Shakespeare's own late plays share many characteristics with our tales of abandoned children – as well as having, in Caliban, the semi-human savage islander of *The Tempest*, his own version of the wild man. He certainly knew Ovid's *Fasti*, as this was one of his sources for *The Rape of Lucrece*, and most likely knew the life of Romulus as it also appeared in North's translation of Plutarch's *Lives*. All the elements we see in the

story of Romulus and Remus are there in these last plays: the abandonment of children; the evocation of the benevolent nurture of 'great creating nature' in *The Winter's Tale*; the impossibility of disguising the
royal nature of the lost child even in the rude, uncultured conditions in
which it finds itself – for the lost child, Perdita, also in *The Winter's Tale*,
'all her acts are queens'; the restoration of the lost child to its family,
and the redemption of a corrupt older generation by the purity of the
found child.

Chapter Two, 'Bodies Without Souls'

1   Digby, 1644: 247.
2   Ibid.: 247–8.
3   Connor, 1698: 1, 342.
4   Ibid.: 343.
5   Ibid.: 343.
6   Ibid.: 346–7.
7   Ibid.: 349.
8   Ibid.: 350.
9   Defoe, 1726: 22.
10 Taylor, 1933: 271.
11 Tickell, 1931: 115–7.
12 Swift, 1963: vol. 3, 128.
13 An Enquiry, 1726: 4.
14 A New Guide to London, 1726: 4–5.
15 An Enquiry, 1726: 3.
16 Van Der Kiste, 1997: 82.
17 An Enquiry, 1726: 3.
18 Ibid.
19 Ibid.: 4.
20 Democritus, 1723: 9–10.
21 The Gentleman's Magazine, 1785: 236.
22 Ashton, 1882: vol. 1, 278.
23 La Mettrie, 1750: 93.
24 Dampier, 1699: vol. 1, 464.
25 Pliny, 1601: 96.
26 Augustine, 1610: 581.
27 Linnæus, 1792: 32.
28 Ibid.: 44–5.
29 Ibid.: 44.

30 This book has just survived the recent spate of de-attributions in the Defoe canon, performed admirably by P. N. Furbank and W. R. Owens, although they only consider the book to be 'probably' by Defoe. See Furbank and Owens, 1998: 221–2.

31 Lee, 1869: vol. I, 413.

32 Ibid.: 414.

33 Wright, 1894: 341.

34 Ibid.

35 Lee, 1869: vol. I, 414.

36 Defoe, 1726: 61.

37 Maximilian Novak argues that this may be Defoe's rebuttal of the earlier feral child text, Abu Bakr Ibn Al-Tufail's medieval text, *The Improvement of Reason, exhibited in the Life of Hai Ebn Yokdan*, recently translated by Simon Ockley (London, 1708). In that book, Hai Ebn Yokdan comes to a knowledge of God purely through the exercise of his own isolated reason.

38 Defoe, 1726: 33–34.

39 Ibid.: 39.

40 Ibid.: 38–9.

41 Ibid.: 66.

42 Ibid.: 69–71.

43 Ibid.: 70.

44 Ibid.: 121.

45 Aitken, 1912: 114.

46 Gentleman's Magazine, 1752: 522.

47 Burnett, 1779–99: vol. 3, 59–68; 368–78.

Chapter Three, 'Lord Monboddo and the Savage Girl'

1 *Savage Girl*, 1768: 4.

2 *Savage Girl*, 1760: 82.

3 *Savage Girl*, 1768: x.

4 A. D.'s introduction to La Condamine, *Journal of a Tour to Italy*, 1753: 18–20.

5 La Condamine, 1747: 26.

6 *Savage Girl*, 1760: 59-60.

7 Ibid.: 27.

8 Boswell, 1785: 83.

9 *Letters on the French Nation*, 1749: 23; 38.

10 *Savage Girl*, 1760: 68–9.

11 Ibid.: 61.

12 Ibid.: 92.

13 Ibid.: 129.

14 *Savage Girl*, 1768: 54–5.

15 Ibid.: 55.

16 Ibid.: v–vii.

17 Ibid.: x–xi.

18 *Savage Girl*, 1760: 139–47.

19 *Savage Girl*, 1768: xi–xii.

20 *Savage Girl*, 1760: 66.

21 Burnett, 1773: 176.

22 Linnæus, 1792: vol. 1, 17.

23 Ibid.: 56.

24 Ibid.: 9.

25 Purchas, 1905–6: vol. 6, 398.

26 Buffon, 1791: vol. 1, 325.

27 Burnett, 1779–99: vol. 4, 28–9.

28 Boswell, 1785: 83.

29 *Savage Girl*, 1768: xvi–xviii.

30 Burnett, 1779–99: vol. 3, 219.

31 White, 1799: 33–4.

32 Burns, 1985: 76. The poems on Eliza Burnett are 'Address to Edinburgh' and 'A Fragment, which was meant for the beginning of an Elegy on the late Miss Burnett of Monboddo', both of which can be found in James Kinsley's edition of *The Poems and Songs of Robert Burns*, published in three volumes by Oxford University Press, 1968: 1, 308–10 and 3, 569–70.

33 Cloyd, 1972: 134.

34 Knight, 1900: 19.

Chapter Four, 'Radical Innocence'

1 Bonaterre, quoted in Lane, 1977: 45.

2 Ibid.: 36–7.

3 Itard, 1802: 22.

4 Lane, 1977: 37.

5 Virey quoted in Lane, 1977: 48.

6 Mercier, 1800: vol. I, 259. Mercier's book is an extraordinary account of the French Revolution written by someone who seems to have been a kind of Roland Barthes before the fact.

7 For Condillac, all our mental ideas derive ultimately from sensations. In the turmoil of post-Revolutionary Paris, another philosopher Destutt-Tracy

had developed Condillac's emphasis on 'ideology' (Tracy's coinage) still
further into a study of the formation of identity through ideas derived from
sensation. In 1795, as a young medical student, Itard may well have attended Tracy's lectures on ideology at the Institut National des Sciences et Arts.
But in any case, Itard had already read and absorbed Condillac at first
hand, for the philosopher's 'psychologism' was at the very heart of medical
practice in France.

8 Condillac, 1756: 171.

9 Ibid.: 175.

10 Itard, 1802: 32.

11 Ibid.: 33.

12 Ibid.: 38–9. This passage is paraphrased from Itard's own words.

13 Ibid.: 40–42.

14 Condillac, 1756: 132.

15 Itard, 1802: 75.

16 Ibid.: 83.

17 Ibid.: 107.

18 Coleridge, 1957: note 1348.

19 Coleridge, 1973: note 3538.

20 Itard, 1932: 73.

21 I am unclear whether this was an additional 150 francs to the usual pension of 500 francs paid by the government to each child at the Institute.

Chapter Five, 'The Child of Europe'

1 Verlaine, 1954: 183.

2 The date of Hauser's first appearance is a subject for debate.
Depending on the source, it may have been 5, 26, or 28 May. In *The True
Story of Kaspar Hauser from Official Documents*, the Duchess of
Cleveland includes an appendix of evidence from Weichmann and others. All the witnesses state that the events took place on Easter Monday –
an interesting mistake (if that's what it is) in view of the later identifica-
tions of Hauser with Christ. I have followed Feuerbach and taken the 26th
as the most likely date.

At the time, the population of Nuremberg in the 1830s was estimated at
around 20,000 (Spencer, 1836: 317), 40,000 (*Southern Germany*, 1837: 54) or,
more likely, between 31,000 and 32,000 inhabitants living in about 3300
houses (Domeier, 1830: 93). All these sources agree that the population had
fallen from a high in the sixteenth century of around 70–80,000.

3 The late war, and the unnatural partition of the empire, gave her

[Nuremberg] up to her ancient enemy, Catholic Bavaria; and now her streets, instead of bales of merchandise, are filled with bands of soldiers; and the sound of martial music is the substitute for gaiety and mirth. (Spencer, 1836: 318).

4 Feuerbach, 1832a: 14.

5 Cleveland, 1893: 2.

6 Feuerbach, 1832b: 15.

7 Money, 1992: 20.

8 Quoted in Feuerbach, 1834: 140–44. (Daumer, 1832a: 52-6).

9 Money, 1992: 20.

10 Binder's discoveries appeared in the form of an official promulgation. This was the first publication of Hauser's story. The account stated that:

He neither knows who he is nor where his home is. It was only at Nuremberg that he came into the world. Here he first learnt that, besides himself and 'the man with whom he had always been', there existed other men and other creatures. As long as he can recollect he had always lived in a hole (a small low apartment which he sometimes calls a cage), where he had always sat upon the ground, with bare feet, and clothed only with a shirt and a pair of breeches. In his apartment he never heard a sound, whether produced by a man, by an animal, or by anything else. He never saw the heavens, nor did there ever appear a brightening (daylight) such as at Nuremberg. He never perceived any difference between day and night, and much less did he ever get a sight of the beautiful lights in the heavens. (Feuerbach, 1832b: 55–6)

11 Jeffrey Masson's translation of Hauser's words in Masson, 1996: 189–90.

12 Masson, 1996: 9.

13 Feuerbach, 1832b: 55–6.

14 Ibid.: 164–5.

15 Evans, 1982: 35.

16 Lang, 1904.

17 Ellenberger, 1994: 78.

18 Gmelin quoted in *Animal Magnetism*, 1839: 19.

19 Bance, 1975: 204. For additional information on Justinus Kerner and Friedericke Hauffer see Henri Ellenberger, *The Discovery of the Unconscious* (London: 1994: 78–81) and Justinus Kerner, *Die Seherin von Prevorst* (Stuttgart and Tübingen: 1829), translated as *The Seeress of Prevorst* (London: 1845).

20 Daumer quoted in Feuerbach, 1834: 153–5.

21 Kerner, 1845: 136.

22 There is a confusion in the chronology here – as elsewhere: the entire Hauser story is very hard to unpick from the numerous contradictory statements made about him. Hauser starts his memoir in early autumn 1829, leading to his attack in October of that year. However, we know that Hauser was writing autobiographical work from September 1828, while living with Daumer (Masson, 1996: 10). Was Hauser starting a new autobiography? Or is there simply uncertainty as to the sequence of events designed to show that the attack was connected to what such a story must reveal?

23 Shengold, 1988: 79.

24 Feuerbach, 1832b: 177–8.

25 Feuerbach, 1846: 166.

26 Domeier, 1830: 95. We know that the better hotels in Nuremberg at the time were Der Baierishe Hof and the Rothes Ross (*Southern Germany*, 1837: 54; Dibdin, 1821: xvii–xviii.

27 Though perhaps Stanhope knew of Hauser long before: certainly the researches of Johannes Mayer in the Chevening archives suggests that Stanhope's interest in Hauser pre-dated his arrival in Nuremberg, and that the interest was connected to negotiations with the royal family of Baden.

28 Cleveland, 1897: 1.

29 Ibid.: 30; Haslip, 1934: 39.

30 Binns, 1845: 451.

31 *Animal Magnetism*, 1839: 49.

32 Cleveland, 1897: 3.

33 Masson, 1996: 215.

34 Lang, 1904: 134.

35 Evans, 1892: 148–9.

36 Evans, 1892: 77.

37 Lübeck quoted in Feuerbach, 1834: 172–3.

38 Masson, 1996: 19–21.

39 Evans, 1892: 49–50.

40 Ibid.: 45.

41 Evans, 1892: 96.

42 Cleveland, 193: 41.

43 Evans, 1892: 112.

44 Stanhope's was not the first book to discredit Hauser. In 1830, Johann Friedrich Karl Merker published a work claiming that Hauser must be an impostor (Kendall, 1992: 214–15).

45 Stanhope, 1836: 39.

46 Stanhope, 1836: 19–20.

47 Lang, 1893: xiii.

48 Lang, 1904: 118–19.

49 Ibid.: 119.

50 Ibid.: 120–21.

51 Ibid.: 121.

52 Stanhope, 1836: 49–50.

53 Ibid.: 58.

54 Cleveland, 1893: 86.

55 Ibid.: 45.

56 John Green, 1840: 35.

57 Kendall, 1992: 218.

58 The epigraph to Feuerbach's book was translated in the first English editions of his book as follows:

    Righteous Heaven, who hast permitted

    All this wo; what fatal crime,

    Was by me, e'en at the time

    Of my hapless birth, committed.

    SIGISMUND

    In Calderon's Life, a Dream

59 Feuerbach, 1832b: 162–3.

60 John Green, 1840: 35.

61 Spencer, 1836: 326.

62 Bance, 1975: 200–201.

63 Sagarra, 1980: 22.

64 Evans, 1892: 113–4.

65 Feuerbach, 1832b: 75–6.

66 Lang, 1893: 121.

Chapter Six, 'The Wolf-Children'

1 Paraphrased from Singh, 1942: xxv.

2 Paraphrased from Singh, 1942: xxix.

3 Ibid.: 4.

4 Ibid.: 5.

5 Ibid.: 8.

6 Ibid.: 11.

7 Ibid.: 14.

8 Ibid.: 19.

9 Ibid.: 31.

10 Ibid.: 53.

11 Ibid.: 60.

12 Ibid.: 100.

13 Kipling, 1990, 1: 7–8, 2: 49 and 2: 71.

14 In *Something of Myself*, Kipling cites his three sources: a tale of Masonic Lions; H. Rider Haggard's *Nada the Lily* (London: 1892); and his own tale of Indian forestry, 'In the Rukh', from *Many Inventions* (London: 1893). Roger Lancelyn Green has identified the tale of Masonic Lions as 'King Lion', a children's story probably written by James Greenwood (Kipling, 1977: 174). In a letter to Edward Everett Hale, 16 January 1895, Kipling mentions the *Jatakamala* and the tales (probably unwritten) of native hunters (Kipling, 1990, 2: 168). A reviewer ('Baron de Book Worm') in *Punch* ('The Jungle Books', 1894) suggested *Uncle Remus* and Aesop's *Fables* as possible sources. Beyond the shared resemblance of these being beast tales this seems unlikely.

While Rudyard Kipling was keen to assert the Indian nature of these tales, it is possible that when he began to write his stories, he used sources even closer to hand. Kipling wrote *The Jungle Books* at Naulahka, his house in Vermont, between 1892 and 1894. It so happens that at this time in New England a series of 'wild man' stories were current: tales of mysterious savages and hairy figures haunting the woods of the north-eastern United States. There was one reported in Connecticut in 1892; one in New York State in 1893; two sightings in 1895; and another in Colebrook, Connecticut, in 1895. The relation of these wild men to Kipling's story may well be coincidental, but it is a matter of interest that the first of them should occur on 11 November 1892, within a hundred miles of Kipling's home near Brattleboro, in the same week that he began to write his Mowgli stories.

15 John Lockwood Kipling, 1891: 313–14.

16 Sterndale, 1884: 233. Kipling certainly made use of other of Sterndale's works, most notably *Denizens of the Jungle* (Calcutta: 1886), in researching the natural history of *The Jungle Books*. It seems likely that R. A. Sterndale's book was a source for both John Lockwood Kipling and *The Jungle Books*. It contains a reference to the Lucknow case, and mentions one of the few facts used by Kipling in 'In the Rukh': that is, that most 'wolf children' die young.

17 Sleeman's mid nineteenth-century pamphlet was reprinted in vol. 12 of *The Zoologist* (London, 1888: 87–98). It is referred to by most writers on wild children from then to the 1920s.

18 Sleeman, 1888: 90.

19 Ibid.: 95–6.

20 There is a likelihood that Kipling read these words: if he did not find it in
the works of the naturalist Sterndale, Kipling's remark in 'In the Rukh', his
first Mowgli story, that wolf-children tend to die young could well be drawn
from Sleeman's pamphlet, which is particularly insistent on that point.
Indeed it may be that this moment of strange grace forms the ultimate
source for the note of wonder in Kipling's Mowgli stories.

21 Tylor, 1863: 21–32.

22 Ibid.: 29.

23 Wolf-Children, 1893: 215–16.

24 Quoted in Ball, 1880: 463.

25 Native evidence, however, for the most part must always be open to suspicion . . . their contention is, moreover, too true, that the average native of
India is ever on the alert to exhibit the wonderful to the Sahib, and noway
particular how or where, so long as a reward is secured. (Stockwell, 1898:
124).

26 Singh, 1942: xv.

27 Ibid.: xxii.

28 Ibid.: xxvii.

29 In *The Management and Medical Treatment of Children in India*,
Edward A. Birch describes the inability of Western children to develop in
the Indian climate beyond the age of five:

> There is a pretty general medical opinion that the Indian climate does
> not in any way injure the health of the European infant in the first year of
> its life; further than this, the conviction is prevalent that with proper pre-
> cautions up to the age of 5 or 6 years the child may be reared nearly as
> satisfactorily in the plains of India as in Europe; but beyond these ages all
> are agreed that physical and moral degeneration occur. The child then
> 'exhibits the necessity for change of climate by emaciating and outgrow-
> ing its strength' (Martin). So profoundly does the climate, after the peri-
> od of immediate childhood, influence the constitution that the effect of a
> more prolonged residence is rendered permanent throughout life . . . Dr.
> K. Mackinnon remarks that even where there is no tangible disease nutri-
> tion and oxygenation do not appear to go on favourably, the skin
> becomes pale, the muscles waste in substance and tone, the joyous spir-
> its of children are wanting, the body is inert, and the mind listless. We
> daily observe evidence that 'the European was not made for the climate,
> nor the climate for him' in attempts to rear children in the plains past a
> certain age. (Birch, 1886: 13–14)

In part, this provided a medical justification for the social practice of sending upper and middle class children back to England for their education at around that age. The idea that children left to grow up in the colonies will degenerate and grow ill appears for instance in the representation of sallow, sickly Mary Lennox in Frances Hodgson Burnett's *The Secret Garden* (1911).

30 Stockwell, 1898: 120.
31 Kipling, 1893: 204.
32 Kipling, 1895: 64.
33 Ibid.: 191.
34 Kipling, 1895: 204.
35 Kipling, 1977: 162.
36 Lupoff, 1965:195.
37 Porges, 1975: 123–4.
38 Porges, 1975: 136.
39 Porges, 1975: 135–6.
40 Burroughs, 1914: 139.
41 Ibid.: 257.
42 Ibid.: 258.
43 Ibid.: 276.

Chapter Seven, 'Where Is Tomorrow, Mrs L.?'

1 Paraphrased from Curtiss, 1977: 19. The following section on Genie is very much indebted to the books on the case by Susan Curtiss and by Russ Rymer. The information in this chapter also derives from press reports in the *Los Angeles Times*, the documentary film on Genie made by Linda Garmon, and conversations with Linda Garmon and Jay Shurley.
2 Rymer, 1994: 18.
3 It is worth noting that the girl's mother ('Irene') disputes a number of the facts presented here. See Rymer, 1994: 191–2.
4 Curtiss, 1977: 3.
5 Ibid.: 3–4.
6 Ibid.: xiii.
7 Ibid.: 9.
8 Ibid.: 10.
9 Rymer, 1994: 60 – and from information drawn from the BBC television documentary, *Horizon*, transmitted on BBC2 on 02/05/1994.
10 Curtiss, 1977: 13.
11 Lenneberg, 1966: 65–9.

12 Aitchison, 1989: 68.

13 'Genie', part of the *Horizon* series on BBC 2, transmitted 02/05/1994.

14 Curtiss, 1977: 15.

15 Ibid.: 35.

16 Rymer, 1994: 62.

17 Ibid.: 58.

18 Curtiss, 1977: xii.

19 Rymer, 1994: 192.

20 Ibid.: 129.

21 Ibid.: 126.

22 Curtiss, 1977: 42.

23 See Karl König, 1995; Pietzner 1983: 8; and Adam Bittleston's introduction to Hauser, 1993.

24 Chatwin, 1989: 233–40.

25 Unpublished letter to the author from Seamus Heaney, 14 May 1999.

Bibliography

Abu Bakr ibn Al-Tufail (1708), *The Improvement of Human Reason, exhibit-ed in the life of Hai Ebn Yokdhan*, trans. Simon Ockley, London: Edmund Powell and I. Morphew.

Aitchison, Jean (1989), *The Articulate Mammal. An Introduction to Psycholinguistics*, third edition, London: Unwin Hyman.

Aitken, George A. (1892), 'Life of Dr. Arbuthnot', in *The Life and Works of John Arbuthnot*, Oxford: Clarendon Press. 1–188.

Allen, Don (1974), *François Truffaut*, London: Secker & Warburg.

Animal Magnetism (1839), *Animal Magnetism Delineated by its Professors: A Review of its History in Germany, France and England*. London: John Churchill.

Annual Register, The (See *Peter the Wild Boy*).

Apollodorus (1921), *The Library*, trans. and ed. James George Frazer, 2 vols, London: Wm. Heinemann.

Arbuthnot, John (1741), *Miscellanies*, Dublin: Edward and John Exshaw.

– (1751), *The Miscellaneous Works of the late Dr Arbuthnot*, 2nd edn., 2 vols., Glasgow: James Carlile.

– (1892), 'Works of Dr. Arbuthnot. Doubtful Works Attributed to Dr. Arbuthnot', in *The Life and Works of Dr. Arbuthnot*, ed. George Aitken, Oxford: Clarendon Press, 191–516.

Arendt, Hannah (1958), *The Human Condition*, Chicago: University of Chicago Press.

– (1979), *The Origins of Totalitarianism*, 1951, San Diego, New York, and London: Harcourt Brace Jovanovich.

– (1990), *On Revolution*, 1964, Harmondsworth: Penguin Books.

Ariès, Philippe (1979), *Centuries of Childhood*, 1960. London: Peregrine Books.

Artin, Alexander von (1892), *Kaspar Hauser: Des Räthsel's Lösung*, Zurich: Caesar Schmidt.

Ashton, John (1882), *Social Life in the Reign of Queen Anne*, vol. 1, London: Chatto & Windus.

Augustine, St (1610), *Of the Citie of God*, trans. John Healey, London: G. Eld.

Auster, Paul (1987), *The New York Trilogy*, 1985/1986. London: Faber and Faber.

Backscheider, Paula (1989), *Daniel Defoe. His Life*, Baltimore: Johns Hopkins University Press.

Bage, Robert (1796), *Hermsprong. Man As He Is Not*, 2 vols., Dublin: Wogan, Byrne, Moore and Rice.

Ball, Valentin (1880), *Jungle Life in India*, London: Thos. de la Rue & Co.

Bance, A. F. (1974–5), 'The Kaspar Hauser Legend and its Literary Survival', in *German Life and Letters*, eds. Leonard Foster, P. F. Ganz, J. C. Middleton, J. M. Ritchie and J. J. White, vol. 28, Oxford: Basil Blackwell, 199–210.

Barbier, Antoine Alexandre (1806–8), *Dictionnaire des ouvrages anonymes et Pseudonymes*, 4 vols., Paris: Imprimerie Bibliographique.

Battell, Andrew (1905), 'The Strange Adventures of Andrew Battell of Leigh in Essex, sent by the Portugals prisoner to Angola, who lived there, and in the adjoining Regions, neere eighteen years', 1625, in *Hakluytus Posthumus, or Purchas his Pilgrimes*, vol. 6, Glasgow: James MacLehose and Sons, 367–406.

Beard, Mary (1996), 'Who Wanted Remus Dead?', *Times Literary Supplement*, No. 4854, 3–4.

Beattie, Lester M. (1935), *John Arbuthnot: Mathematician and Satirist*, Cambridge, MA: Harvard University Press.

Bernheimer, Robert (1952), *Wild Men in the Middle Ages*, Cambridge, MA: Harvard University Press.

Bettelheim, Bruno (1972), *The Empty Fortress: Infantile Autism and the Birth of the Self*, New York: The Free Press.

Binns, Edward (1845), *The Anatomy of Sleep*, London: James Churchill.

Birch, Edward A. (1886), *The Management and Medical Treatment of Children in India*, Calcutta: Thacker, Spink & Co.

Black, Jeremy (1992), *The British Abroad: The Grand Tour in the Eighteenth Century*, New York: St Martin's Press.

Blumenbach, Johann Friedrich (1865), *The Anthropological Treatises of Johann Friedrich Blumenbach*, trans. Thomas Bendyshe, London: Longman, Green, Longman, Roberts & Green.

Bonaterre, Pierre-Joseph (1977), 'Historical Notice on the Sauvage de l'Aveyron', 1800, in Lane (1977), 33–48.

Bord, Janet and Colin (1982), *The Bigfoot Chronicle*, London: Granada.

Boswell, James (1767), *Essence of the Douglas Cause*, London.

– (1785), *The Journal of a Tour to the Hebrides*, London.

– (1953), *Life of Samuel Johnson*, 1791, ed. R. W. Chapman, Oxford: Oxford University Press.

– (1955), *Boswell on the Grand Tour*, New Haven: Yale University Press.

Boswell, John (1989),*The Kindness of Strangers. The Abandonment of Children in Western Europe from late Antiquity to the Renaissance*, 1988, London: Allen Lane.

Bremmer, J. N. and N. M. Horsfall (1987), *Roman Myth and Mythography*, London: University of London Institute of Classical Studies, Bulletin Supplement 52.

Brooke, Chris (1999),'Boy Who Was Raised By Monkeys', *Daily Mail*, Thursday 23 September 1999.

Brown, Iain Gordon (1986), 'A Character of Lord Monboddo', in *Notes and Queries*, eds. L. G. Black, D. Hewitt, E. G. Stanley, vol. 231/vol. 33, no. 4, Oxford: Oxford University Press, 523–4.

Buffon, Comte de (Georges-Louis Leclerc) (1791a), *Natural History, General and Particular*, 1753, trans. William Smellie, 3rd edn., 9 vols., London: A. Strahan and T.Cadell.

– (1791b), *The System of Natural History*, 2 vols., Perth: R. Morison and Son.

Burnett, Frances Hodgson (1911), *The Secret Garden*, London: William Heinemann.

Burnett, James (1768), 'Preface', in *An Account of a Savage Girl Caught Wild in the Woods of Champagne*, Edinburgh: A. Kincaid and J. Bell, iii–xviii.

– (1773), *Of the Origin and Progress of Language*, vol. 1, Edinburgh: A. Kincaid and W. Creech. London: T. Cadell.

– (1779–99), *Antient Metaphysics: or, the Science of Universals*, 6 vols, vol. 1: 1779, vol. 2: 1782, vol. 3: 1784, vol. 4: 1795, vol. 5: 1797, vol. 6: 1799, vols. 1–3, Edinburgh: J. Balfour, London: T. Cadell; vol. 4, Edinburgh: Bell & Bradfute, London: T. Cadell; vols. 5–6, Edinburgh: Bell & Bradfute, London: W. Davies.

Burnett, James, et al. (1789), *Curious Thoughts on the History of Man* (including work by Lord Kames, Dr Dunbar, and Montesquieu), London: G. Kearsley.

'Burnett, James' (1886), *Dictionary of National Biography*, vol. 7, ed. Leslie Stephen, London: Smith, Elder & Co., 412–14.

Burns, Robert (1968), *The Poems and Songs of Robert Burns*, 3 vols., Oxford: Oxford University Press.

– (1985), *The Letters of Robert Burns*, ed. J. De Lancey Ferguson, 2nd edn, 2 vols., Oxford: Clarendon Press.

Burroughs, Edgar Rice (1914), *Tarzan of the Apes*, New York: A. L. Burt Company.

– (1915), *The Return of Tarzan*, London: C. F. Cazenove.

– (1925), *The Cave Girl*, Chicago: A. C. McClurg & Co.

Burton, John Hill (1846), *Life and Correspondence of David Hume*, Edinburgh: William Tait.

Calderón de la Barca, Pedro (1961), 'Life is a Dream', in *Six Plays*, 1635, trans. Denis Florence, Revd Henry Wells, New York: Las Américas Publishing Company, 13–95.

Camerarius, Phillipus (1609), *Operae Horarum Subcisivarum, sive Meditationes Historicae*, Frankfurt: Petri Kopffij.

Candland, Douglas Keith (1993), *Feral Children and Clever Animals: Reflections on Human Nature*, New York and Oxford: Oxford University Press.

Caraboo (1817), *Caraboo, Caraboo. The Singular Adventures of Mary Baker, Alias Princess of Javasu*, London: A. Topping.

Carr, William (1991), *A History of Germany, 1815–1990*, 4th edn., London and New York: Edward Arnold.

Carrington, Charles (1970), *Rudyard Kipling: His Life and Work*, 1955, Harmondsworth: Penguin Books.

Case of Archibald Douglas, The (1769), *The Case of Archibald Douglas*, Edinburgh.

Cato (1986), *Les Origines*, Paris: Société D'Edition 'Les Belles Lettres'.

Chapple, Eliot Dismore, and Carleton Stevens Coon (1947), *Principles of Anthropology*, London: Jonathan Cape.

Chatwin, Bruce (1989), *What Am I Doing Here?* Harmondsworth: Penguin Books.

Cheselden, William (1726), *The Anatomy of the Human Body*, 3rd ed., London: W. Bowyer.

Chesterton, G. K. (1905), *Heretics*, London: Bodley Head.

Cleveland, Catherine Lucy Wilhelmina, Duchess of (1893), *The True Story of Kaspar Hauser from Official Documents*, London: Macmillan and Co.

– (1897), *The Life and Letters of Lady Hester Stanhope*, London: William Clowes and Sons.

Cloyd, E. L. (1972), *James Burnett, Lord Monboddo*, Oxford: Clarendon Press.

Cole, William (1951), *A Journal of My Journey to Paris in the Year 1765*, London: Constable & Co.

Coleridge, Samuel Taylor (1828), 'Zapolya', in *The Poetical Works of S. T. Coleridge*, vol. 2, London: William Pickering, 237–370.

– (1956), *Collected Letters of Samuel Taylor Coleridge*, ed. Earl Leslie Griggs, vol. 4, Oxford: Clarendon Press.

– (1957), *The Notebooks of Samuel Taylor Coleridge. 1794–1804*, vol. 1, ed.

Kathleen Coburn, London: Routledge & Kegan Paul.

– (1962), *The Notebooks of Samuel Taylor Coleridge. 1804–1808*, vol. 2, ed. Kathleen Coburn, London: Routledge & Kegan Paul.

– (1971), *Collected Letters of Samuel Taylor Coleridge*, ed. Earl Leslie Griggs, vol. 6, Oxford: Clarendon Press.

– (1973), *The Notebooks of Samuel Taylor Coleridge. 1804–1819*, vol. 3, ed. Kathleen Coburn, London: Routledge & Kegan Paul.

Condillac, Etienne Bonnot De (1746), *Essai Sur L'Origine des Connaissances Humaines*, 2 tom., Amsterdam: Pierre Mortier.

– (1755), *Traité des Animaux*, Amsterdam: De Bure and Jombert.

– (1756), *An Essay on the Origin of Human Knowledge Being a Supplement to Mr Locke's Essay on the Human Understanding*, trans. Thomas Nugent, London: J. Nourse.

Connor, Bernard (1697), *Evangelium medici, seu Medicinae mystica: de suspensis naturae legibus, sive de miraculis*, London: Richard Wellington.

– (1698), *The History of Poland in Several Letters to Persons of Quality*, 2 vols., London: Dan. Brown and A. Roper.

Considerations (1767), *Considerations on the Douglas Cause*, London: J. Wilkie.

Constantine, David (1994), *Caspar Hauser*, Newcastle: Bloodaxe Books.

Cope, Edward Drinker (1896), *The Primary Factors of Organic Evolution*, Chicago: Open Court Publishing.

Cornell, T. J. (1995), *The Beginnings of Rome*, London and New York: Routledge.

Crisp, C. G. (1972), *François Truffaut*, London: November Books.

Curiosités De Paris (1771), *Curiosités De Paris*. Paris.

Curtiss, Susan (1977), *Genie: A Psycholinguistic Study of a Modern-Day Wild Child*, New York: Academic Press.

Dampier, William (1699), *A New Voyage Around the World*, vol. 1, London: James Knapton.

Darnton, Robert (1968), *Mesmerism and the End of the Enlightenment in France*, Cambridge, MA: Harvard University Press.

– (1985), *The Great Cat Massacre and other Episodes in French Cultural History*, 1984, London: Allen Lane.

Daumer, G. F. (see: Feuerbach 1834: 121–59).

– (1832a) *Mittheilungen über Kaspar Hauser*, 1st edn, Nürnberg: Heinrich Haubernstrider.

– (1832b), *Mittheilungen über Kaspar Hauser*, 2nd edn., Nürnberg: Heinrich Haubernstrider.

Davie, Donald (1963), *The Language of Science and the Language of Literature,1700–1740*, London and New York: Sheed and Ward.

Day, Thomas (1788), 'The History of Little Jack', in *The Children's Miscellany*, London: John Stockdale, 1–58.

Defoe, Daniel (1719), *The Dumb Philosopher; or Great Britain's Wonder*, London: Thomas Bickerton.

– (1724), *The Fortunate Mistress*, London: T. Warner.

– (1726), *Mere Nature Delineated: or, a Body Without a Soul*, London: T. Warner.

– (1983), *The Life and Strange Surprizing Adventures of Robinson Crusoe, of York, Mariner*, 1719, ed. J. Donald Crowley (1972), Oxford: Oxford University Press.

– (1989), *The Fortunes and Misfortunes of the Famous Moll Flanders, &c.*, 1722, ed. David Blewett, Harmondsworth: Penguin Books.

Democritus (1723), *Democritus, The Laughing Philosopher's Trip Into England*, Third Edition, London: Sam Briscoe.

Derrida, Jacques (1980), *The Archeology of the Frivolous*, 1976, trans. John P. Leavey, Pittsburgh: Duquesne University Press.

Descartes, René (1970), *Philosophical Writings*, ed. and trans. Elizabeth Anscombe and Peter Thomas Geach, London: Thomas Nelson and Sons.

Devil to Pay, The (1727), *The Devil to Pay at St. James's: or, A Full and True Account of a Most Horrible and Bloody Battle Between Madam Faustina and Madam Cuzzoni*, London: A. Moore.

Dibdin, Thomas Frognall (1821), *A Bibliographical, Antiquarian and Picturesque Tour in France and Germany*, vol. III London: Shakespeare Press.

Dickinson, H. T. (1970), *Bolingbroke*, London: Constable & Company.

Dickson, Arthur (1929), *Valentine and Orson: A Study in Late Medieval Romance*, New York: Columbia University Press.

Digby, Kenelm (1644), *Two Treatises: In One of Which, the Nature of Bodies; in the Other, the Nature of Man's Soule, is Looked into: in way of Discovery of the Immortality of Reasonable Soules*, Paris: Gilles Blaizot.

Domeier, Edward Augustus (1830), *A Descriptive Road-Book of Germany*, London: Samuel Leigh.

Douglas, Norman (1917), *South Wind*, London: Martin Secker.

Dudley, Edward, and Maximilian Novak, eds. (1972), *The Wild Man Within*.

An Image in Western Thought from the Renaissance to Romanticism, Pittsburgh: University of Pittsburgh Press.

Ellenberger, Henri (1994), *The Discovery of the Unconscious: the History and Evolution of Dynamic Psychiatry*, 1970, London: Fontana Press.

Ellis, G. Harold (1912), 'Fetichism in Children', in *Aspects of Child Life and Education*, ed. G. S. Hall, Boston: Ginn and Company, 287–99.

Ellis, Havelock (1890), *The Criminal*, London: Walter Scott.

Enquiry How the Wild Youth, An (1726a), *An Enquiry How the Wild Youth, Lately taken in the Woods near Hanover, (and now brought over to England) could be there left, and by what Creature he could be suckled, nursed, and brought up*, London: H. Parker.

– (1726b), *An Enquiry How the Wild Youth, Lately taken in the Woods near Hanover, (and now brought over to England) could be there left, and by what Creature he could be suckled, nursed, and brought up*, London: H. Parker.

Equiano, Olaudah (1997), *Interesting Narrative*, Harmondsworth: Penguin Books.

Etat ou Tableau de la Ville de Paris (1760), *Etat ou Tableau de la Ville de Paris*, Paris.

Evans, Elizabeth Edson (1875), *The Abuse of Maternity*, Philadelphia: J. B. Lippincott & Co.

– (1892a), *The Story of Kaspar Hauser from Authentic Records*, London: Swan Sonnenschein & Co.

– (1892b), *A History of Religions*, New York: Truth Seeker Co.

– (1893), *The Story of Louis XVII of France*, London: Sonnenschein & Co.

– (1895a), *Confession*, London: Swan Sonnenschein & Co.

– (1895b), *Transplanted Manners*, London: Swan Sonnenschein & Co.

– (1897), *Ferdinand Lassalle and Helene von Dönniges*, London: Swan Sonnenschein & Co.

Faustina (1726), *Faustina: or the Roman Songstress, A Satyr, on the Luxury and Effeminacy of the Age*, London: J. Roberts.

Feuerbach, Anselm Ritter von (1832), *Kaspar Hauser. Beispiel eines Verbrechens am Seelenleben des Menschen*, Ansbach: J. M. Dollfuss.

– (1832), *Caspar Hauser. An Account of an Individual Kept in a Dungeon, Separated from all Communication with the World, from Early Childhood to about the Age of Seventeen*, trans. Henning Gottfried Linberg, Boston: Allen and Ticknor.

– (1834), *Caspar Hauser. An Account of an Individual Kept in a Dungeon, Separated from all Communications with the World, from Early Childhood to about the Age of Seventeen. With a Memoir of the Author. To which are added Further Details*, by G. F. Daumer and Schmidt Von Lübeck, 2nd edn., London: Simpkin and Marshall.

– (1846), *Narratives of Remarkable Criminal Trials*, 1808, trans. Lady Duff Gordon, London: John Murray.

– (1981), *Kaspar Hauser. Beispiel eines Verbrechens am Seelenleben des Menschen*, ed. Helmut Bender, Waldkirch: Waldkircher Verlagsgesellschaft.

Fletcher, John (1976), 'The Faithful Shepherdess', ed. Cyrus Hoy, *The Dramatic Works in the Beaumont and Fletcher Canon*, gen. ed. Freedson Bowers, Cambridge: Cambridge University Press, 483–612.

Flynn, Carol Houlihan (1990), *The Body in Swift and Defoe*, Cambridge: Cambridge University Press.

Fox, William Sherwood (1916), *The Mythology of All Races*, vol. 1, Boston: Marshall Jones Company.

Frazer, Sir James George (1907–15), *The Golden Bough*, 12 vols., 3rd edn., London: Macmillan & Co.

– (1929), *Publii Ovidii Nasonis. Fastorum Libri Sex*, vol. 2, ed. and trans. with a commentary by Sir James George Frazer, London: Macmillan and Co.

Freud, Sigmund (1955), 'Analysis of a Phobia in a Five-Year-Old Boy', ('Little Hans'), *The Standard Edition of the Complete Psychological Works of Sigmund Freud*, 1909, trans. James and Alix Strachey, vol. 10, London: Hogarth Press. 1–149.

– (1957), 'Totem and Taboo', *The Standard Edition of the Complete Psychological Works of Sigmund Freud*, 1913, trans. James Strachey, vol. 13, London: Hogarth Press, vii–xv/1–161.

– (1959), '"Civilized" Sexual Morality and Modern Nervous Illness', *The Standard Edition of the Complete Psychological Works of Sigmund Freud*, 1908, trans. James Strachey, vol. 9, London: Hogarth Press, 177–204.

– (1979a), 'Psychoanalytic Notes on an Autobiographical Account of a Case of Paranoia' ('Schreber'), *The Pelican Freud Library*, 1911 trans. James Strachey, vol. 9, Harmondsworth: Penguin Books, 129–223.

– (1979b), 'From the History of an Infantile Neurosis' ('The Wolf Man'), *The Pelican Freud Library*, 1918, trans. James Strachey, vol. 9, Harmondsworth: Penguin Books, 224–336.

Furbank, P. N. and W. R. Owens (1988), *The Canonisation of Daniel Defoe*, New Haven and London: Yale University Press.

– (1994), *Defoe De-Attributions: A Critique of J. R. Moore's Checklist*, London and Rio Grande: Hambledon Press.

– (1998), *A Critical Biography of Daniel Defoe*, London: Pickering & Chatto.

Gall, Franz Jospeh, and Johann Caspar Spurzheim (1810), *Anatomie et Physiologie du Système Nerveux en Général, et du Cerveau en Particulier*, vol. 2, Paris: F. Schoell.

Gay, John (1716), *Trivia*, London: Bernod Lintott.

'Genie' (transmitted 02/05/1994), *Horizon*: 'Genie', BBC 2, written and directed by Linda Garmon.

Gesell, Arnold (1940), *Wolf Child and Human Child*, New York and London: Harper & Brothers Publishers.

Gibbon, Edward (1796), *Miscellaneous Works of Edward Gibbon, Esquire*, London: A. Strahan and T. Cadell.

Gilroy, Paul (1993), *The Black Atlantic*, London and New York: Verso.

Glendinning, Victoria (1998), *Jonathan Swift*, London: Hutchinson.

Goldsmid, Edmund (1886), *Un-natural History, of Myths of Ancient Science*, 4 vols., Edinburgh: Collectanea Adamantea.

Gore-Browne, Robert (1953), *Chancellor Thurlow. The Life and Times of an XVIIIth Century Lawyer*, London: Hamish Hamilton.

Great Britain's Vade Mecum (1720), *Great Britain's Vade Mecum*, London.

Green, John (1840), *Kaspar Hauser, or the Power of External Circumstances*, Manchester: A. Heywood.

Green, Roger Lancelyn, ed. (1971), *Rudyard Kipling: the Critical Heritage*. London: Routledge and Kegan Paul.

Greg, Walter (1906), *Pastoral Poetry and Pastoral Drama*, London: A. H. Bullen.

Greig, J. Y. T. (1985), *The Letters of David Hume*, New York and London: Garland Publishing.

Grunwell, Pamela (1987), *Clinical Phonology*, 2nd edn., London: Chapman & Hall.

Guillet, Cephas (1900), 'Recapitulation and Education', in *The Pedagogical Seminary*, ed. G. S. Hall, vol. 7, Worcester, Massachusetts: Louis N. Wilson, 397–445.

Gunn, Thom (1994), *Collected Poems*, New York: Farrar, Straus & Giroux.

Gutch, James Matthew (1817), *Caraboo: a narrative of a singular imposition*. London: Baldwin, Cradock and Joy.

Gutzkow, Carl Ferdinand (1870), *Die Söhne Pestalozzi's*, Berlin: Otto Zante.

Hagen, Victor W. von (1949), *South America Called Them*, London: Robert Hale.

Hamerow, Theodore (1958), *Restoration Revolution Reaction: Economics and Politics in Germany, 1815–1871*, Princeton, New Jersey: Princeton University Press.

Haslip, Joan (1934), *Lady Hester Stanhope*, London: Cobden-Sanderson.

Hatton, Ragnhild (1978), *George I: Elector and King*, London: Thames and Hudson.

Hauser, Kaspar (1993), *Kaspar Hauser Speaks For Himself*, from Daumer (1832a), introduction by Adam Bittleston, afterword by Barach Luke Urieli, ed. Andrea Damico Gibson, trans.William B. Forward, Botton Village: Camphill Press.

Headlam, Cecil (1899), *The Story of Nuremberg*, London: J. M. Dent & Co.

Heaney, Seamus (1998), *Opened Ground. Poems 1966–1996*, London: Faber and Faber.

Hecquet, Madame (see *Savage Girl*).

Herbert-Brown, Geraldine (1994), *Ovid and the Fasti: An Historical Study*, Oxford: Clarendon Press.

Herder, Johann Gottfreid (1803), *Outlines of a Philosophy of the History of Man*, trans. T.Churchill, 2 vols., London: J. Johnson.

Hewett, Sir John (1938), *Jungle Trails In Northern India*, London: Methuen and Company.

Hine, Ellen McNiven (1979), *A Critical Study of Condillac's Traité des Systèmes*, The Hague, Boston, and London: Martinus Nijhoff.

Honig, Edwin (1972), *Calderón and the Seizures of Honor*, Cambridge, MA: Harvard University Press.

Husband, Timothy (1980), *The Wild Man: Medieval Myth and Symbolism*, New York: Metropolitan Museum of Art.

Huxley, Thomas Henry (1863), *Evidence as to Man's Place in Nature*, London: Williams and Norgate.

Itard, Jean Marc Gaspard (1801), *De l'Education d'un Homme Sauvage, ou des Premiers Dévelopements Physiques et Moraux du Jeune Sauvage de l'Aveyron*, Paris: Gouyon.

– (1802), *An Historical Account of the Discovery and Education of a Savage Man, of the First Developments, Physical and Moral, of the Young Savage Caught in the Woods near Aveyron, in the Year 1798*, trans. Nogent, London: Richard Phillips.

– (1932), *The Wild Boy of Aveyron (Rapports et Mémoires sur le Sauvage de l'Aveyron)*, trans. by George and Muriel Humphrey, New York: Century Co.

It Cannot Rain but it Pours (1726a), *It Cannot Rain but it Pours: or, London Strow'd with Rarities*, London: J. Roberts.

– (1726b), *It Cannot Rain but it Pours: or, the First Part of London Strow'd with Rarities*, London: J. Roberts.

James, M. R., ed. (1928), *The Bestiary*, London: Roxburghe Club.

Jeffereys, D. (1743), *A Journal from London to Rome, by way of Paris*, London: W. Owen and T. James.

Jones, Peter, ed. (1988), *Philosophy and Science in the Scottish Enlightenment*, Edinburgh: John Donald Publishers Ltd., 145–68.

'The Jungle Books' (1894), review in the *Athenaeum Journal*, no. 3477, London: John C. Francis, 766.

– (1894), review in *Punch*, vol. 106, London: Punch Office, 286.

Kames, Lord. Henry Home (1778), *Sketches of the History of Man*, 2nd edn., vol. 1, Edinburgh: W. Creech.

Karlin, Daniel (1987), 'Introduction', *The Jungle Books*, Harmondsworth: Penguin Books, 7–29.

Kellog, W. N. and L. A. Kellog (1933), *The Ape and the Child*, New York and London: Whittlesey House.

Kendall, Joshua (1992), 'Kaspar Hauser in Literature', in John Money 1992: 213–63.

Kerner, Justinus (1829), *Die Seherin von Prevorst*, Stuttgart and Tübingen: J. S. Cottaschen Buchhandlung.

– (1845), *The Seeress of Prevorst*, trans. Mrs Crowe, London: J. C. Moore.

Keir, James (1791), *An Account of the Life and Writings of Thomas Day, Esq.*, London.

Kipling, John Lockwood (1891), *Beast and Man in India*, London: Macmillan and Co.

Kipling, Rudyard (1891), *Plain Tales from the Hills*, 1888, 3rd edn., London: Macmillan and Co.

– (1893), *Many Inventions*, London: Macmillan and Co.

– (1894), *The Jungle Book*, London: Macmillan and Co.

– (1895), *The Second Jungle Book*, London: Macmillan and Co.

– (1901), *Kim*, London: Macmillan and Co.

– (1904), *Traffics and Discoveries*, London: Macmillan and Co.

– (1917), *Just So Stories*, 1902, London: Macmillan and Co.

– (1937), *The Jungle Books*, Sussex Edition, London: Macmillan & Co.

– (1940), *Collected Poems*, London: Hodder & Stoughton.
– (1977), *Something of Myself*, 1937, ed. Robert Hampson, Harmondsworth: Penguin Books.
– (1987a), *The Day's Work*, 1898, ed. Constantine Phipps, Harmondsworth: Penguin Books.
– (1987b), *A Diversity of Creatures*, 1917, ed. Paul Driver, Harmondsworth: Penguin Books.
– (1987c), *Life's Handicap*, 1891, ed. P. N. Furbank, Harmondsworth: Penguin Books.
– (1987d), *Puck of Pook's Hill*, 1906, ed. Sarah Wintle, Harmondsworth: Penguin Books.
– (1987e), *Rewards and Fairies*, 1910, ed. Roger Lewis, Harmondsworth: Penguin Books.
– (1987f), *Stalky and Co.*, 1899, ed. Isabel Quigley, Oxford: Oxford World's Classics.
– (1988a), *The Light That Failed*, 1891, ed. John Lyon, Harmondsworth: Penguin Books.
– (1988b), *Wee Willie Winkie*, 1895, ed. Hugh Haughton, Harmondsworth: Penguin Books.
– (1990), *The Letters of Rudyard Kipling, 1865–1936*, ed. Thomas Pinney, vols. 1 and 2, Basingstoke: Macmillan.
Kipling, Rudyard and C. R. L. Fletcher (1911), *A School History of England*, Oxford: Clarendon Press.
Kirkby, John (1745), *The Capacity and Extent of the Human Understanding*, (*Automathes*), London: R. Manby and H. Shute Cox.
Knight, William (1900), *Lord Monboddo and Some of his Contemporaries*, London: John Murray.
Koenig, Henrici Conradi (1730), *De Hominum Inter Feras Educatorum Statu Naturali Solitario*, Hanover: Holwein.
König, Karl (1995), *A Christmas Story*, including 'The Story of Kaspar Hauser', 1961, Botton Village: Camphill Press.
Kramnick, Issac (1968), *Bolingbroke and his Circle: the Politics of Nostalgia in the age of Walpole*, Cambridge, MA: Harvard University Press.
Kroeber, Theodora (1976), *Ishi in Two Worlds: A Biography of The Last Wild Indian in North America*, Berkeley & Los Angeles: University of California Press.

La Condamine, Charles Marie de (1745), *Relation abrégée d'un voyage fait dans l'intérieur de l'Amérique Méridionale*, Paris: Pissot.

– (1747), *A Succint Abridgment of a Voyage Made Within the Inland Parts of South America*, London: E. Withers.

– (1751), *Journal du Voyage Fait Ordre du Roi a l'Équator*, Paris: L'Imprimerie Royale.

– (1753), *Journal of a Tour to Italy*, London: T. Lewis.

– (1755) (see *Savage Girl*).

– (1755), *A Discourse on Inoculation, Read Before the Royal Academy of Sciences at Paris, the 24th of April, 1754*, London: P. Vaillant.

Lane, Harlan (1977), *The Wild Boy of Aveyron*, London: George Allen & Unwin.

– (1988), *When the Mind Hears*, 1984, Harmondsworth: Penguin Books.

Lang, Andrew (1893), *The True Story Book*, London: Longman, Green and Co.

– (1904), *Historical Mysteries*, London: Smith, Elder & Co.

Lee, William (1869), *Daniel Defoe: His Life, and Recently Discovered Writings: Extending from 1716 to 1729*, 3 vols., London: John Camden Hotten.

Lenneberg, Eric, ed. (1966), *New Directions in the Study of Language*, Cambridge, Mass: MIT Press.

Les Rues et Les Environs De Paris (1745), *Les Rues et Les Environs De Paris*, Paris.

Le Sueur, Achille Ambroise Anatole (1909), 'La Condamine – D'Après ses Papiers Inédits', in *Mémoires de L'Académie des Sciences, des Lettres et des Arts D'Amiens*, vol. 56, Amiens: Yvert & Tellier, 1–80.

Letters on the French Nation (1749), *Letters on the French Nation*, London.

Linnæus, Charles (1792), *The Animal Kingdom or Zoological System of the Celebrated Sir Charles Linnæus*, 1735 etc., trans. with additions by Robert Kerr, London: J. Murray.

Liou-Gille, Bernadette (1980), *Cultes 'Héroiques' Romains*, Paris: Société D'Edition 'Les Belles Lettres'.

Livy (1925), *History*, vol. 1, trans. B. O. Foster, London: Wm Heinemann.

Loomis, C. Grant (1948), *White Magic. An Introduction to the Folklore of Christian Legend*, Cambridge, Mass.: Mediaeval Academy of America.

Los Angeles Times (1970), articles on Genie from 17 to 24 November.

Lovejoy, Arthur O., and George Boas (1935), *Primitivism and Related Ideas in Antiquity*, Baltimore: Johns Hopkins Press.

Lübeck, Schmidt von (see 'Feuerbach' 1834: 161–73).

Lupoff, Richard A. (1965), *Edgar Rice Burroughs: Master of Adventure*, New York: Canaveral Press.

Lyly, John (1902), 'The Speeches and Honorable Entertainment giuen to the Queenes Maiestie in Progresse, at Cowdrey in Sussex, by the right Honorable the *Lord Montacute* (1591)', *The Complete Works of John Lyly*, ed. R. Warwick Bond, vol. 1, Oxford: Clarendon Press, 421–30.

– (1902), 'Speeches Delivered to Her Maiestie This Last Progresse, at the Right Honorable the Lady Rvussels, at Bissam, the Right Honorable the Lorde Chandos, at Sudley, at the Right Honorable the Lord Norris, at Ricorte', *The Complete Works of John Lyly*, ed. R. Warwick Bond, vol. 1, Oxford: Clarendon Press, 471–90.

McKay, Margaret (1990), 'Peacock, Monboddo, and the Swedish Connection', in *Notes and Queries*, eds. L. G. Black, D. Hewitt, and E. G. Stanley, vol. 235/vol. 37, no. 4,.422–4.

Mackensie, Paul (1981–2), 'Kaspar Hauser in England: The First Hundred Years', in *German Life and Letters*, vol. 35, Oxford: Basil Blackwell, 118–37.

– (1993), 'Kaspar's Wooden Horse: A Metaphor of Childhood?' *Modern Language Review*, vol. 88, London: Modern Humanities Research Association, 905–11.

Maclean, Charles (1977), *The Wolf Children*, London: Allen Lane.

Malson, Lucien (1972), *Wolf Children*, 1964, trans. Edmund Fawcett, Peter Ayrton and Joan White, London: NLB.

Mandelstam, Osip (1991), *The Collected Critical Prose and Letters*, trans. Jane Gary Harris and Constance Link, ed. Jane Gary Harris, London: Collins Harvill.

Manifesto of Lord Peter, The (1726), *The Manifesto of Lord Peter*, London: J. Roberts.

Masson, Jeffrey Moussaieff (1996), *The Wild Child: The Unsolved Mystery of Kaspar Hauser*, New York: Simon & Schuster.

Mayer, Johannes (1988), *Philip Henry Lord Stanhope: Der Gegenspieler Kaspar Hausers*, Stuttgart: Urachhaus.

Mayer, Johannes and Peter Tradowsky (1984), *Hauser: Das Kind von Europa*, Stuttgart: Urachhaus.

'Member of the Craft, A' (1874), *The Text Book of Freemasonary*, London: Reeves and Turner.

Memorial (1766), *Memorial for Archibald Douglas*, Edinburgh.

Mericer, M. (1800), *New Picture of Paris*, 2 vols., London: H. D. Symonds.

Merleau-Ponty, Maurice (1973), *Consciousness and the Acquisiton of Language*, trans. Hugh Silverman, Evanston: Northwestern University Press.

– (1975), *Les Relations Avec Autrui Chez L'Enfant*, 1951, Paris: Centre de Documentation Universitaire.

Mettrie, Julien Jan, Offray de la (1750), *Man A Machine*, 1748, 2nd edn., London: G. Smith.

Mills, Maldwyn, ed. (1973), *Six Middle English Romances*, London, Melbourne and Toronto: Dent.

Money, John (1992), *The Kaspar Hauser Syndrome of 'Psychosocial Dwarfism'*, Buffalo: Prometheus Books.

Montaigne, Michel de (1904–6), *The Essayes of Michael Lord of Montaigne*, trans. John Florio, 3 vols., Oxford: Oxford University Press.

Montesquieu, Charles Louis de Secondat, Baron de (1722), *Lettres Persanes*, 1721, trans. Ozell, 2 vols., London: Jacob Tonson.

Most Wonderful Wonder, The (1726), *The Most Wonderful Wonder that ever Appear'd to the Wonder of the British Nation*, London: A. Moore.

Mucedorus (1598), *A Most Pleasant Comedie of* Mucedorus *the Kings sonne of* Valentia *and* Amadine *the Kings daughter of* Arragon, *with the merie conceites of* Mouse, London: William Jones.

Mucedorus (1610), *A Most Pleasant Comedie of* Mucedorus *the Kings sonne of* Valentia, *and* Amadine *the King's daughter of Arragon*, London: William Jones.

New Guide to London, A (1726), *A New Guide to London*, London.

New Review of London, A (1723), *A New Review of London*, London.

Nokes, David (1985), *Jonathan Swift, A Hypocrite Reversed*, Oxford: Oxford University Press.

Novak, Maximilian (1963), *Defoe and the Nature of Man*, Oxford: Oxford University Press.

– (1972), 'The Wild Man Come to Tea', Dudley and Novak, 1972: 183–222.

Octavian (1973), 'Octavian', *Six Middle English Romances*, ed. Maldwyn Mills, London: J. M. Dent & Sons, 75–124.

Ogburn, W. F. and M. K. Bose (1959), 'On the Trail of the Wolf Children', in *Genetic Psychology Monographs*, vol. 60: 117–93.

Ovid (1584), *The XV Bookes of P. Ovidius Naso, Entitled Metamorphoses*, trans. Arthur Golding, London: John Windet and Thomas Tudson.

– (1929), *Publii Ovidii Nasonis. Fastorum Libri Sex*, ed. and trans. Sir James George Frazer, vol. 1, London: Macmillan and Co.

Page, Norman (1984), *A Kipling Companion*, London: Macmillan Press.

Parker, Alexander (1988), *The Mind and Art of Calderón*, Cambridge: Cambridge University Press.

Pausanias (1794), *The Description of Greece*, trans. Tom Taylor, 3 vols., London: R. Faulder.

Peacock, Thomas Love (1817), *Melincourt*, 3 vols., London: T. Hookham.

Peter the Wild Boy (1787), 'A Particular Account of *Peter the Wild Boy*, extracted from the Parish Register of *North Church*, in the County of *Hertford*'. *The Annual Register, or a View of the History, Politics, and Literature, for the Years 1784 and 1785*. London: J. Dodsley, 'Characters', 43–5.

Pietzner, Carlo (1983), *Who Was Kaspar Hauser?*, Oxford: Floris Press.

Pinel, Phillipe (1806), *A Treatise on Insanity*, trans. D. D. Davis, Sheffield: Caddel and Davis.

Pliny (Plinius Secundus) (1601), *The Historie of the World*, trans. Philemon Holland, 2 tom., London: Adam Islip.

Plutarch (1718), *Plutarch's Morals*, 5th edn., 5 vols., London: W. Taylor.

– (1895), *Plutarch's Lives of the Noble Grecians and Romans*, 1579, trans. Thomas North, vol. 1, London: David Nutt.

– (1914), *Plutarch's Lives*, vol. 1, trans. Bernadotte Perrin, London: William Heinemann.

Porges, Irwin (1975), *Edgar Rice Burroughs: The Man who Created Tarzan*, Utah: Brigham Young University Press.

Potkay, Adam, and Sandra Burr, eds. (1995), *Black Atlantic Writers of the Eighteenth Century*, London: Macmillan Press.

Poucet, Jacques (1985), *Les Origines de Rome*, Brussells: Facultés Universitaires Saint Louis.

Proofs in the Conjoined Processes (1766), *Proofs in the Conjoined Processes . . . Against the Person Pretending to be Archibald Stewart, alias Douglas*, Edinburgh.

Pseudo-Aurélius, Victor (1983), *Les Origines du Peuple Romain*, Paris: Société D'Edition 'Les Belles Lettres'.

Purchas, Samuel (1905–6), *Hakluytus Posthumus, or Purchas His Pilgrimes*, 1625, 20 vols., Glasgow: James MacLehose and Sons.

R., A. (1760), *The Curiosities of Paris*, London.

Racine, Louis (1808), *Oeuvres*, 6 vols., Paris: C. Lebeau.

Raleigh, Sir Walter (1617), *The History of the World*, London.

Robinson, Gwennah (1975), *The Book of Hemel Hempstead & Berhamstead*, Chesham, Buckinghamshire: Barracuda Books Ltd.

Rousseau, Jean-Jacques (1817), *Essai sur L'Origine des Langues, où il est parlé de la Mélodie, et de L'Imitation musicale*, Paris: A. Belin.

– (1953), *Confessions*, 1781, trans. J. M. Cohen, Harmondsworth: Penguin Books.

– (1973), *The Social Contract and Discourses*, trans. G. D. H. Cole, revised J. H. Brumfitt and John C. Hall, London: J. M. Dent and Sons.

– (1984), *A Discourse on Inequality*, 1755, trans. Maurice Cranston, Harmondsworth: Penguin Books.

– (1986), *The First and Second Discourses Together with the Replies to Critics and Essay on the Origin of Languages*, ed. and trans. Victor Gourevitch, New York: Perennial Library.

– (1991), *Emile*, 1762, trans. Allan Bloom, Harmondsworth: Penguin Books.

Rymer, Russ (1994), *Genie: A Scientific Tragedy*, Harmondsworth: Penguin Books.

Sackville, Thomas, and Thomas Norton (1570), *The Tragidie of Ferrex and Porrex*, London: John Daye.

Sagarra, Eda (1980), *An Introduction to Nineteenth Century Germany*, London: Longman.

Sampath, Ursula (1991), *Kaspar Hauser: A Modern Metaphor*, Columbia, SC: Camden House.

Savage Girl (1731), 'Lettre écrite de Châlons, en Champagne, le 9 Decembre 1731, par M. A M. N . . . au sujet de la Fille sauvage, trouvée aux environs de cette Ville'/ 'Extrait d'une Lettre sur le même sujet', *Mercure de France*, vol. for December 1731, Paris, 2983–91.

Savage Girl (1755), *Histoire d'une Jeune Fille Sauvage, Trouvée dans les Bois à l'âge de dix ans*, Paris: Madame Hecquet.

Savage Girl (1760), *The History of a Savage Girl, Caught Wild in the Woods of Champagne*, London: R. Dursley, T. Davison, T. Manson, C. Bland, and P. Jones.

Savage Girl (1768), *An Account of a Savage Girl, Caught Wild in the Woods of Champagne*, trans. William Robertson, Edinburgh: A. Kincaid and J. Bell. See also Burnett, J.

Savage Girl (1820a), *La Belle Sauvage. The True and Surprising History of a Savage Girl, Found Wild in the Woods of Champagne, by Mons. D'Epinoy, and Presented to the Queen of Poland*, London: J. Bailey.

Savage Girl (1820b), *Savage Girl*, Newcastle: T. Marshall.

Savage Girl (1821a), *The Surprising Savage Girl, who was Caught Wild in the Woods of Champagne, a Province in France*, Falkirk: T. Johnston.

Savage Girl (1821b), *The Surprising Savage Girl, who was Caught Wild in the*

Woods of Champagne, a Province in France, Glasgow: Robert Hutchison.

Savage Girl (1824), *The Surprising Savage Girl, Who was Caught Wild in the Woods of Champagne, a Province in France*, Falkirk: T. Johnston.

Savage Girl (1970), *Histoire d'une jeune fille sauvage trouvée dans les bois à l'âge de six ans*, 1755, ed. Franck Tinland, Paris: Editions Ducros.

Seabrook, William B. (1931), *Jungle Ways*, London: George G. Harrap.

Shakespeare, William (1974), *The Riverside Shakespeare*, ed. G. Blakemore Evans, Boston: Houghton Mifflin Company, 1564–1605.

Shattuck, Roger (1980), *The Forbidden Experiment*, London: Quartet Books.

Shengold, Leonard (1988), *Halo in the Sky: Observations on Anality and Defense*, New York and London: Guilford Press.

Shirren, A. J. (1960), *Daniel Defoe in Stoke Newington*, Stoke Newington: Stoke Newington Public Libraries Committee.

Silverman, Kaja (1981–2), 'Kaspar Hauser's "Terrible Fall" into Narrative', in *New German Critique*, New York, 73–93.

Singh, J. A. L. and Robert Zingg (1942), *Wolf-Children and Feral Man*, 1939, New York: Harper Row.

Sleeman, W. H. (1888), 'An Account of Wolves Nurturing Children in their Dens', *The Zoologist*, vol. 12, ed. J. E. Harting, London: Simpkin, Marshall & Co., 87–98; 221.

Smith, Adam (1774), *The Theory of Moral Sentiments*, 1759, London: W. Strahan, J. and F. Rivington, W. Johnston, T. Longman, and J. Cadell; Edinburgh: W. Creech.

Smith, N. V. (1989), *The Twitter Machine*, Oxford: Basil Blackwell.

Smollett, Tobias (1766), *Travels Through France and Italy*, London: R. Baldwin.

Sophocles (1917), 'Tyro', *The Fragments of Sophocles*, ed. A. C. Pearson, vol. 2, Cambridge: Cambridge University Press, 270–90.

Southern Germany (1837), *A Handbook for Travellers in Southern Germany*, London: John Murray and Son.

Speeches and Judgement (1768), *The Speeches and Judgement of the Right Honourable The Lords of Council and Session in Scotland, Upon the Important Cause, his Grace George-James Duke of Hamilton and others, Pursuers Against Archibald Douglas, Defender*, Edinburgh.

Spencer, Edmund (1836), *Sketches of Germany and the Germans*, Second Edition, London: Whittaker & Co.

Spenser, Edmund (1909), 'The Faerie Queene', *The Poetical Works of Edmund Spenser*, 1590; 1595, vol. 1 and 2, ed. J. C. Smith, Oxford: Clarendon Press.

Squires, Paul C. (1927), 'Wolf Children of India', in *The American Journal of Psychology*, vol. 38, New York: Cornell University, 313–15.

Stanhope, Philip Henry, 4th Earl of (1828), *A Letter to the Owners and Occupiers of Sheep Farms*, London: James Ridgway.

– (1834), *Letters from Switzerland, 1833*, Carlsruhe: W.Hasper.

– (1836), *Tracts Relating to Caspar Hauser*, London: James S. Hodson.

Steedman, Carolyn (1995), *Strange Dislocations: Childhood and the Idea of Human Interiority, 1780–1930*, London: Virago Press.

Sterndale, Robert Armitage (1884), *Natural History of the Mammalia of India and Ceylon*, Calcutta: Thacker, Spink, and Co.

– (1886), *Denizens of the Jungle*, Calcutta: Thacker, Spink, and Co.

Sterndale, R. A. and E. H. A. (Edward Hamilton Aitken) (1894), *A Naturalist on the Prowl*, London: W. Thacker & Co.

Steuart, A. Francis (1909), *The Douglas Cause*, Edinburgh: William Hodge & Co.

Stockwell, George Archie (1898), 'Wolf-Children', in *Lippincott's Monthly Magazine*, vol. LXI, January issue, Philadelphia: J. B. Lippincott Company.

Stoler, John (1984), *Daniel Defoe: An Annotated Bibliography of Modern Criticism, 1900–1980*, New York and London: Garland Publishing.

Stone, Lawrence (1979), *The Family, Sex and Marriage in England, 1500–1800*, Harmondsworth: Pelican Books.

Sutherland, James (1937), *Defoe*, London: Methuen & Co.

Swift, Jonathan (1704), *A Tale of A Tub. The Battle of the Books. A Discourse Concerning the Mechanical Operation of the Spirit*, London: John Nutt.

– (1730), *A Modest Proposal for Preventing the Children of Poor People from being a Burthen to their Parents or the Country, and for Making them Beneficial to the Publick*, 1729, 3rd edn., Dublin: Weaver Bickerton.

– (1963), *The Correspondence of Jonathan Swift*, ed. Harold Williams, vol. 3, Oxford: Clarendon Press.

– (1967), *Gulliver's Travels (Travels into Several Remote Nations of the World)*, 1726, Harmondsworth: Penguin Books.

Taylor, W. D. (1933), *Jonathan Swift: A Critical Essay*, London: Peter Davies.

Tennant, C. M. (1938), *Peter the Wild Boy*, London: James Clarke & Co.

Thomas, Hugh (1997), *The Slave Trade*, London: Papermac.

Thomas, Ian (1998), 'The Boy of Six Who Lived With A Pack of Stray Dogs', in *Daily Mail*, Monday 20 July 1998.

Thomas, Keith (1984), *Man and the Natural World: Changing Attitudes in England, 1500–1800*, 1983, Harmondsworth: Penguin Books.

Thompson, Stith (1955–7), *Motif Index of Folk Literature*, 5 vols., Copenhagen: Rosenhilde and Bagger.

Tickell, Richard Eustace (1931), *Thomas Tickell and the Eighteenth-Century Poets*, London: Constable & Co.

Tinland, Franck (1970), 'Préface', *Histoire d'une jeune fille sauvage trouvée dans les bois à l'âge de dix ans*, Paris: Editions Ducrox, 7–42.

Tonkin, Humphrey (1972), *Spenser's Courteous Pastoral. Book VI of The Faerie Queene*, Oxford: Clarendon Press.

Torgovnick, Marianna (1990), *Gone Primitive: Savage Intellects, Modern Lives*, Chicago and London: University of Chicago Press.

Tracy, Destutt (1801), *Projet D'Eléments D'Idéologie à L'Usage des Ecoles Centrales de la République Française*, Paris: Debray.

– (1817), *A Treatise on Political Economy, to Which is Prefixed a Supplement to a Preceding Work on the Understanding, or Elements of Ideology*, trans. Thomas Jefferson, Georgetown, DC: Joseph Milligan.

Trilling, Lionel (1940), 'Kipling', *The Liberal Imagination*, London: Martin Secker and Warburg, 118–128.

Tulpius, Nicolaus (1671), *Observationes Medicae*, Amsterdam: Daniel Elzevir.

Tylor, Edward Burnet (1863), 'Wild Men and Beast Children', in *The Anthropological Review*, vol. 1, London: Trubner & Co., 21–32.

– (1871), *Primitive Culture: Researches into the Development of Mythology, Philosophy, Religion, Art and Customs*, 2 vols., London: John Murray.

Tyson, Edward (1699), *Orang-Outang, sive Homo Sylvestris: or, the Anatomy of a Pygmie*, London: Thomas Bennet and Daniel Brown.

Urban, Sylvanus (1751), *The Gentleman's Magazine, and Historical Chronicle*, vol. 21, London: Edw. Cave, 522.

– (1785), *The Gentleman's Magazine: and Historical Chronicle*, vol. 55, London: David Henry, Part the First:113–14; 236, Part the Second: 851–3.

Valentine and Orson (1825?), *The Famous and Wonderful History of Valentine and Orson*. Banbury: T. Cheney.

Valentine and Orson (1826), *The Famous History of Valentine and Orson*, London: J. F. Dove.

Valentine and Orson (1937), *Valentine and Orson, 1550*, trans. Henry Watson, ed. Arthur Dickson. London: Early English Text Society.

Van Der Kiste, John (1997), *King George II and Queen Caroline*, Stroud: Sutton.

Verlaine, Paul (1954), *Œuvres Poétiques Complètes*, Paris: Librarie Gallimard.

Virgil (1958), *The Aeneid*, trans. W. F. Jackson Knight, revised edn., Harmondsworth: Penguin Books.

– (1966), *Aeneid VII–XII. Minor Poems*, trans. H. Rushton Fairclough, revised edn. London: William Heinemann.

Vivitur Ingenio (1726), *Vivitur Ingenio: Being a Collection of Elegant, Moral, Satirical, and Comical Thoughts, on Various Subjects: as Love and Gallantry, Poetry and Politicks, Religion and History, &c.*, London: J. Roberts.

Voltaire, Francois Marie Arouet de (1738), *Eléments de la Philosophie de Neuton*, Amsterdam: Etienne Ledet & Compagnie.

– (1964), *Zadig/L'Ingénu*, 1747/1767, trans. John Butt, Harmondsworth: Penguin Books.

Walsh, Jill Paton (1998), *Knowledge of Angels*, London: Black Swan. (Formerly published by Green Bay Press.)

Wassermann, Jakob (1908), *Caspar Hauser oder die Trägheit des Herzens*, Stuttgart and Leipzig.

– (1938), *Caspar Hauser,* trans. Caroline Newton, London: George Allen & Unwin.

Watt, Ian (1957), *The Rise of the Novel. Studies in Defoe, Richardson and Fielding*, London: Chatto & Windus.

Welsford, Enid (1927), *The Court Masque*, Cambridge: Cambridge University Press.

White, Charles (1799), *An Account of the Regular Gradation in Men, and in Different Animals and Vegetables; and from the Former to the Latter*, London: C. Dilly.

White, T. H. (1954), *The Book of Beasts, being a Translation from a Latin Bestiary of the Twelfth Century*, London: Jonathan Cape.

Whitling, H. J. (1850), *Pictures of Nuremberg*, London: Richard Bentley.

Whitney, Lois (1934), *Primitivism and the Idea of Progress*, Baltimore: Johns Hopkins Press.

Wilson, William (1830), *Memoirs of the Life and Times of Daniel De Foe*, 3 vols., London: Hurst, Chance, and Co.

Wiseman, Timothy Peter (1995), *Remus, a Roman Myth*, Cambridge: Cambridge University Press.

Wokler, Robert (1988), 'Apes and Races in the Scottish Enlightenment: Monboddo and Kames on the Nature of Man', in *Philosophy and Science in the Scottish Enlightenment*, ed. Peter Jones, Edinburgh: John Donald Publishers Ltd, 145–68.

Wolf-Children (1893), 'Wolf-Children', in *North Indian Notes and Queries*, vol. 2, no. 12, Allahabad: 'Pioneer Press', 215–16.

Wright, Thomas (1894), *The Life of Daniel Defoe*, London: Cassell and Company.

Young, Kimball (1942), *Sociology: A Study of Society and Culture*, New York: American Book Company.

Z., A. (1754), *A Five Weeks Tour to Paris*, London.

Index